"In this detailed, well-written book, Richard H. Hiers explores the meaning of the creation, the sovereignty of God, humans' place in the world and relations with other creatures and landscapes, and ethical guidelines for treatment of nature that emerge from biblical texts. *Nature and Creation* is important reading for biblical scholars, environmental ethicists, and people of faith interested in a careful, critical evaluation of what biblical texts have to say about human relations and obligations to the rest of nature."

—Anna L. Peterson
Professor of religion, University of Florida

"In *Nature and Creation*, Richard H. Hiers offers a thorough treatment of the Bible's account of creation, other creatures, and their relation to both God and humanity. There are breakthrough readings here, including on the contested issue of human dominion over creation. Overall, Hiers shows that the Bible offers a treasure trove of resources for Christian ecological ethics. I highly commend this crucial work."

—David P. Gushee
Professor of Christian ethics, Mercer University

"In this book, the accomplished biblical scholar Richard H. Hiers expertly searches the entire Bible to prove the thesis that God's creation gives a value and importance to all created terrestrial life and not just human life."

—Charles E. Curran
Professor of human values, Southern Methodist University

"Richard H. Hiers goes behind contemporary policy discussions about environmental ethics, offering both lay and professional students of the Bible a carefully catalogued and annotated compendium of passages revealing the unique triangle of relationships between God, the wider creation, and human beings. Exploring texts from diverse Christian canons in short, accessible sections, Hiers thoughtfully reflects on environmental issues from creation as a divine agent to the land sabbatical and humane treatment of animals."

—Marie Fallinger
Former editor, *Journal of Law and Religion*

Nature and Creation

Nature and Creation

Biblical Perspectives on Life Here on Planet Earth

RICHARD H. HIERS

WIPF & STOCK · Eugene, Oregon

NATURE AND CREATION
Biblical Perspectives on Life Here on Planet Earth

Copyright © 2023 Richard H. Hiers. All rights reserved. Except for brief quotations in critical publications or reviews, no part of this book may be reproduced in any manner without prior written permission from the publisher. Write: Permissions, Wipf and Stock Publishers, 199 W. 8th Ave., Suite 3, Eugene, OR 97401.

Wipf & Stock
An Imprint of Wipf and Stock Publishers
199 W. 8th Ave., Suite 3
Eugene, OR 97401

www.wipfandstock.com

PAPERBACK ISBN: 978-1-6667-5778-1
HARDCOVER ISBN: 978-1-6667-5779-8
EBOOK ISBN: 978-1-6667-5780-4

VERSION NUMBER 041323

Unless otherwise noted, Scripture quotations are from the New Revised Standard Version of the Bible, copyright © 1989, National Council of Churches of Christ in the United States of America. Used by permission. All rights reserved.

The Revised Standard Version of the Bible is copyright © 1946, 1952, and 1971, National Council of Churches of Christ in the United States of America. Used by permission. All rights reserved worldwide.

Quotations from the present writer's article "Reverence for Life," posted in *Forum on Religion and Ecology* (2001), are used here by permission from Mary Evelyn Tucker, *Forum* editor.

"The LORD is good to all,
and his compassion is over all that he has made."

Ps 145:9

Contents

Preface | xiii
Acknowledgments | xxi
Abbreviations | xxiii
Prologue | xxvii

Introduction | 1

PART ONE: YHWH/God, the Created World, and All Creation | 21

CHAPTER 1

YHWH/God's Good Creation | 23
  A. YHWH/God: Creator of All That Is | 23
  B. All Creation and All Creatures Are Good | 28
  C. All Creation and All Creatures Are YHWH/God's: He Is Owner of All | 30

CHAPTER 2

YHWH/God as Ruler or Sovereign over All Creation and All Creatures | 33
  A. YHWH/God's Sovereignty over and through Creation | 33
  B. YHWH/God's Compassionate Care for the Earth, the Land, and All Creatures | 36
    1. The Earth—the Land | 37
    2. YHWH/God's Continuing Care for the Land—Providing Water for the Earth | 37

3. YHWH/God Sends Rain, Providing for Humans and Other Creatures | 39
4. Initial Blessings: "Be Fruitful and Multiply" | 41
5. YHWH/God Saves Endangered Species from the Great Flood | 43
6. The Everlasting Covenant between YHWH/God and Every Living Creature of All Flesh | 44
7. YHWH/God's Continuing Care for All Creatures | 45

CHAPTER 3

All Creatures Call Upon, Pray To, Praise, Bless, and Rejoice before YHWH/God | 50

   A. All Creatures Cry or Pray to YHWH/God | 50
   B. All Creatures Praise, Bless, and Rejoice before YHWH/God | 52

PART TWO: YHWH/God, the Creation, All Creatures, and Human Beings | 57

CHAPTER 4

The Primordial Commandments and the P Covenant with Noah and with "Every Living Creature of All Flesh" | 59

   A. On Being Fruitful, Multiplying, Filling and Subduing the Earth, and Having Dominion | 59
   B. After Vegetarianism: Respecting the Life of Animals Killed for Food | 65
   C. Genesis 9:8–17: The P Covenant with Noah and with Every Living Creature of All Flesh | 67

CHAPTER 5

Animal Sacrifices | 71

   A. Sacrificial Laws: Animal Sacrifices | 72
      1. Consecration of the Firstborn: One of the Earliest Laws | 73
         Consecration of Firstborn Israelites and Their Cattle to YHWH/God | 75
      2. Other Laws Governing Animal Sacrifice and Slaughter | 76
         a. The Deuteronomic Reform: Worship in One Place; Secular Slaughter and Respect for Sacrificial Animals' Life | 77

    i. Deuteronomy 12:1—13:1: Sacrificial Worship in Only the One Place | 77
    i. Deuteronomy 12:15-16, 20-25: Secular Slaughter and Reverence for Life | 79
   b. New Sacrificial Offerings in the Priestly Code | 80
    i. Ordination of Priests and Other Occasions | 80
    ii. Sacrifices to Heal or Purify | 81
    iii. Leviticus 16:1–34: Sacrifices and the Day of Atonement | 72
    iv. Leviticus 17:1–9: Bloodguilt for Killing Animals Other Than as Gifts Offered to YHWH/God | 82
    v. Leviticus 17:10–14: Animals' Blood and Reverence for Life | 83
   c. Animal Sacrifice Laws: Concluding Observation | 85
  B. Opposition to Animal Sacrifices | 86
   1. Psalms | 86
   2. Wisdom Writings | 88
   3. Prophets | 89
   4. Old Testament Apocrypha/Deuterocanonical Scriptures | 94
   5. New Testament | 95
    a. Jesus Traditions | 95
    b. The Early Church | 97

CHAPTER 6

Humans and Other Creatures: Much Alike in Many Ways | 99
  A. Common Sources: The Same Ground and the Same Spirit or Breath | 100
  B. Humans and Other Creatures: A Common Fate | 102
  C. In the Meantime: Humans and Other Living Things Alike Are Subject to Divine Judgment | 104

CHAPTER 7

Images of God, Humans, and Other Creatures | 110
  A. The Image of God in Humans and in Other Creatures | 110
  B. Humans Compared with Other Living Beings | 113

CHAPTER 8

Observation and Appreciation of Creation and all Living Beings | 121

A. Observation and Appreciation of "Nature" | 122
   1. Genesis and the Law: "Clean" and "Unclean" | 122
   2. The Book of Job | 123
   3. Psalms | 125
   4. "Solomonic" Wisdom Writings | 125
   5. Proverbs 30: The Sayings of Agur | 131
   6. Sirach, the Letter of Jeremiah, and 4 Maccabees | 132
   7. Sayings of Jesus | 135
B. Other Creatures as Models for Human Emulation | 137

CHAPTER 9

Caring for Creation: Biblical Faith and Environmental Ethics | 141
   A. Caring for the Land, Plants, and Trees | 141
      1. Land Ethics | 142
         a. The Land Is YHWH/God's, Not Israel's or Any People's | 143
         b. Israel's Contingent Possession of the Good Land | 145
         c. Against Pollution of the Land | 149
         d. Tilling the Ground | 152
         e. Sabbath Rest for the Land | 155
      2. Abundant Gifts of the Land: For YHWH/God, People, and Other Creatures | 157
         a. The Land of Milk and Honey | 157
         b. Abundant Harvests but Only on Condition of Continuing Fidelity | 158
         c. Responding to YHWH/God and to Persons in Need | 160
            i. Offerings to YHWH | 161
            ii. Provisions for Persons in Need | 161
      3. Care for Trees and Vegetation | 164
         a. New Orchards | 165
         b. Of Trees and War | 166
         c. Trees and Asherim | 166
   B. Care for Other Animate Creatures: The Ethics of Reverence for Life | 167
      1. Biblical Narratives | 167
         a. Preserving Biodiversity: Noah, the Ark, and the Animals | 168
         b. Other Biblical Narratives | 170
      2. Humane Treatment Legislation | 171

a. Newborn Bull Calves, Lambs, Kids, and Their Mothers | 172
       b. On Not Boiling a Kid in Its Mother's Milk | 172
       c. Affirmative Duties to Care for Lost or Distressed Domestic Animals | 173
       d. Conservation: Birds and Their Young | 174
       e. On Not Muzzling Oxen Treading Grain | 175
       f. Sabbath Days and Years of Rest for the Benefit of Cattle and Wildlife | 176
          i. The Sabbath Day of Rest | 176
          ii. The Sabbath Year of Rest | 177
    3. Other Biblical Traditions | 178

CHAPTER 10

Other Creatures as YHWH/God's Agents
in His Dealings with Humans | 182

  A. Creatures Helping Humans | 182
  B. Other Creatures as Agents of YHWH/God's Judgment | 188
    1. Acts of Judgment against Individuals | 188
    2. Acts of Judgment against Nations or Peoples in Past and Present Times | 190
    3. YHWH/God's Agents in Future Time or Times of Judgment against Nations or Peoples | 191

CHAPTER 11

Conditions of Life in the New or Messianic Age | 197

  A. Plants, Harvests, and Trees | 199
  B. People, Animals, and Other Creatures | 204

CHAPTER 12

Summary and Concluding Reflections | 215

  A. Summary | 215
  B. Concluding Reflections | 226

Bibliography | 235

Preface

BACK IN THE MID-1940S, I used to visit the Fels Planetarium in Philadelphia. One of the shows presented a number of theories as to how the world, or life on this world, would come to an end. The astronomy lecturer presented several scary scenarios. For instance, that as Earth's rotation slowed, the moon's gravitational pull would raise enormous seas twice a day that would sweep over most or all land areas, making them uninhabitable for all but sea creatures.

Or that in time, as the moon's mass increases under the weight of colliding asteroids and other accumulated space debris, it would gradually come nearer and nearer to the Earth, with multiple catastrophic consequences. Even before any totally destructive eventual collision, its gravitational pull would produce huge waves that would surge around the Earth, washing away the land and everything upon it.

And, as it came closer to the Earth, the moon's increased gravitational attraction would also produce monster earthquakes and volcanic eruptions, the latter spewing toxic smoke and gases that would choke out all breathing life-forms and, by blocking sunlight, bring about a deep freeze that would kill most or all remaining vegetation and animate life.

Or that a huge meteor, or asteroid, could come crashing into the Earth, again with disastrous consequences for the planet and all life on Earth.

Or that the sun would gradually cool, this time bringing about a permanent deep freeze that no life could survive. Or, alternatively, the sun might explode and turn into a supernova that would shatter and scorch our entire solar system. Or that in time, the

Earth, our solar system, and perhaps our entire galaxy would all disappear into one of those mysterious and ominous "black holes."

After an hour—that seemed more like a day—when most people in the planetarium audience were now fidgeting anxiously in their seats, the kindly lecturer would bring us relief by pointing out that none of these dread catastrophes was likely to occur in the next million or so years. Then, as the planetarium lights gradually came on, we begin to feel that we could go on with our lives as usual, and now need concern ourselves only with the familiar challenges presented by living in the world as we then knew it.

No one in that audience could have imagined that within but a few decades, humankind would find ways to bring about the end of life on Earth, all by ourselves.[1]

Now in the twenty-first century, new catastrophic scenarios are all around us. Imminent catastrophes, not just things that might happen sometime in the far distant future. These new, human-made catastrophes are already happening, so far, mainly coming incrementally, rather than with a big bang. Because so many of us still live in comfort and, we think, security, we are inclined to ignore or deny what is already happening and to pay but little attention to our scientists' expectations that worse (or the worst) is yet to come.

Here are some of these more recent scenarios.[2] Several result from climate change, now known to derive from the last few

1. "We're living on a planet where everything is connected—where the heartbreaking disappearance of animals and plants is putting all life on a path toward destruction and collapse." Kieren Suckling, executive director, Center for Biological Diversity, letter to members dated April 2022.

2. For continuing reports and commentary, see magazines, journals, reports, and newsletters published by American Rivers, the Animal Welfare Institute, Bat Conservation International, the Center for Biological Diversity, Earth Island Institute, Earthjustice, the Environmental Defense Fund, Florida Defenders of the Environment, Forest Service Employees for Environmental Ethics, Greenpeace, Marine Mammal Association, Montana WIlderness Association, National Audubon Society, National Parks and Conservation Association, National Parks Foundation, National Wildlife Association, Natural Resources Defense Council, Nature Conservancy, Northern Alaska Environmental Center, Ocean Conservancy, Pacifica Environmental, Rain Forest Alliance, Sea Turtle Conservancy, Sierra Club, Southern Utah Wilderness Alliance, Vital Grounds Foundation, Waterkeepers Alliance, Wild Montana, Wilderness Society, Wilderness Watch, World Wildlife Fund, Yosemite Conservancy,

centuries of human activity, sometimes referred to as the Industrial Revolution. The consequences of those activities now threaten the lives of nearly all living species. For instance, the world is getting not just warmer but hotter—much hotter.

Heat is causing deadly droughts that impact agriculture, dry up wells, ponds, streams, lakes, and rivers, and produce temperatures—already sometimes as high as 100–130°F—that neither humans, domestic animals, nor wildlife can survive.[3] Such heat sometimes creates dust storms, cyclones, and strong storms and hurricanes with devasting embedded tornados. And catastrophic flooding. Overheated oceans, lakes, rivers, streams, and ponds now spawn various deadly microorganisms, such as "red tide" that depletes aquatic oxygen, making them harmful and deadly to humans and most other creatures. These intense periods of heat and drought can, in turn, produce torrential rains and floods that wash away people, domestic animals, wildlife, trees, and agricultural soil. Drought also can fuel severe fires that destroy hundreds of square miles of forests, putting enormous amounts of carbon back into the atmosphere, further reducing the Earth's capacity to absorb and store the already excessive amounts of atmospheric CO_2.[4] Heat and drought have also given rise to vast forest fires all over the world, now the new normal. These fires, along with clear cutting ancient rain forests and millions of square miles of woodland, have also raised the amounts of carbon dioxide throughout Earth's atmosphere, with foreseeably disastrous consequences for all animate life.[5] This heat/drought/fire/storm/flood cycle already

---

and many other organizations concerned with the Earth's environment and the beings that live here. As to prevention of animal abuse, publications by such organizations as Animal Legal Defense Fund, Farm Sanctuary, Humane Society of the United States, People for the Ethical Treatment of Animals.

3. See "Is It Already 2050?" See also Pulver and Rice, "Baked Up?": "'I can't imagine what these heat waves will be like in the future,' University of Georgia meteorologist Marshall Shepherd told *USA Today*. . . . Temperatures in the US could rise 3–12 degrees by the end of the century, according to the National Oceanic and Atmospheric Administration. . . . More than 9,000 temperature records were broken around the world in July [2022], nearly 6,000 of them in the U.S., according to the National Climate Change Center."

4. See Buck, "Carbon Removal Is Essential."

5. Most dramatically, perhaps, the millions of acres deliberately burned and

has devastated millions of acres of ranch and farmland necessary for production of basic human food sources.

Heat, together with intense sunlight, accidental leaks and indiscriminate application of thousands of toxic chemicals developed beginning in the 1950s, and repeated major aquatic oil spills, has already destroyed huge swaths of once flourishing ocean phytoplankton, needed critically in order to maintain the O_2/CO_2 cycle that supplies the breathable air we and other living things need to survive.

Farmland and wildlife have also been decimated by human activities like paving millions of square miles of streets and highways, shopping malls, and mega-housing developments, covering over with asphalt and concrete what once was productive soil and destroying native pollinators. So that now bees, butterflies, and many other pollinating insects are on the verge of extinction.

Many, if not all, other living species are at risk too. Often because of other kinds of misguided governmental activities that once were thought helpful or at least harmless. For instance, draining swamps and estuaries, breeding places for aquatic life, essential food sources for humans and wildlife. Or by the BLM's continuing, expensive, yet pointless efforts to remove topsoil and vegetation from western wilderness lands.[6] And by the U.S. Forest Service's criminally clumsy fire mitigation activities.[7] And, despite Rachel Carson's classic *Silent Spring*, by continuing use of many kinds of highly toxic pesticides and herbicides in agriculture and around homes and gardens.

In these and many other ways, humans today choose to ignore or deny the cumulative effects of seemingly innocent practices that poison and pollute the Earth's air, land, and water. The prevailing assumption seems to be, and long to have been, that nature can and

---

cleared throughout much of the Amazon rain forests. Not only there but elsewhere, in all of Earth's wide bounds.

6. "Crucially, large-scale vegetation removal is a backward step when it comes to mitigating the worst impacts of climate change. These practices decrease soil stability, reduce fire resiliency, hasten the spread of invasive species, and produce dust that accelerates snowmelt in the Colorado Rockies, worsening the already cataclysmic future of drought and desertification." Marienfeld, "Missing the Forest," 7.

7. See "Wildfire Mitigation."

will somehow adjust to whatever we do, not only with our sewage, garbage, plastic, other biodegradable and nonbiodegradable pollutants, and trash, but with highly toxic and hazardous materials. in effect, that Mother Nature will be so obliging as to clean up after us. She did so for most of the history of humankind but now is signaling that she has had enough of doing that.

Those who profit from farming, ranching, mining coal, extracting gas and oil, and other polluting industries generally seem to believe that they have the right to do whatever they please, so long as they are making money. So, for example, if they can profit by dumping toxic or hazardous waste materials into nearby streams, rivers, lakes, and seas rather than spend money in order to safely dispose of such waste, they feel entitled to do so.

This kind of practice sometimes is justified as "externalizing the costs of production." Meaning that people and wildlife downstream have to pay for it by becoming sick and dying before their time. In other words, the polluters reap the profits, while those downstream have to pay by suffering the consequences.

Polluters of all kinds, whether of air, water, or land, often try to justify "externalizing" *their* production costs by invoking the magic of "cost-benefit analysis." The benefit to them, they say, is greater than the costs to those downwind, downstream, or next door, so that makes it all right. Not surprisingly, polluting industries and agriculturalists deeply resent and oppose efforts by "the government"—read citizens' well-being represented by local, state, or federal legislative and regulatory agencies—to shift the burden of paying for clean-up, *from* the people or industries *doing* the polluting to those harmed by it and *to* taxpayers. In their view, the value of the people and animals adversely affected by their pollution is so minimal that they can easily be left out of the equation.

In such circles, regulations are considered inherently evil and un-American. Consequently, hopefully announced goals for soon achieving significant percentage reductions in quantities of greenhouse gases and toxic or hazardous pollutants largely remain unfulfilled and unlikely ever to be achieved. That is to say, absent some kind of religious conversion or moral transvaluation of values and goals, whereby more people come to understand and believe that that human life and the lives of all the creatures living in the good world the Lord God made are more important than acquiring maximum power, glory, and wealth for themselves.

Two additional, perhaps the most catastrophic, end-of-world scenarios attributable to human activity are often forgotten or repressed. One, of course, is the continuing, exponential multiplication of human populations, which already exceed the Earth's carrying capacity.[8] The other is the peril of present and future warfare, especially the tragic consequences of accidental, unthinking, desperate, or intentional use of nuclear weapons.

Rather than address these emerging catastrophic crises, it is easier—for those not yet experiencing their debilitating and lethal effects—to avoid facing up to them. All-too-familiar responses: blame the messenger, ignore or deny the obvious reality, change the subject, or blithely assume that "science and technology" will solve all such problems, so why should we worry or do anything about them?

Rather than face up to the present and near future, many people try to escape from these fears—or responsibilities. Some by indulging in alcohol, drugs, and various kinds of diversion and entertainment. People also try to escape by immersing themselves in the illusion that the current and pending environmental catastrophes won't touch *them*, just those people living in poor undeveloped countries, or people in different racial or ethnic communities, or some later generation. Or just animals. As if environmental degradation and destruction were someone else's problem. And as if, for better either or worse, we weren't already all "in it" together.

A few scientists and engineers seriously propose that "we" (meaning the very wealthy) can escape from this world's problems and fears by constructing, moving to, and inhabiting huge,

---

8. "If every person in the world were to consume the same number of resources required for an American lifestyle, we would need five planet earths to draw from." Massie, "Moral Dilemma of Growth," 32. Many years ago, in their now classic *Limits to Growth*, Meadows et al. red-flagged the question of Earth's carrying capacity. They noted what happens when wildlife herds multiply beyond available resources: sudden, dramatic population collapse. The human herd that peoples the earth—now over eight billion of us—is already beginning to experience the early stages of such collapse. For example, in the form of millions of "climate refugees."

self-sustaining, plexiglass structures located out in space, and thereby leave behind our Earth and all its troubles. The present author grew up just two doors away from Phil Nolan, creator of the once famous *Buck Rogers* comic strips. These comics featured people living in condominium-size rocket ships, occasionally jetting out to board small orbiting asteroids. But even here, all was not well. The arch villain, Killer Kane, was intent on causing grief and destruction even in this outer world. Thus, frequent scenes depicted death ray fights between Kane and the strip's namesake hero, Buck Rogers. My little friends and I used to play star wars with model rocket ships and ray guns that the Nolans kindly shared with us.

The latter-day, but also nearly forgotten *Star Wars* films—probably inspired by the *Buck Rogers* strip—even more graphically demonstrated that human proclivities toward violence would not be likely to change for the better, even if people could escape Earth's evils for some synthetic heavenly paradise. Because it would still be populated by people.[9] A famous saying from the comic strip sage Pogo says it all: "We have met the enemy and he is us." Or as the biblical sage Sirach put it: "What race is good? The human race ... What race is evil? The human race ... ." Or as expressed in Jewish tradition: humans are continually prompted by two conflicting "inclinations": *ha yetzer ha tov* and *ha yetzer ha rah*—the good inclination and the bad or evil inclination.

The biblical "handwriting on the wall" sends an all-too-clear message for people in our times who try to ignore, deny, or just don't care about the environmental crises all around us: "You have been weighed in the balance and are found wanting."[10]

---

9. It has been suggested that the fact that our planet Earth is more than a light-year's distance from the nearest, possibly populated, neighboring solar system out there in space is one further evidence of the Creator's providential wisdom. Whatever damage and destruction the human race may inflict upon our own solar system cannot extend to those of others.

10. Cf. the prologue to the biblical flood story: "The LORD saw that the wickedness of man was great in the earth, and that every imagination of the thoughts of his heart was only evil continually. And the LORD was sorry that he had made man on the earth, and it grieved him to his heart. So the LORD said, 'I will blot out man whom I have made from the face of the ground, man and beast and creeping things and birds of the air, for I am sorry that I have made them.'" Gen 6:5–7 RSV.

Or is there still time for us to turn around, to repent and change our ways?

The chapters that follow point to not just a few but a multitude of biblical witnesses testifying to the profound meaning and value of the creation and all terrestrial life, human and otherwise, that God has given us to share in this good world he made and continues to create.

These biblical beliefs and values can also be seen as offering an urgent message for people in our times to be thankful for God's world, and to honor it in our thoughts and deeds. In biblical faith, the Earth and all creatures on Earth that do dwell *matter*.

Acknowledgments

I HERE WISH TO express my thanks to and for my many teachers, mentors, colleagues, fellow students, and friends, for their inspiration and encouragement over many years. Particularly:

Biblical studies: Melissa Aubin, John M. Bullard, Millar Burrows, Martin Buss, Anthony Buzzard, John B. Carman, Henry Carrigan, Brevard S. Childs, Erich Dinkler, Morton S. Enslin, Theodor H. Gaster, John Hollar, Leander E. Keck, Charles F. Kennedy, Susan Lewis, Thomas W. Ogletree, Paul Meyer, David Glen Rose, Jack Sanders, Jack Sasson, Paul Schubert, D. Moody Smith, Robert Spivey, Krister Stendahl, Phyllis Trible, and Amos N. Wilder

Ethics and social ethics: Joseph Allen, Barbara Andolsen, E. Wight Bakke, Waldo Beach, Robert N. Bellah, David J. Black, William E. Brown, Polly Stone Buck, Lisa Sowle Cahill, David and Jean Chalmers, William Sloane Coffin, Joseph Crist, Margaret Cubine, Charles E. Curran, Manning Dauer, John Dollard, Duncan Ferguson, Ralph Fisher, Gregory Flint, Perry Foote, Ralph Gabriel, David P. Gushee, James M. Gustafson, Norvin Hein, Vernon Jensen, J. Ray Jones, Ralph Kimbrough, Violet Lindbeck, William F. May, Charles McCoy, T. Ballard Morton, Eric J. Mount, William Muehl, James Nelson, H. Richard Niebuhr, Liston Pope, David Potter, Michael H. Radelet, Russell and Deborah Reynolds, Jeffrey Rubin, Donald and Peggy L. Shriver, Ralph Turner, Gwendolyn Zoharah Simmons, Harry Smith, Harold M. Stahmer, George Todd, Kenneth Underwood, and Bennet Willeford

Law and social policy: James C. Adkins, Frank S. Alexander, Fletcher and Nancy Baldwin, John R. Brown, Mary Ellen Caldwell, Richard Carnell, Jonathan R. Cohen, Stuart Cohn, Darryl Deaktor, Spencer Ervin Jr., Marie Failinger, E. Clinton Gardner, Patrick Higginbotham, E. Roy Hunt, Robert and Lisa Jerry, Earnest Jones, Jeffrey Lewis, Joseph Little, Frank Maloney, Richard Matasar, Robert Mautz, Francis McCoy, Jon Mills, Robert Moffat, Robert Mounts, William K. Muir, Winston Nagan, Stephen C. O'Connell, Walter Probert, James Quarles, Frank T. Read, Sharon Rush, Frederick Shenkman, Marc H. Shivers, Paula Stahmer, Douglas Sturm, Howard Vogel, Kathleen Waits, Charles Longstreet Weltner III, Raymond Westbrook, Walter Weyrauch, Jerre S. Williams, Jim Williams, Norma Coindreau Williams, and John Minor Wisdom

Creation, plants, animals, and reverence for life: Virginia Allen, Henry Clark, Fredrick J. Doolittle, John Hart, Dieter T. Hessel, Jane Gale, Mildred, Peter, and Rebecca Hiers, Jackson Lee Ice, Suzanne Lewis, Mary Midgley, Anna L. Peterson, Francine Robinson, Erna, Helen, and Magnus Stender, Sibley Towner, Gene Tucker, and Mary Evelyn Tucker

None of whom are responsible for any errors, minor or egregious, that may be found in this book.

Abbreviations

ABD	*Anchor Bible Dictionary*
Add Esth	Additions to Esther
BCE	Before Common Era (BC)
Bel	Bel and the Dragon
CE	Common Era (AD)
1–2 Chron	1–2 Chronicles
Col	Colossians
1–2 Cor	1–2 Corinthians
D	Deuteronomic Code
Dan	Daniel
Deut	Deuteronomy
DH	Deuteronomic history or tradition
E	Northern or Israelite tradition
Eccl	Ecclesiastes (Qoheleth)
Ecclus	Ecclesiasticus (Sirach)
Ep Jer	Epistle (Letter) of Jeremiah
Eph	Ephesians
1–3 Esd	1–3 Esdras
Esth	Esther
Ezek	Ezekiel

Exod	Exodus
Gal	Galatians
Gen	Genesis
H	Holiness Code
Hab	Habakkuk
Heb	Hebrews
Heb.	Hebrew text
Hos	Hosea
IDB	*Interpreter's Bible Dictionary*
IDBSup	*Interpreter's Bible Dictionary Supplemental Volume*
Isa	Isaiah
J	Southern or Judahite tradition
Jas	James
Jdt	Judith
Jer	Jeremiah
JSOTSup	Journal for the Study of the Old Testament Supplement Series
Judg	Judges
1–2 Kgs	1–2 Kings
KJV	King James Version
Lam	Lamentations
Lev	Leviticus
1–4 Macc	1–4 Maccabees
Mal	Malachi
Matt	Matthew
Mic	Micah
Nah	Nahum
Neh	Nehemiah

NOAB-NRSV	*New Oxford Annotated Bible, New Revised Standard Version*
NOAB-RSV	*New Oxford Annotated Bible, Revised Standard Version*
NRSV	New Revised Standard Version
NT	New Testament
Num	Numbers
OT	Old Testament
P	Priestly tradition
PC	Priestly Code
1–2 Pet	1–2 Peter
Phil	Philippians
Pr Man	Prayer of Manasseh
Prov	Proverbs
Ps, Pss	Psalm, Psalms
Qoh	Qoheleth (Ecclesiastes)
RD	Ritual Decalogue
Rev	Revelation
Rom	Romans
RSV	Revised Standard Version
1–2 Sam	1–2 Samuel
Sg Three	Prayer of Azariah and the Song of the Three Young Men
Sir	Sirach (Ecclesiasticus)
Song	Song of Solomon (Canticles)
Sus	Susanna
1–2 Tim	1–2 Timothy
Wis	Wisdom of Solomon
YHWH	Tetragrammaton, representing the divine name

Zech	Zechariah
Zeph	Zephaniah

Prologue

According to the Gospels, Jesus often expressed his deep appreciation of nature—that is, the creation and the creatures God made and cares for: humans, birds and other animals, green fields and flowers. With some exceptions, however, most of the New Testament writers and the apostolic fathers focused their attention on human life in this world and the next but showed little or no interest in the present world or other life-forms that share it as their home. This lack of interest may have derived, at least in part, from their expectation that the present world would soon pass away and be replaced by a new world, where God's rule or kingdom would be manifested and all creation would finally be at peace.

The earliest notable Christian moves toward appreciation and concern for other living thing were those of two major late twelfth- and thirteen-century figures: St. Francis of Assisi and St. Thomas Aquinas. Drawing from the earlier medieval model of the "great chain of being" (God at the top, then angels, then humans, then animals, then plants, and, finally, minerals), Aquinas maintained that not only humans but also animals and plants have souls, and that not only humans but animals, too, could enter to heaven. St. Francis clearly and explicitly loved animals, all kinds of creatures that God had made, and both practiced and advocated concern for their welfare.

Beginning as early as the eighteenth centuries, a number of voices have been heard insisting that not only human beings' but other species' lives and well-being are of great importance, and that human beings are morally obliged to treat them accordingly. For instance, and notably, Thomas Paine, Michel de Montaigne, Francois

Voltaire, Jeremy Bentham, Arthur Schopenhauer, the poet Percy Bysshe Shelley, and John Stuart Mill. And more recently, and just as emphatically, Albert Schweitzer and Mary Midgley.

Until recent times, however, Protestant theology and ethics have focused almost exclusively on the human species, and virtually ignored the rest of creation. Only a few of the prominent twentieth-century Protestant theologians[11] had much to say about God's concern for animals, trees, and other plants, or the kind of relations with them incumbent on humans.

"The environment," meaning all those places on our planet where humans and other life-forms reside, came in for closer attention early in the second half of the twentieth century. In those years, it became obvious, especially to thoughtful natural scientists, that many species of living beings were on the verge of extinction, and that human activities were fast exhausting, degrading, and destroying many of the conditions necessary for sustaining life here on the Earth. Rachel Carson, the Club of Rome group, and E. O. Wilson were among the first to sound the alarm.

At first, their alarms were met with angry denial by many of those involved in the production and sale of toxic hazardous chemicals that had recently been developed as pesticides and herbicides. But others responded by beginning to practice and promote organic farming, or at least more cautious use of chemical fertilizers and pesticides. Another response focused on the increasingly obvious consequences of human overpopulation, a problem flagged centuries earlier by Thomas Malthus. Yet another kind of response, all too familiar, was to look for somebody to blame.

This last response was exemplified by historian Lynn White's condemnation of Christianity and its Bible.[12] Particularly its Bible, and more particularly those verses early in the book of Genesis where it is said that God granted humans "dominion" over the other creatures he had created, and instructed humans to "be fruitful and multiply." Although White's thesis has (properly) been

---

11. Notable exceptions: Tillich, *Shaking of the Foundations*, 76–86; and Gustafson, *Sense of the Divine*.

12. The biblical texts White considered dispositive for his argument appeared first, several hundred years earlier, in what would later be called Jewish Scriptures.

subjected to severe criticism, he should be credited with prompting many Christian, Jewish, Islamic, and secular scholars to look more closely at the book of Genesis and other biblical writings, and to try to understand not only what those writings meant to people in biblical times but also their implications and relevance for understanding and responding to present-day environmental concerns and crises.

These questions are addressed as part of the present book, particularly in footnotes that cite to and often quote from some of the many excellent studies by post-White exegetes and commentators. It is notable that many of these studies describe and apply biblical insights regarding environmental crises not only in America but also to equally or even more urgent environmental crises elsewhere, particularly in contemporary Africa.

However, the present book focuses primarily on biblical texts themselves and their meanings and messages for people in biblical times. Our primary purpose here is to identify and consider those biblical texts that have to do with any and all kinds of relations between—or among—God, humans, and the rest of creation, particularly other living beings.

Many of these texts have received considerable attention since publication of White's challenging essays. What is different about the present study is that it goes beyond the early chapters in the book of Genesis and takes into consideration hundreds of pertinent biblical texts. These texts reflect a wide range of understandings regarding relations between the creation and other living beings; between God and humans; and between and among humanity, the creation, and other life-forms. Chapter headings and subheadings indicate the topics considered here. Many of these topics have received little or no attention in other studies.

A final note: serious attention to these texts and issues is not something new under the sun. Careful studies by Christian scholars date back several centuries. For example, those by the anonymous G. G. (1622), William Drummond (1838), and J. W. Dawson (1875). These, and most of the more recent studies referenced here, are well worth close reading today. Which illustrates an important point in regard to literature—scholarly and otherwise—namely, that the most recent is not necessarily the best.

The Bible itself, though written many centuries ago, is not on that account antiquated and therefore irrelevant in present time. We find and suggest that the Bible still has much to say, if read with a view to understanding it not only as ancient history, legend, law, and literature, but also as a treasury of insights, beliefs, and reflections by faithful and wise people: people who felt called upon to express and record the ways they had experienced and come to understand God's purposes in creating the world and his intention to care for it, for humankind, and for all other living things he created and continues to create.

Introduction

IN RECENT YEARS, NUMEROUS—IF not innumerable—published studies have described and analyzed Western religious traditions and understandings relating to nature, and in particular, the Earth's ecosystems and the living beings they sustain. A few decades ago, it was suggested that modern attitudes that promote the degradation and destruction of nature and other living beings somehow derived from the Bible of Judaism and Christianity. It is now generally recognized that this supposition is too simplistic.[1] Taken as a whole, the Bible presents a much more positive appreciation and affirmation of the importance and value of all creation and all living things than generally assumed by Christians and most others. To be sure, Christianity too often has tended toward anthropocentrism, that is, excessive or even exclusive concern for human well-being, whether in this world or in the life to come.[2] Many of the fine studies cited in the footnotes to this book examine traditional, recent, and current Christian reflections on contemporary environmental issues. A number of these studies identify and examine important biblical texts relating to nature, particularly living beings. But a full

1. See below, ch. 4A. Also, see generally Bouma-Prediger, *For the Beauty*, 76–86; and Oelschlaeger, *Caring for Creation*, 22–27. Christian clergy and laypersons played major roles in eighteenth- and nineteenth-century British animal protection movements and societies. See Preece and Li, *Rights of Animals*, xix, xxxv–xliv.

2. For a brief but excellent discussion of the theocentric vs. anthropocentric character of biblical faith and ethics, see McAfee, "Ecology and Biblical Studies." And see Sturm, *Solidarity and Suffering*, 253–87, pointing to the limits of anthropocentrism, and urging that considerations of deep ecology and social justice undergird recognition of our participation in the communal ground of all existence. As to anthropocentric—and egoistic—tendencies of secular humanism, understood as a *religion*, see Ehrenfeld, *Arrogance of Humanism*; and J. Cobb, *Is It Too Late*, 39–40, 91–97.

and systematic description of the broader range of relevant biblical texts has yet to appear. The present book undertakes to provide such an account. Its main goal is to put before readers the pertinent biblical texts themselves, with a minimum of commentary, so that readers can draw their own conclusions as to the meaning of these texts and their possible relevance as to contemporary issues or concerns. Some of these concerns are discussed briefly, especially in footnotes, which often refer readers to excellent secondary studies where they can be examined more fully.

As groundwork for this study, each biblical "book" or writing was examined closely, and recurrent concerns or themes were identified. The outline or structure of the present book is based upon these findings. Several biblical texts relate to more than one topic or theme. Consequently, some texts are considered more than once. A few particularly pertinent biblical texts are quoted at considerable length.

* * *

Some preliminary background matters should be mentioned briefly before turning to these topics and themes.[3] The pages that follow in this introductory chapter summarize the following preliminary questions: First, the meaning and extent of the biblical "canon." Second, various hypothetical sources incorporated in the present biblical text. Next, the English translations from which biblical quotations here are drawn. Then, certain stylistic matters, including the somewhat problematic question, how to represent the divine name, and some general comments about interpreting the substance of biblical faith, which is sometimes called "biblical theology." And finally, a brief discussion of biblical faith and ethics. This introduction concludes with a short summary of the topics examined in the chapters that follow.

Many issues and texts considered here involve somewhat complicated literary and historical, as well as theological questions.

---

3. Readers already familiar with these background matters or not interested in them may wish to skip ahead to the following chapters, which attempt to describe the substance of biblical texts relating to our topic.

Readers may wish to make use of one or more of the many excellent study Bibles and single or multivolume modern Bible commentaries and Bible dictionaries now available. Occasionally footnote references are made to discussions and commentaries in the pages of the *New Oxford Annotated Bible* edition of the NRSV,[4] referred to here as the *NOAB-NRSV*.

THE BIBLICAL CANON

Will the real Bible stand up? This question is implicit in discussions or arguments about reading "the Bible" in public schools. The problem is that not everyone has the same Bible.[5] For Jews, the Bible, Tanach, or "Hebrew Scriptures," includes only those "books" or writings that Christians refer to as "the Old Testament." In Jewish circles, these books are categorized and arranged differently: first the Torah (Law), then the Nevi'im (Prophets, also including Joshua, Judges, 1 and 2 Samuel, and 1 and 2 Kings), and then the Ketuvim (Writings, consisting of all the other books). According to legend, Jewish authorities decided which books should be included in Jewish Scripture at a gathering held at Jamnia, around 90 CE.[6] At that time, if not later, a number of writings or books, most of which were then known only in Greek versions, were excluded from the Jewish canon. The term "canon" refers to those writings officially recognized as constituting Scripture in a particular religious community.

Many of the excluded writings continued to be regarded as part of Christian Scriptures, which also included the Jewish Scriptures so recognized at Jamnia. Together, these writings later came to be known in Christian circles as "the Old Testament." The writings which, in time, formed "the New Testament" were being composed during the period between the middle of the first and the early

---

4. Coogan, *New Oxford Annotated Bible*. In this study Bible, pages are numbered separately for the Hebrew Bible (HB), Old Testament Apocrypha (AP), New Testament (NT), and essays at the back of the volume (ES).

5. See *NOAB-NRSV*, 453–60 ES; and Richard Hiers, *Trinity Guide to Bible*, 18–21.

6. The present book follows the conventional and inclusive practice of designating the Common Era as CE, and the earlier eras BCE, that is, Before the Common Era.

second centuries CE. A number of other Christian writings were in circulation during the first several centuries CE. For some time, it remained to be determined which of these should be accorded the status of Scripture. To address this problem, beginning in the latter part of the second century CE, various bishops and other church leaders began to keep lists of writings they thought should be included or excluded. Consensus eventually was reached, and by the end of the Council of Chalcedon in 450 CE, it had been determined that those writings it now contains would constitute the New Testament.

Christians continued to use Greek versions of the Old Testament, particularly the Septuagint, as Scripture. In time, Greek became less familiar to Christians living in the Mediterranean world, while Latin was becoming the common language for people of many nationalities. In the late fourth century CE, the scholarly monk Jerome undertook to translate both the Old and New Testaments into Latin. The result of his efforts came to be known as "the Vulgate," so named because it was written in Latin, the "vulgar," i.e., common, language of the Western world at the time. Jerome considered several of the writings found in the Septuagint somewhat less authoritative, though still important. These he characterized as "deuterocanonical." The Vulgate remained the most influential version of Scripture for much of Western Christianity for many centuries.

In the sixteenth century CE, Martin Luther, who was to become, so to speak, the father of the Protestant Reformation, concluded that several of the writings included in the Vulgate had been composed well after the lifetime of their purported authors and that, perhaps for other reasons as well, they should no longer be regarded as Scripture. In effect, Luther reverted to the Jewish canon as settled at Jamnia, so far as the Old Testament was concerned. Luther valued the other writings, however, and included many of them in his translation of the Bible into German, but under a secondary category, eventually designated as the Old Testament Apocrypha. Protestant churches have generally followed Luther's lead in this regard. At the Council of Trent, later in the sixteenth century, Roman Catholic authorities reaffirmed Jerome's

Vulgate as their official Bible and recognized Jerome's deuterocanonical books as fully scriptural, except First Esdras and the Prayer of Manasseh.

In the meantime, Eastern Christianity continued to use Greek and also Slavonic versions of the Bible, which contained certain other writings that, in time, were characterized as either apocrypha or appendix. These included 3 and 4 Maccabees and Ps 151, as well as 1 and 2 Esdras and the Prayer of Manasseh.[7]

For purposes of the present study, the Bible or the biblical canon is understood inclusively: that is, as including all writings considered Scripture in Judaism, as well as those classified as deuterocanonical or apocryphal, or at least as part of an appendix in one or more of the branches of contemporary Christianity, along with the writings that constitute what Christians call the New Testament. These writings are all included in the *NOAB-NRSV*.

BIBLICAL "SOURCES"

Not all biblical scholars agree that the Bible was derived from earlier sources or strands of tradition. Many faithful readers believe that the Bible was divinely inspired or revealed by God verbatim, and written down in its present form all at one time. These readers may wish to pass lightly over references made in this book to such "sources." *What is important in any case is what is said in the biblical texts themselves.*

Nevertheless, there is some consensus among many biblical scholars about certain hypothetical early sources, that is, written or oral traditions, which, in time, presumably, were combined and edited so as to form the ancient texts that constitute the basis for modern translations of the Bible. Recognizing that certain texts may reflect particular historical circumstances or characteristic concerns can sometimes suggest meanings that otherwise might be overlooked. Distinctive understandings or perspectives often

---

7. These and several other ancient books or writings apparently had been considered as Scripture in some early Jewish or early Christian circles. Modern translations and commentaries on these writings are available in Charlesworth, *Old Testament Pseudepigrapha*.

seem to be associated with certain strands of tradition or sources. For instance, as will be seen, certain biblical traditions evaluate animal sacrifices quite differently.[8]

Two sources (or edited collections of tradition) are commonly thought to underlie the first several chapters of the book of Genesis. One of these, commonly designated J, probably recorded southern or Judahite traditions. This tradition generally refers to God by the Hebrew divine name *YHWH*,[9] usually translated in English as "the Lord." This source may have been composed as early as the tenth or ninth century BCE. The other hypothetical source, P,[10] uses the divine name *Elohim*, translated in English versions as "God." The letter P stands for "priestly," because it is thought that those who composed or edited this source were priests who were particularly interested in such matters as priests' prerogatives, rituals, and sacrificial offerings. P tradition is thought to have been collected or written down during the sixth or fifth centuries BCE.[11]

The main sources for biblical law are the several law codes that have been identified in the books of Exodus, Leviticus, Numbers, and Deuteronomy. Although those codes are found in these four books, they are not identical or coextensive with any of them. Codes also are to be distinguished from individual laws.

A law code may be defined as a collection of laws intended to be operative at any given time in a particular social system. It is not surprising to find embedded in biblical tradition a number of

---

8. See below, ch. 5.

9. These four letters transliterate the underlying Hebrew consonants, referred to sometimes as the Tetragrammaton. In traditional Judaism, this name is not to be pronounced, and an altogether different term (*adonai*, often pronounced *adonoi*), is used when reading aloud. Biblical translators commonly substitute the term the Lord for YHWH. The names Jehovah and Yahweh represent attempts to pronounce the Tetragrammaton. These names are not used in this book, except in occasional quotations from secondary studies.

10. P narrative tradition has been identified in all of the first four books of the Bible, Genesis through Leviticus.

11. Another hypothetical source, E, is thought to appear later in Genesis, and to run through several following "books" of the Bible. This source also uses the divine name *Elohim*. For further discussion of these and other hypothetical sources, as well as a sketch of biblical history and other matters of background interest, see Richard Hiers, *Trinity Guide to Bible*, 14–18; and *NOAB*-NRSV, 3–6 HB; 460–71 ES; and 507–25 ES.

law codes that draw upon many centuries of Israelite, Judahite, and Jewish experience. These biblical codes are all represented as versions of the laws given by God (or YHWH) to Moses at Mt. Sinai (or Mt. Horeb), and then transmitted by him to the people of Israel during several decades of their wandering in "the wilderness" after leaving Egypt but before entering into the land of Canaan. Biblical scholars do not entirely agree as to the extent and dating of these codes, so the descriptions here should be considered tentative. For purposes of this study, interest is directed primarily to the content or substance of biblical tradition, not to historical, textual, or literary analysis.

The earliest and shortest of these collections, the so-called Ritual Decalogue (or RD), is contained in Exod 34:11–28. The first comprehensive collection, the Covenant Code (CC), also known as the Book of the Covenant, is found in Exod 20:1—23:33. The CC may date from as early as the twelfth or eleventh century BCE.

A few laws set out in the Covenant Code evidently were incorporated later into the Deuteronomic Code (D), which is usually identified as Deut 5:1–21 and 12:1—26:19. The Deuteronomic Code may have been written down only a century or two after the Covenant Code. However, a number of the provisions found in Deut 12–19 and 26 were probably added subsequently in connection with the Deuteronomic reform, a major institutional innovation carried out late in the seventh century BCE. This innovation established Jerusalem as the only place where YHWH/God could be worshiped with sacrificial offerings, called for the closing of all other shrines, and established a number of new institutions or practices in order to accommodate these arrangements.[12]

The next codification can be dated around the middle of the seventh century BCE. This is the Holiness Code (H), found in Leviticus 18–26.[13] The Holiness Code does not require that sacrificial worship take place only in Jerusalem; and it refers twice to plural "sanctuaries" (Lev 21:23; 26:31). It may, therefore, have

12. See Richard Hiers, *Trinity Guide to Bible*, 53–54.

13. Interpreters often include Lev 17 in the Holiness Code. Because of its affinity to characteristic priestly motifs, however, that chapter is considered part of the Priestly Code in this book.

been set down prior to the Deuteronomic reform. Parts of the Holiness Code, however, may have been edited or revised by P, or the priestly editors, who refer twice to the "tent of meeting,"[14] a term signifying what P tradition visualized as a portable prototype of the later Jerusalem temple. Priestly tradition held that the Israelites took this tent around with them during their journey through the wilderness following their escape from Egypt.[15] Ritual purity, sexual propriety, and social welfare are leading concerns in H.

The most recent and extensive collection of laws is commonly characterized as the Priestly Code (PC). It is thought to have been written down during the late sixth or fifth century BCE, under the auspices of priests who were then serving at the Jerusalem temple. It is so named because its provisions typically refer to sacrificial offerings and other procedures and ceremonies in which priests figured prominently. The so-called Priestly Code includes all laws contained in Exod 24:1 through Num 36:13, except those attributable to the RD and H. Because it is so extensive, it might be characterized more aptly as the Priestly Legislation.

Laws relating to nature and respect or reverence for life are found in all of these biblical law codes. Occasionally it is possible to trace certain developments or changes in specific laws where earlier versions appear to have been modified or abandoned, and new provisions added. As will be seen, many other types of biblical writings also provide insights into the biblical understanding and appreciation for nature and life lived in its midst. Namely, Old Testament narratives, psalms, wisdom books, prophets, and a number of New Testament texts.

QUOTATIONS AND LANGUAGE

In the present study, quotations from the Bible usually are taken from the New Revised Standard Version, occasionally drawing on alternative translations indicated in NRSV footnotes. Like most

---

14. Lev 19:21; 24:13.

15. P tradition seems to have understood that beginning in the wilderness period, the people of Israel always worshiped in just one place, namely, this portable "tent" or "tabernacle."

other modern Bible translations, this version necessarily is based upon hundreds of early manuscripts written in a number of ancient languages, including Hebrew and Greek.[16] There are several other excellent modern translations, but the NRSV generally provides English readers a close approximation to the meaning of the underlying ancient manuscripts.[17] The NRSV translators attempted to use gender-inclusive language where such inclusion is implicit in the biblical context or where such inclusive language appeals to modern sensibilities. Readers often find it instructive to compare two or more different translations of a given text.

The Hebrew terms typically used for the divine name (*YHWH* or *Elohim*) do not, as such, specify gender.[18] Throughout biblical tradition, however, God is generally referred to in male terms, and this book generally uses such language in discussing what is found in biblical texts. In biblical perspective, however, God was sometimes thought of in ways that embrace both male and female, or that transcend concepts of gender altogether.[19]

THE OLD AND NEW TESTAMENTS, AND BIBLICAL THEOLOGY

Modern Christians differ in their understandings as to the authority of the Old Testament. Marcion of Padua (or Sinope), ca. 140 CE, is distinguished by having been the first "heretic" known to have been so identified in the history of Christianity. Marcion

16. See "Translations of the Bible into English," in *NOAB*-NRSV, 466–71 ES.

17. The Revised Standard Version sometimes provides a more literal rendering of the language found in the ancient texts. This text is available, among other places, in May and Metzger, *Oxford Annotated Bible*. In some instances, the present writer has chosen variant readings found in the RSV in order to bring out additional relevant connotations and meanings. In such instances, the quoted text is placed between brackets or noted in parentheses.

18. The Greek term *theos*, used in Greek versions of the Bible, is masculine in form, as is the Greek *ho kurios*, translated as "the Lord."

19. See Gen 1:27 and 5:1–2, suggesting that the "image" or "likeness" of God embraced both "male and female." See also Hos 13:8, comparing God to a female "bear robbed of her cubs." A number of other texts also associate female gender with God. See, e.g., Prov 8:1–32; Isa 49:15; and Wis 7:24—8:1. See generally Trible, *God and Rhetoric*.

urged that the Old Testament (along with the God there revealed or described) should be abandoned altogether, and that Christians should regard only certain writings (some of which came to be included in the New Testament) as their Scripture.[20] Other Christian interpreters believe that the Old Testament was largely fulfilled in the person of Jesus or in the events described in the New Testament, and so, as such, has little, if any, continuing relevance or authority. Still others regard the Old Testament as an inspired writing, or at least as a source of profound insights as to God and God's relations with the created world, humankind, and all other created beings. There are many other perspectives, particularly as to the authority of biblical law.

The present book recognizes that readers may hold differing views as to whether Old Testament texts should be understood as relevant or authoritative in modern times, and does not address that question.[21] It is observed, however, that Christian Bibles do include both the Old Testament and the New Testament, and that many also include, at least within the penumbra of Scripture, some or all of the deuterocanonicals or apocryphal Old Testament writings. The present objective is to put before readers the principal

---

20. Some modern Christians, perhaps intending to avoid offending Jewish sensibilities, refer to the Old Testament as the Hebrew Scriptures, and to the New Testament as the Christian Scriptures. This nomenclature might imply that those who use it no longer consider the Old Testament part of Christian Scriptures. Moreover, it is inapt. The Christian Old Testament is not identical with the Hebrew Scriptures or the Scriptures of Judaism. The writings in each are arranged in different sequences. Christian Bibles often include the Old Testament Apocrypha or deuterocanonicals, while Jewish Scriptures never do. Christian Bibles are generally translated into English or other modern languages, while, unless translated, the Hebrew Scriptures are in Hebrew—and Aramaic. Modern Christian translations of the Old Testament draw on other ancient manuscript sources, such as the Syriac, Vulgate, Septuagint, and Dead Sea Scrolls (referred to in RSV and NRSV footnotes as "other ancient versions"). At any rate, Christian Scriptures comprise both the Old Testament and the New Testament, not just the latter.

21. But see Mastaler, *Woven Together*, 96–97: "Christians ought to draw on their ancient biblical stories as a source for inspiration and illumination for a life lived well in the world today. To do so is to read them in ways that are responsible to the signs of the times in which we live. Christians can and must reclaim an ancient sense of what it means to be a person before their God, before others, and before the whole family of creation, but in ways that are informed by what the hard and social sciences tell us about the world and also about what it means to be human."

biblical texts relating to "nature," that is, as understood in biblical faith, the whole creation.[22] As will be seen, these texts consistently express appreciation of the created world and all kinds of living things. Some texts explicitly affirm the goodness of this world and of the many kinds of living beings who dwell upon it. And many of the texts advocate what we now refer to as "environmental ethics" or the ethics of "reverence for life."[23]

The approach followed here proceeds along the lines of "biblical theology" as described many years ago by Krister Stendahl.[24] In brief, the point is to recognize the theological and normative beliefs and affirmations set out in biblical texts, understood in their historical and cultural contexts. This approach leaves it to the reader, socially located in whichever religious or secular community she may be, to reflect for herself upon the relevance of the biblical beliefs and affirmations or values described here. The present book occasionally mentions some possible implications, particularly in footnote references, but does not undertake a theological-normative analysis as to possible applications of biblical texts for contemporary ethics and social policy issues. Many of the authors or sources cited in footnotes do offer important suggestions as to these matters.

BIBLICAL FAITH AND ETHICS

Ethics necessarily is based upon some kind of faith. People act on the basis of what they believe and experience as meaningful and valuable. Humanistic or anthropocentric ethics is grounded on the belief that human beings are of the highest importance. Those who so believe respond by acting in caring ways for other human beings.

---

22. See Murphy, *Haunted by Paradise*, xvi-xvii: "Jews focus on Old Testament ethics and Christians on New Testament ethics. I will insist that there is no Old Testament or New Testament ethics—only a unified biblical ethics. Of course, Jews, Orthodox Christians, Catholics, and Protestants have their own distinctive Bibles, containing partly different books."

23. In this book, reverence or respect for life is understood as a way of expressing appreciation for or concern about living beings, human, other creatures, and also trees and plant life.

24. Stendahl, "Biblical Theology, Contemporary."

For some such humanists, nature is seen either as enemy territory to be "conquered"[25] or as raw material to be exploited for human benefit, whether now or at some future time. In notable contrast, biblical ethics is grounded on the belief that God is the Creator of all that exists, that God values and cares for his entire creation, and that human beings and all other kinds of beings have meaning and value in relation to him. In biblical faith, the appropriate reciprocal response of those who so believe is to regard and act affirmatively toward all that God has made and cares for.[26]

* * *

THEMES OR TOPICS CONSIDERED IN THE FOLLOWING CHAPTERS

A great many biblical texts focus upon God's relationship to both the creation and the creatures that he has brought, and continues to bring, into being. The chapters in part 1 focus on texts that primarily have to do with God's relationships with the nonhuman world, including what we call nature, particularly living beings, and the nonhuman world's relationships with God. In these texts, human beings play only incidental roles, at most serving God's purposes in regard to other living things.

Chapter 1 initially considers a variety of texts that identify and affirm God as Creator of all that is. Implicit in the understanding of God as Creator is a positive view of nature: of the world, indeed, of the entire cosmos. This positive view extends especially to living beings. Several texts explicitly affirm the goodness of all that exists. This affirmation is at the heart of the biblical ethic of care for

---

25. See Ehrenfeld, *Arrogance of Humanism*. The illogical and illusory character of the idea that humans should or even can engage in the "conquest of nature" also was critiqued many decades ago by Lewis, *Abolition of Man*.

26. See Asamoah-Gyado, "Foreword," xii: "The natural world has largely been ignored as a subject of theological education and Christian spirituality. . . . The underlying thesis of the biblical scholarship in this volume is that the Bible has much to say about ecotheology and that continued desacralization would spell the doom for the whole of humanity."

all creation. Lest there be any doubt about it, several biblical texts identify God as the One to whom all creation and all creatures belong. For instance, the psalmist proclaims:

> The heavens are yours, the earth also is yours,
> the world and all that is in it—you have founded them.
> (Ps 89:11)

Chapter 2 examines numerous texts that acknowledge and celebrate God's sovereignty or dominion over all creation and all creatures. Many of these texts have to do with God's compassionate care for the earth or the land, and for all kinds of creatures "of all flesh." In contrast to what may be all too typically human indifference to other creatures, Sirach, also known as Ecclesiasticus, summarizes the inclusive character of divine caring as follows:

> The compassion of human beings is for their neighbors,
> but the compassion of the Lord is for every living thing.
> (Sir 18:13)

Chapter 3 draws attention to a large number of texts that for the most part have been neglected in studies of biblical understandings of nature and environmental ethics. These are texts that declare that the heavens, the earth, and the sea glorify God; moreover, that all kinds of living creatures pray to or praise God for giving them food and water, or for his wondrous ways and for the joy of being. These texts are not to be dismissed as simply anthropomorphic projections. They express an appreciation for the direct relationship other beings have with the Source of their being. Psalm 150:6, which concludes not only that psalm but the entire book of Psalms, epitomizes this latter theme:

> Let everything that breathes praise YHWH!
> Praise YHWH!

In part 2 attention turns to texts relating to the place of human beings in the world of other living beings. Proponents of "dominion theology" and ecologically oriented critics of biblical religion alike sometimes assume or assert that biblical ethics is entirely anthropocentric: that other kinds of creatures are understood to exist only to serve human purposes. A few biblical texts provide some grounds for this idea. But a great many other texts present a quite different picture of relationships between human beings and other creatures before God and under his dominion.

Chapter 4 reviews a number of texts found in the early chapters of Genesis that describe various kinds of interactions between God, humans, and other creatures. A few of these texts have received considerable attention in recent discussions of biblical faith and environmental ethics. It is observed here that the much-cited words "be fruitful and multiply" apply not only to the primordial progenitors of humankind but also to the ancient forebears of all other creatures of land, sea, and air. Also, it is noteworthy that, read in their biblical contexts, these texts referred to the situation of humankind and other species only in antiquity. These texts were not repeated as instructions or commands calling for perpetual and unlimited multiplication in either later biblical or subsequent historical time.

As the stories are told in Genesis, both before and during the era of the biblical flood, humans and other animate creatures were vegetarians. Afterwards, humans were told that they might eat other creatures. But they were not to eat the blood of animals killed for food. Their blood must be returned the Creator, for the animals' blood constituted their life, and that was to be respected and preserved. Moreover, as the story is told, following the flood, God made the famous "rainbow" covenant not only with humans but, as stated several times in Gen 9, with all other creatures as well. Genesis 9:16 typifies these statements; here God promises:

> When the [rain]bow is in the clouds, I will see it and remember the everlasting covenant between [me] and every living creature of all flesh that is on the earth.

Chapter 5 examines biblical traditions regarding animal sacrifices. Paradoxically, these laws showed profound concern and respect for the "life" of the animals sacrificed. Their life was associated with their blood, which was not to be eaten but, rather, returned to God. Important as sacrifices were in certain portions of biblical tradition, however, many other biblical writings express strong opposition to the whole theory and practice of animal sacrifice. All creatures already belong to God, who, it was said, does not need or desire sacrificial offerings. This theme is affirmed explicitly, for example, in Ps 50:9–12:

> I will not accept a bull from your house,
>   or goats from your folds.
> For every wild animal of the forest is mine,
>   [as are] the cattle on a thousand hills.
> I know all the birds of the air,
>   and all that moves in the field is mine.
> If I were hungry, I would not tell you;
>   for the world and all that is in it is mine.

Chapter 6 considers a number of biblical texts that recognize that humans and other creatures are closely related and have much in common. All alike come from the earth or ground, and all alike return to it. All share the same breath or spirit given them by God. And all are subject to divine judgment. Moreover, it is often the sad, if unjust, fate of other creatures to suffer the consequences of human wickedness or depravity. A quotation from the prophet Hosea illustrates this connection. The people of Israel had violated their covenant relationship with YHWH/God and broken many of his commandments:

> Therefore, the land mourns,
>   and all who live in it languish,
> together with the wild animals,
>   and the birds of the air,
> even the fish of the sea are perishing. (Hos 4:3)

Chapter 7 focuses on biblical texts that compare God with humans *and* with a variety of animals and other creatures. It is sometimes said that the biblical image of God is anthropomorphic: that God is represented in the image of humanity. Actually, only a few texts attribute human features to God. On the other hand, several texts represent God as being like other creatures in various ways. A number of texts also suggest comparisons between humans and animals or birds, or even between humans and plants, flowers, or trees. Some of these comparisons express disapproval of the ways of both humans and the animals they resemble.[27] But many texts underscore admirable traits in other creatures (also in plants, flowers, and trees) in ways that are complimentary when attributed to humans. For instance, Prov 5:18 advises husbands:

> Rejoice in the wife of your youth,
> a lovely deer, a graceful doe.

Chapter 8 examines another feature of biblical tradition that has largely been neglected. There we consider several texts indicating that people in biblical times were interested and careful observers of the flora and fauna about them. Such texts often make clear a sense of profound appreciation and sometimes awe. Both directly and indirectly, biblical tradition calls for interest in and concern about nature. Plants and animals were not simply regarded as grist for human mills. Some texts suggest that people would do well to listen to or adopt the ways of other creatures. For instance, Job, responding to the dubious advice of his purported friends, tells them:

> [Just] ask the animals, and they will teach you;
>   the birds of the air, and they will tell you;
> ask the plants of the earth, and they will teach you;
> and the fish of the sea will declare to you. (Job 12:7–8)[28]

Chapter 9 explores numerous texts that more explicitly concern what we now would call "environmental ethics": texts that spell out what people should or should not do in relation to the Earth and other living beings. The first part of this chapter examines what might be called the biblical "land ethic," as well as texts relating to agricultural practices, distribution of the fruit of various kinds of harvests, and care of trees. The second part focuses

---

27. No texts, however, refer disparagingly to humans as "behaving like animals." In the Bible, animal behavior is never characterized as gross, disgusting, or immoral. Humans are seen to be like animals in many positive ways. And to be depraved in their own ways.

28. Job's response here follows what is perhaps the most sardonic line in the Bible, where Job addresses these self-righteous but—as it turns out—deluded critics: "No doubt you are the people, and wisdom will die with you" (Job 12:1). See Job 42:7, where YHWH says to the "friends": "You have not spoken of me what is right, as my servant Job has."

on biblical laws, narratives, and other texts that refer specifically to human involvement with other animate species. Both kinds of concerns are exemplified in Lev 25:1–7:

> YHWH spoke to Moses on Mount Sinai, saying: Speak to the people of Israel and say to them: When you enter the land that I am giving you, the land shall observe a Sabbath for YHWH. Six years you shall sow your field, and six years you shall prune your vineyard, and gather in their yield; but in the seventh year there shall be a Sabbath of complete rest for the land, a Sabbath for YHWH; you shall not sow your field or prune your vineyard. You shall not reap the aftergrowth of your harvest or gather the grapes of your unpruned vine: it shall be a year of complete rest for the land. You may eat what the land yields during its Sabbath—you, your male and female slaves, your hired [. . .] laborers [and the sojourners] who live with you; for your [cattle] also, and for the wild animals that are in your land all its yield shall be for food.

Chapter 10 looks at another strangely neglected feature of biblical tradition: the many texts that see *other* creatures as agents of God in dealing with people. Usually, biblical tradition is thought to focus on human activity: what humans do or should do, or do not or should not do. Several texts, however, represent other creatures as agents of God's beneficent purposes in dealing with people. Conversely, other creatures often are represented as agents of divine judgment *against* persons or against entire nations, including the people of Israel. Moses, for instance, is said to have warned his fellow Israelites what would happen if they failed to obey the laws YHWH/God had given them:

> Your corpses shall be food for every bird of the air, and the animals of the earth,
> and there shall be no one to frighten them away. (Deut 28:26)

Chapter 11 concludes by turning to texts that depict various aspects of the natural—or supernatural—conditions expected to characterize life in the future or messianic age. Other biblical terms for this era include "the coming age," "the age to come," "the world to come," "the "new world," and "the kingdom of God." As will be seen, references to this future age or era do not always or necessarily mention the presence of a (or the) messiah. Many of these texts anticipate that not only people but also all kinds of other creatures will be present and enjoy life in the coming age.

Some New Testament texts look for the establishment of God's kingdom either on earth or upon a greatly transformed earth. Other texts look for a new heaven and a new earth, and still others expect the righteous to be taken up into the air or heaven. Old Testament expectations generally look for the fulfillment of life in the coming age on this earth. There would continue to be harvests, but then in great abundance—as if the primordial curse upon the ground had been removed.[29] There would be trees, some quite remarkable ones. And there would be animals and other creatures of all kinds, as many as came off the "ark" after the flood. Then, after the flood, God made his "everlasting covenant" with all these creatures. The prophet Hosea likewise declared that in the future, God would establish a covenant of peace with all kinds of creatures:

> I will make for them a covenant on that day with the wild animals, the birds of the air, and the creeping things of the ground; and I will abolish the bow, the sword, and war from the land; and I will make you lie down in safety. (Hos 2:18)

* * *

A few years ago, an observant biblical scholar wrote:

> The most important contribution biblical scholarship has to make to theological education and religious studies in the area of the environment, is to bring greater methodological sophistication to the exegetical component of theological and ethical reflection. As long as the primary religions of the West form the core of theological education and a part of the religious studies curriculum, and as long as the Bible remains the foundational document of those religions, exegesis of the Bible will be an inescapable task, arguably the first task, and the work of biblical scholars will remain the point of departure

---

29. See Gen 3:17–19; 4:11–12; cf. Gen 8:21.

for theological and ethical reflection on the environment for the foreseeable future.[30]

---

30. McAfee, "Ecology and Biblical Studies," 41. Several scholars have made significant contributions towards accomplishing this task. For example: Anderson, *From Creation*; Austin, *Hope for the Land*; Barr, "Man and Nature"; Gushee, *Sacredness of Human Life*, 388–410; Malchow, "Contrasting Views of Nature"; Rolston, "Bible and Ecology"; Santmire, *Travail of Nature*, ch. 10; Simkins, *Creator and Creation*; and Steck, *World and Environment*. Many other important studies are referred to in the bibliography at the end of the present book. See also Hessel, "Bibliography," listing over seven hundred titles relating to pertinent biblical themes and texts.

PART ONE

YHWH/God, the Created World, and All Creation

In the beginning, God created the heavens and the earth. The earth was without form and void, and darkness was upon the face of the deep; and the spirit of God was moving over the face of the waters. . . .

And God saw everything that he had made, and behold, it was very good. (Gen 1:1–2, 31 RSV)

Then God said to Noah and to his sons with him, "As for me, I am establishing my covenant with you and your descendants after you, and with every living creature that is with you, the birds, the domestic animals, and every animal of the earth with you, as many as came out of the ark, every animal of the earth.[1] I establish my covenant with you, that never again shall all flesh be cut off by the waters of a flood, and never again shall there be a flood to destroy the earth." God said, "This is the sign of the covenant that I make between me and you and every living creature that is with you, for all future generations. I have set my bow in the clouds, and it shall be a sign of the covenant between me and the earth. When I bring clouds over the earth and the bow is seen in the clouds, I will remember my covenant that is between me and you and every

---

1. The translation given here quotes the Hebrew version. In Hebrew, repetition indicates emphasis. The RSV and NRSV translations, which are based on Greek versions, omit the second reference to "every animal of the earth."

living creature of all flesh; and the waters shall never again become a flood to destroy all flesh. When the bow is in the clouds, I will see it and remember the everlasting covenant between God and every living creature of all flesh that is on the earth." God said to Noah, "This is the sign of the covenant that I have established between me and all flesh that is on the earth." (Gen 9:8–17)

Biblical tradition repeatedly affirms that YHWH/God is the Creator of and Sovereign over all that exists.[2] Numerous texts declare that all that he made—all creation and all creatures—are his, and so all belong to him. YHWH/God's concern for the well-being of the whole creation comes to expression again and again: his care and compassion for the land itself and for all kinds of living beings—not only domestic animals but also wildlife—and for trees. A narrative early in the book of Genesis sets out the covenant that YHWH/God said that he established not only with Noah and his descendants but also with all kinds of living creatures and their descendants for all future generations to come.

Both implicitly and explicitly, biblical tradition affirms the goodness of the created world and of all the living beings YHWH/God has brought into existence. God's sovereignty or dominion over all creation is affirmed in several ways. And a considerable number of texts depict a wide range of creatures relating directly to God: looking, praying, or crying to, and blessing and rejoicing in him. Some texts even say that the land rejoices in him—or in times of disaster, mourns or grieves over what has happened. All these texts have to do with direct relationships between God and the creation and creatures that he made. It is perhaps striking that so many biblical texts concern these relationships, without reference to the role or place of human beings, as if to say that God does not need human beings in order to be God.[3] Such texts will be examined here in part 1 of this book.

---

2. As will be seen, certain NT texts also ascribe a role in creation to Christ, and/or affirm his sovereignty or dominion in or at the end of history.

3. Human beings are considered in pt. 1, but only to the extent that they function as agents of God's purposes in saving all kinds of species from extinction during the great flood. See ch. 2B5. The significance of human activity in connection with the flood is considered again in pt. 2, where the emphasis is on human relationships with

CHAPTER 1

YHWH/God's Good Creation

ALTHOUGH THE POINT MAY be obvious, it should not be overlooked that according to biblical tradition, all that exists was created by God. No evil being had anything to do with the creation; nor was the world made by some deity who happened to be having a fit or tantrum. Nor is the world thought to be illusory or unreal. Several biblical texts state explicitly what is already implicit in recognition of God as Creator of all that is: namely, that everything that is, is good, and that all creation belongs to him. God is also acknowledged as Sovereign or Lord over all creation; moreover, God is understood as compassionate, caring for the creation and for all the creatures he has made. An important feature of biblical faith often neglected is the corollary understanding that all kinds of creatures—not only humans—have a direct relationship with God: praying to him, praising and blessing him, and rejoicing before him.

A. YHWH/GOD: CREATOR OF ALL THAT IS

Throughout biblical tradition, God is affirmed and praised as the Creator of all that exists: the entire cosmos, the heavens, the earth,

---

and responsibilities in regard to other species.

and all living beings.[1] This understanding is expressed at the very beginning of the Bible in the two Genesis creation stories.[2] The P creation story (Gen 1:1—2:4a) details God's creation of all that is over the course of six days: his calling forth light and darkness, and the firmament or heaven above; his separating the seas from the dry lands; his calling on the earth to bring forth plants and trees of all kinds; his making the sun, the moon, and the stars, and setting them in the heavens; his calling on the waters to bring forth all kinds of sea creatures and birds, and calling on the earth, again, this time to bring forth all kinds of earth creatures, including wildlife, cattle, and "everything that creeps upon the ground"; and finally, creating humankind, both male and female.

The J creation story that follows (Gen 2:4b–24), presents a different sequence; and some features of the P creation story are not specifically mentioned. Here, everything is said to have taken place in a single day. The story begins, "In the day that YHWH/God made the earth and the heavens..." After doing so, YHWH/God watered the earth; formed the first man from the watered ground and "breathed into his nostrils the breath of life"; then planted a garden and made a variety of trees to grow there; put the man in the garden; afterwards made all kinds of animals and birds to keep him company; and, finally, made the first woman from the man's rib.[3] Both creation stories give expression to the mystery of life: YHWH/God had created so many different and remarkable living

---

1. See Berry, *Sex, Economy*, 196–97: "If we read the Bible... we will discover that humans do not own the world or any part of it.... We will discover that God made not only the parts of Creation that we humans understand and approve but all of it.... And so we must credit God with the making of biting and stinging insects, poisonous serpents, weeds, poisonous weeds, dangerous beasts, and disease-causing micro-organisms. That we may disapprove of these things does not mean that God is in error or that He ceded some of the work of Creation to Satan; it means that we are deficient in wholeness, harmony, and understanding—that is, we are 'fallen.'"

2. Genesis 1:1–10 can be read to suggest that God worked with preexisting materials, which he then separated, respectively, into waters above the firmament (or heaven), waters below the firmament, and the seas. See *NOAB-NRSV* translation.

3. In this account, it is not said that God made or separated the seas from the dry lands, though four rivers are named; nor is there any mention of his calling into being the sun, moon, and stars, or specific reference to his creating "every creeping thing that creeps upon the earth."

things. It was beyond the power of humans to do so—as is still the case in modern and purportedly postmodern times.

That God created everything that exists is celebrated again and again in the psalms[4] and throughout the Bible. For example, in Ps 33:6–9:

> By the word of YHWH the heavens were made,
> and all their host by the breath of his mouth.
> He gathered the waters of the sea as in a bottle;
> he put the deeps in storehouses.

Or again, in Isaiah:

> For thus says YHWH,
> Who created the heavens
> (he is God!),
> who formed the earth and made it
> (he established it;
> he did not create it a chaos,
> he formed it to be inhabited!)
> I am YHWH and there is no other. (Isa 45:18)

Likewise, Ezra exclaims in praise to God: "You . . . alone have made heavens, the heaven of heavens, with all their host, the earth and all that is on it, the seas and all that is in them. To all of them you give life" (Neh 9:6).[5]

Biblical tradition views creation not only as something that occurred in the distant past, but also as a continuing process in which YHWH/God is engaged. Thus, for example, the prophet Isaiah speaks on behalf of YHWH/God in the present tense: "I form light and create darkness, I make weal and create woe; I YHWH do all these things" (Isa 45:7). So also Jer 31:35:

> Thus says YHWH who gives the sun for light by day
> and the fixed order of the moon
> and the stars for light at night,

---

4. See also, e.g., Pss 74:12–17; 89:11–12; 95:4–5; 102:25; 121:2; 124:8; and 136:4–9.

5. See also Job 26:7–10; 38–1–11; Isa 40:12; 42:5; 45:12; 48:13; Jer 10:12; 27:5; Jonah 1:9; Sir 16:26–30; 18:1–2; Bel v. 5; Pr Man, vv. 2–3; Rom 1:19–20; and Rev 14:6–7. As to biblical creation stories and other OT texts seen as a basis for understanding and critiquing specific contemporary environmental crises, see, e.g., Kalugila, "Old Testament Insights"; and Fihavango, "Quest for Ecotheology."

> who stirs up the sea so that its waves roar—
> YHWH of hosts is his name.

Thus from the standpoint of biblical tradition, creation is ongoing, a continuing process, not just something that happened long ago.[6] YHWH/God made things in the past and continues to make things, to do things, to create, in the present. Other texts similarly describe divine creative action in the present tense. Amos wrote—or spoke:

> For lo, the one who forms the mountains, creates the wind,
> reveals his thoughts to mortals.
> makes the morning darkness,
> and treads on the heights of the earth—
> YHWH, the God of hosts, is his name! (Amos 4:13)[7]

Likewise, Job, speaking in praise of God:

> He stretches out [the north] over the void,
> and hangs the earth upon nothing.
> He binds up the waters in his thick clouds,
> and the cloud is not torn open by them. (Job 26:7–8)

Here as in many of the other biblical texts quoted here, God's creation is seen as an ongoing process: God is still creating.[8] In Sir 43:26, the wisdom sage declares: "By his word all things hold together."[9] Similarly, the Wisdom of Solomon says "the spirit of the Lord has filled the world" and "holds all things together" (Wis 1:7).[10]

Some New Testament texts attribute such activity to also Christ, again using the present tense. Thus, Paul wrote: "For us there is one God, the Father, from whom are all things and for

---

6. See also J. Cobb, *Is It Too Late*, 105–6.

7. See also Amos 5:8–9. Strangely, proponents of "creationism" tend to visualize the creation as something that happened entirely in the past, as if—as eighteenth-century Deists also assumed—divine creative activity had ceased long ago.

8. As pointed out by Dawson, *Nature and the Bible*, 53–55, 113–45.

9. See also Isa 48:13.

10. See also Wis 7:24—8:1. A few New Testament texts represent Christ as the one who fills all things. See Eph 1:23 and 4:10.

whom we exist, and one Lord, Jesus Christ, though whom are all things and through whom we exist."[11]

Certain NT texts also ascribe a role in the creation to Christ. For instance, in John's Gospel, it is said that "all things were made through him, and without him was not anything made that was made" (John 1:3). The same understanding is expressed in Col 1:15–6: "He is the image of the invisible God, the first born of all creation, for in him all things in heaven and on earth were created, things visible and invisible, . . . all things have been created through him and for him." This affirmation also appears in Heb 1:2, where Christ is said to be the "Son" through whom God "also created the worlds." These texts may represent efforts by early Christians to reinterpret Prov 8:22–31, which describes Wisdom as YHWH's companion when he (YHWH) created the cosmos. However, none of the first three Gospels suggests that Jesus had been, or believed himself to have been, present at or involved in the creation. Other NT texts attribute the creation to God, without referring to Christ.[12] In any case, such texts see "all things" as divine creations and, at least by implication, ultimately valued and valuable.[13]

---

11. 1 Cor 8:6. See also Col 1:17 and Heb 1:3a; compare Heb 2:10. See generally Bouma-Prediger, *For the Beauty*, 105–10; and McFague, "Ecological Christianity." As to the incarnation as a basis for appreciating and affirming the value of "all living and material things," see Hill, *Christian Faith and Environment*, 98–106.

12. See, e.g., Paul, as quoted in Acts 14:15 and 17:24; Eph 3:9; 1 Tim 4:4; and Rev 14:6–7. So, also, implicitly, Rom 1:18–23. This understanding later came to expression in the Nicene Creed: "I believe in one God the Father Almighty, Maker of heaven and earth, And of all things visible and invisible." It goes on, somewhat ambiguously, to affirm that "all things were made," but whether by "God the Father" or "the Lord Jesus Christ" is grammatically unclear. The Apostles' Creed's affirmation, "I believe in God the Father Almighty, Maker of heaven and earth," makes no mention of Jesus Christ in connection with the creation or making of heaven and earth.

13. Commenting on Col 1:15–17, Mwombeki writes: "Christ is therefore a unifying force who continues to play a providential role in the continuance of creation of all things. Having established this truth, it follows that any violence to the harmony of the universe, any action on our part, which disrupts the ecosystem, which necessarily makes life disharmonious, is violence against Christ himself." Mwombeki, "Ecology in New Testament," page number unavailable.

B. ALL CREATION AND ALL CREATURES ARE GOOD

Since it was understood that YHWH/God created all that exists, it could have been assumed that all that exists is good. Several texts so affirm in explicit terms. In biblical perspective, the created, material world is never seen as evil, nor is its creation ever viewed as a mistake.[14] Instead, the created world and the creatures who inhabit it are characterized specifically as "good."[15]

The first creation story sets the tone. Six times in the course of creating the cosmos, this narrative affirms that God saw that what he had made "was good."[16] This is said with respect to "vegetation . . . plants yielding seed, and fruit trees of every kind on earth that bear fruit with the seed in it" (Gen 1:11–12); "the great sea monsters, and every living creature that moves, of every kind, with which the waters swarm, and every winged bird of every kind" (Gen 1:21); and "the wild animals of the earth of every kind,

---

14. Biblical tradition does, of course, acknowledge the occurrence of injustice, suffering, and tragedy. See, e.g., the books of Job, Ecclesiastes, and 2 Esdras. But such evils are never understood to derive from the creation itself. Some NT texts say that the earth has been taken over temporarily by Satan or the devil. See, e.g., Matt 4:1–4; John 12:31; 1 John 5:19; and Rev 12:7–12.

15. See Berry, *Sex, Economy*, 97: "[If we read the Bible] . . . we will discover that God found the world, as He made it, to be good, that He made it for His pleasure, and that He continues to love it and to find it worthy, despite its reduction and corruption by us. People who quote John 3:16 as an easy formula for getting to Heaven neglect to see the great difficulty implied in the statement that the advent of Christ was made possible by God's love for the world—not for God's love for Heaven or for the world as it might be but for the world as it was and is." Cf. Hart, *Sacramental Commons*, 75–76: "All creation has intrinsic value that is independent of a human-assigned instrumental value based on a human-assigned assessment of a being's potential benefits for human life and livelihood." And see Heide, *My Father's World*, 144: "What is extraordinary about each of these creative acts is that when God looked at what He had done, He knew it was good. Each act of God's creation was completed with care. . . . He lovingly desired that the plants and animals should be formed with special attention given to their biological functions and their place within the entire picture of creation." See also C. Wright, *Old Testament Ethics*, 508.

16. Gen 1:3, 10, 12, 18, 22, and 24. See Johnson, "Losing and Finding Creaton," 15: "If the earth is indeed God's creation, a sacrament of the glory of God with its own intrinsic value, then, for those of the Christian persuasion, ongoing destruction of Earth bears the mark of deep sinfulness. Through greed, self-interest, ignorance, and injustice, human beings are bringing violent disfigurement and death to this living, evolving planet that God created as 'very good' (Gen 1:31)."

and the cattle of every kind, and everything that creeps upon the ground of every kind" (Gen 1:25). Lest it be thought that any creatures or other created entities might be excluded by omission from these enumerations, the narrative eliminates any possible doubt with its concluding summary: "God saw everything he had made, and indeed, it was very good" (Gen 1:31a).

Other biblical texts likewise consistently affirm the goodness of the created world. According to Exod 3:8, YHWH described the land of promise as "a good and broad land." Again, all kinds of creatures are said to be good, here by "Solomon":

> For he created all things that they might exist;
> the [creatures] of the world are wholesome,
> there is no destructive poison in them. (Wis 1:14)

Similarly, in Wis 11:24—12:1, it is said to and of God:

> For you love all things that exist,
> and detest none of the things that you have made. . . .
> You spare all things, for they are yours,
> O Lord, you who love the living.
> For your immortal spirit is in all things.

Sirach likewise identified the divine basis for affirming the goodness of all created beings:

> When the Lord created his works from the beginning,
> and in making them, determined their boundaries
> he arranged his works in an eternal order,
>   and their elements for all generations. . . .
> Then the Lord looked upon the earth,
> and filled it with his good things.
> With all kinds of living beings he covered its surface,
>   and into it they must return. (Sir 16:26–30)[17]

Certain NT texts likewise affirm the goodness of the creation, for example, 1 Tim 4:4: "For everything created by God is good, and nothing is to be rejected, provided it is received with thanksgiving." In the Synoptic Gospels, Jesus's appreciation of the created

---

17. See also Sir 39:16: "All the works of the Lord are very good"; see also Sir 39:25–34 and Sir 43.

world is expressed not only in his sayings about the birds of the air and the lilies of the field[18] but also, perhaps, in his sojourn with "the wild animals" in "the wilderness" just before the beginning of his public ministry.[19]

C. ALL CREATION AND ALL CREATURES ARE YHWH/GOD'S: HE IS OWNER OF ALL

Since it was believed that YHWH/God had created all that exists and found it good, it might be expected that he also would be regarded as the sole owner of all that is. Several texts so state in explicit terms. Some refer to the entire cosmos, others to the earth or the land or the seas, and others to some or all living beings.

Deuteronomy 10:14 is one of the texts affirming YHWH/God's ownership of the entire cosmos or creation: "Heaven and the heaven of heavens belong to YHWH your God, [along with] the earth, with all that is in it." Thus also Ps 89:11: "The heavens are yours, the earth also is yours; the world and all that is in it—you have founded them." Several texts focus on the world or the earth, together with all its inhabitants. For example, Ps 24:1: "The earth is YHWH's and all that is in it, the world and those who live in it."[20] Jeremiah 27:5–6 says that YHWH/God, in exercising his sovereignty, might choose to give "the earth, with the people and animals that are on the earth" temporarily to a human sovereign (here Nebuchadnezzar). Similarly, Ps 115:16 suggests: "The heavens are YHWH's heavens, but the earth he has given to human beings." But, at most, only temporarily. Nearly all other biblical texts affirm and insist that the earth is YHWH's.[21] For instance, Exod

---

18. Matt 6:26, 28–30; Luke 12:24, 27–28.

19. Mark 1:12b. The context suggests that these wild animals, along with "the angels," "ministered to" Jesus either during or after his temptation by Satan. The scene may have been understood as foreshadowing the messianic age to come. In the future messianic age, it was expected that human beings and wild animals would live together in peace. See below, ch. 11.

20. See Berry, *Sex, Economy*, 96: "If we read the Bible . . . we will discover that we do not own the world or any part of it: 'The earth is the Lord's, and the fullness thereof: the world and they that dwell therein.'" See also Maguire, *Moral Creed*, 67–68.

21. See Lagat, *Christian Faith*, 14: "The things that people tend to think of as our

9:29, where Moses, speaking to Pharaoh, says, "I will stretch out my hands to YHWH; the thunder will cease, and there will be no more hail, so that you may know that the earth is YHWH's." Likewise, in Exod 19:5, YHWH tells Moses, "Indeed, the whole earth is mine." Again, in Lev 25:23, while giving the law to Moses, YHWH declares: "The land shall not be sold in perpetuity, for the land is mine." That YHWH is sovereign owner of all the earth is also affirmed in Josh 3:11 and 13 where YHWH is said to be "the Lord of all the earth." Not only the earth, but also the sea is said to be his:

> In his hand are the depths of the earth;
> the heights of the mountains are his also.
> The sea is his, for he made it;
> and the dry land, which his hands have formed. (Ps 95:4–5)

Such texts affirm in general terms that everything YHWH/God created is his. Other texts specifically refer to birds and animals, both domestic and wildlife, as belonging to him. Various sacrificial ordinances state that all firstborn "cattle" or farm animals are his.[22] But not just firstborn animals:

> For every wild animal of the forest is mine,
> [also] the cattle on a thousand hills.
> I know all the birds of the air,
> and all that moves in the field is mine. . . .
> For the world and all that is in it is mine. (Ps 50:10–12)[23]

Indeed, "all living things" belong to the Lord. (Wis 11:26). Judith also affirms that all creatures are God's in her song or psalm: "Let all your creatures serve you, / for you spoke, and they were made, / you sent forth your spirit, / and it formed them" (Jdt 16:14). Psalm

---

'resources' are actually elements of a creation belonging to God. God the owner gives them graciously to his people, not to a few capitalists. Not to a few owners for their own selfish pleasure. The resource was given to all people and all generations for their sustenance."

22. E.g., Exod 34:19. See below, ch. 5A1.

23. See McAfee, "Ecology and Biblical Studies," 37, commenting on this text: "Divine creation of the world presumes divine ownership of the same." If the earth belongs to God, it does not then belong to humans to ravage or exploit however we may so desire. See Gary Hirshberg, quoted in Underwood, "10 Fixes," 56: "We have to stop treating the earth as a wholly-owned subsidiary of our economy."

104:16 affirms that trees also belong to YHWH/God; here in its context, the expression "the trees of YHWH" evidently refers to all trees. Summing up, Ps 104 declares that all that YHWH has made and all living creatures belong to him:

> O YHWH, how manifold are your works!
> In wisdom you have made them all;
> the earth is full of your creatures.
> Yonder is the sea, great and wide,
> creeping things innumerable are there,
> living things both small and great.
> There go the ships,
> and Leviathan that you formed to sport in it. (Ps 104:24–26)

All creatures, whether great like Leviathan, or small like "creeping things," were created in order to enjoy their own lives before YHWH's presence. Because God created everything that exists, it is not surprising that biblical tradition consistently affirms that all that is belongs to him.[24]

People also belong to God: "Know that YHWH is God! It is he that made us, and we are his; we are his people and the sheep of his pasture" (Ps 100:3; also Ps 95:6–7). Biblical understandings of the complex relationships between YHWH/God, the creation, human beings, and other creatures as well are considered below in part 2.

The two chapters that follow immediately again focus on biblical texts concerned primarily with interactions between YHWH/God, creation, and all kinds of life-forms other than human. This first chapter has examined texts that celebrate and otherwise refer to the creation and other creatures. The next chapter turns to texts that affirm YHWH/God's continuing rule, sovereignty, or dominion over all that he has made.

---

24. See Lagat, *Christian Faith*, 81–82: "Ken Ghanakan observes that the connection between land and [the] God-Israel relation clearly communicated to Israel that God was the owner of the land. . . . In fact, God says, 'the land is mine and you are but aliens and my tenants' (Lev 25:23); and He refers to it clearly as 'my land' (Jer 2:7; 16:18)."

CHAPTER 2

YHWH/God as Ruler or Sovereign over All Creation and All Creatures

IN BIBLICAL FAITH, YHWH/GOD is understood not only as the Creator of all that is but also as Ruler or Sovereign over all creation. The English term "the LORD," commonly used in translations as substitute for the divine name YHWH, aptly expresses this understanding.[1] YHWH/God's sovereignty or dominion is affirmed throughout biblical traditions. This sovereignty is represented in different ways. It is implicit in numerous descriptions of what YHWH/God has done and what he does in and through creation. It is expressed in many texts that describe his concern and compassionate care for the creatures he brought into being. And, as will be seen later in ch. 10, many biblical texts portray animals and other creatures as agents of YHWH/God's sovereignty in his dealings with human beings.

A. YHWH/GOD'S SOVEREIGNTY OVER AND THROUGH CREATION

In both the Genesis flood and the Exodus "Red Sea" stories, and also later in the story of Jonah, YHWH/God is seen controlling

---

1. Biblical texts sometimes identify YHWH/God as "Lord" or "the Lord" (Heb. *adon*; Gk. *kurios*).

what in modern times might be called the "forces of nature" in order to bring about his own purposes. These stories refer to such forces as floodwaters, rain, "the "fountains of the great deep,"[2] and wind and raging sea (Jonah 1:4–15).[3] The plagues inflicted upon Egypt likewise were understood as expressions of YHWH/God's sovereignty: frogs, gnats, and flies (Exod 8:1–24),[4] hail and locusts (Exod 9:25; 10:1–19), among other phenomena. In the book of Joshua, YHWH, who is twice named "Lord of all the earth" (Josh 3:11, 13), is said to have sent "the hornet" to drive out various indigenous peoples (Josh 24:12).[5]

Several of the psalms celebrate YHWH/God's rule over nature or creation. He silences "the roaring of the seas, the roaring of their waves, waters and enriches the earth, providing [grain for all]," and crowns the year with his "bounty" (Ps 65:6–13). Psalm 135 expresses such understanding in both broad and particular terms:

> Whatever YHWH pleases, he does,
>   in heaven and on earth,
>   in the seas and all deeps.
> He it is who makes the clouds rise at the end of the earth;
>   he makes lightnings for the rain
>   and brings out the wind from his storehouses. (Ps 135:6–7)[6]

Prophetic texts likewise depict YHWH/God's sovereignty over nature, which frequently takes the form of catastrophic judgment against nations or peoples—particularly against Israel or Judah. Drought is one such expression of divine judgment.[7] Wis-

---

2. Gen 6:17; 7:4—8:5.

3. See also Exod 14:21 (wind and sea); Job 38:8–15, 22–38 (the sea, morning, snow and hail, light, the east wind, rain, dew, ice, hoarfrost, constellations, clouds, and lightning); and Amos 4:7–9 (rain, blight, mildew, and locusts). See also Job 36:27—37:18; Jer 10:13; 51:15–16; and Mal 3:10–12.

4. So also Ps 105:30–35.

5. So also Exod 23:28 ("hornets") and Deut 7:20. Although commentators often suggest otherwise, there is no textual basis for supposing that "hornet" in these texts was meant to symbolize human forces.

6. See also Pss 93, 97, and 99, which affirm YHWH/God's reign or rule over the cosmos and also, perhaps, over all nations. See also Ps 96:12.

7. See, e.g., Jer 3:1–3; 14:1–4; Amos 4:7–8; Hag 1:10; Mal 3:7–12.

dom writings likewise affirm YHWH/God's sovereignty over all creation, which he uses to bring about his purposes:

> For the creation, serving you who made it,
>   exerts itself to punish the unrighteous,
>   and in kindness relaxes on behalf
>   of those who trust in you. (Wis 16:24)[8]

This kind of understanding is aptly expressed in the Letter of Jeremiah vv. 60–63:

> For sun and moon and stars are bright and when sent to do service they are obedient. So also, the lightning, when it flashes, is widely seen; and the wind likewise blows in every land. When God commands the clouds to go over the whole world, they carry out his command. And the fire sent from above to consume mountains and woods does what it is ordered.

YHWH/God's sovereignty is sometimes referred to as his "dominion," "rule," or "kingdom" (Heb. *malkuth* or *mamlakah*). His dominion extends to nations and history as well as to the created world.

> All the ends of the earth shall remember and turn to YHWH;
> and all the families of the nations shall worship before him.
> For dominion belongs to YHWH,
>   and he rules over the nations. (Ps 22:28)[9]

Or, again, in Ps 145:13: "Your kingdom is an everlasting kingdom, and your dominion endures throughout all generations."[10] In the story of Bel and the Dragon, Daniel links YHWH/God's creation with his dominion. Asked why he does not worship Bel, the Babylonian deity, Daniel responds, "Because I do not revere idols made with hands, but the living God, who created heaven and earth and has dominion over all living creatures" (Bel v. 5).[11]

---

8. See also Wis 16:5–10 and Sir 39:16–34. Other texts in which various creatures are said to function as agents of YHWH/God in assisting or punishing humans are considered below in ch. 10.

9. Ps 22:28–29 in the Hebrew text.

10. See also Ps 103:19: "YHWH has established his throne in the heavens / and his kingdom rules over all."

11. See also Ps 103:22. One NT text ascribes "dominion" or, more precisely, a

B. YHWH/GOD'S COMPASSIONATE CARE FOR THE EARTH, THE LAND, AND ALL CREATURES

A great many biblical texts describe YHWH/God's sovereignty or dominion over creation by affirming and celebrating his compassion and care for all kinds of living things. This compassionate care is affirmed both in general terms and in describing his responses to particular created entities and living beings.[12]

Psalm 145:9 declares YHWH/God's compassion for all creation: "YHWH is good to all, and his compassion is over all that he has made." Another text underscores his compassion for all living beings—in contrast to exclusively humanistic proclivities:

> The compassion of human beings is for their neighbors,
>   but the compassion of the Lord is for every living thing.
>   (Sir 18:13)

That this should be so is not surprising, for, as will be recalled, according to Gen 1:3–31, God created all living beings and also found them not only "good" but "very good."

A similar affirmation is found in Wisdom of Solomon. Addressing YHWH/God in prayer, this wisdom writer declares:

> For you love all things that exist,
> and detest none of the things that you have made. . . .
> You spare all things, for they are yours,
> O Lord, you who love the living.
> For your immortal spirit is in all things. (Wis 11:24—12:1)

As will be seen in what follows, YHWH/God's compassion for the creation is expressed in his care for the earth or the land and

---

place "far above all rule and authority and power and dominion" to the risen Christ (Eph 1:20–22). See also Phil 2:9–11 and 3:20–21. The Hebrew term transliterated as "messiah" and translated into Greek as *Christos* and into English as "Christ" means "the anointed one" or "king."

12. See Dawson, *Nature and the Bible*, 39: "A third and recognized [point of importance] in the Bible is the welfare and happiness of all the lower animals. [God] listens to the young ravens when they cry, and provides for the sparrows, while he feeds 'all the creeping things innumerable' of the great and wide sea. This also, science must recognize, not only because of the wonderful and complicated adaptations of all parts of nature to each other, but [also] because of those vast geological periods in which the earth was tenanted by the lower animals alone."

the vegetation that grows upon it, and for wildlife and domestic animals alike. In Genesis, at the beginning of the biblical narrative, he is said to have made a covenant with all living creatures "for all generations" (Gen 9:8–17). The prophet Hosea declares that YHWH/God would make a covenant "with the wild animals, the birds of the air, and the creeping things of the ground" at the beginning of the messianic age (Hos 2:18). A large number of texts anticipate the presence of nonhuman creatures in the coming messianic age.[13]

1. The Earth—the Land

YHWH/God's care for the earth or the land and plants that grow upon it is set forth throughout biblical tradition. The J or second creation story (Gen 2:4b–24) says that YHWH/God himself "planted a garden in Eden" and there "made to grow every tree that is pleasant to the sight and good for food."[14] In Gen 9:13, it is said that the rainbow was God's sign of the covenant between himself and "the earth." In Joel, YHWH/God himself is said to address the land with reassurance: "Fear not, O soil; be glad and rejoice, for YHWH has done great things!" (Joel 2:21). Jesus's saying about the lilies of the field expresses wonder as to how God adorns the ground: "Consider the lilies of the field, how they grow; they neither toil nor spin, yet I tell you, even Solomon in all his glory was not clothed like one of these" (Matt 6:28b–29).[15]

2. YHWH/God's Continuing Care for the Land—Providing Water for the Earth

A number of other biblical texts also refer to YHWH/God's care for the land, focusing on his watering it with rain from heaven.

---

13. See below, ch. 11.

14. The man's assigned task, "to till" the garden "and keep it" (Gen 2:17), will be considered again below, ch. 11A1d.

15. See also Luke 12:27.

The land to which the people of Israel were going after their long sojourn in Egypt was said to be

> a land of hills and valleys, watered by rain from the sky, a land that YHWH your God looks after. The eyes of YHWH your God are always on it, from the beginning of the year to the end of the year. (Deut 11:11–12)

YHWH/God's care is not confined to the land of Israel, nor does he water the land only for human benefit. Replying "out of the whirlwind" to Job's complaints (Job 38:1), YHWH asks Job:

> Who has cut a channel for the torrents of rain,
>   and a way for the thunderbolt,
> to bring rain on *a land where no one lives,*
>   *on the desert, which is empty of human life,*
> *to satisfy the waste and desolate land,*
>   and to make the ground put forth grass? (Job 38:25–27)[16]

Likewise, Job's "friend," Eliphaz, affirms as a matter of common faith: "[God] gives rain on the earth and sends waters on the fields" (Job 5:10).

---

16. Emphasis added. See also Deut 32:2, in the Song or Psalm of Moses, where the psalmist alludes to "the gentle rain on grass like showers on new growth." See also Job 37:11–13:

> He loads the thick cloud with moisture; the clouds scatter his lightning. They turn round and round by his guidance, to accomplish all that he commands them on the face of the habitable world. Whether for correction, or for his land, or for love, he causes it to happen.

See generally G. Tucker, "Rain on a Land." See also McKibben, *End of Nature*, 75–76: "In recent years, many theologians have contended that the Bible demands a careful 'stewardship' of the planet instead of a careless subjugation, [pointing out] that immediately after giving man dominion over the earth, God instructed him to 'cultivate and keep it.' But actually, I think, the Scriptures go much deeper. The Old Testament contains in many places, but especially in the book of Job, one of the most far-reaching defenses ever written of wilderness, of nature free from the hand of man. . . . God seems to be insisting that we are not the center of the universe, that he is quite happy if it rains where there are no people—that God is quite happy with *places* where there are no people, a radical departure from our most ingrained notions." Compare the familiar philosophical conundrum: Does a tree falling in the forest make a sound if no one hears it? This is a conundrum only to those who think inside the box of anthropocentrism, as if sounds are made only when heard by human ears.

The psalmist, in turn, praises YHWH/God for visiting, watering, and enriching the earth:

> You visit the earth and water it,
> you greatly enrich it;
> the river of God is full of water;
> you provide the people with their grain,
> for so you have prepared it.
> You water its furrows abundantly,
> settling its ridges,
> softening it with showers,
> and blessing its growth.
> You crown the year with your bounty;
> your wagon tracks overflow with richness.
> The pastures of the wilderness overflow,
> the hills gird themselves with joy,
> the meadows clothe themselves with flocks,
> the valleys deck themselves with grain,
> they shout and sing together for joy. (Ps 65:9–13)

Many other texts also rejoice and praise YHWH/God for sending rain upon the earth.[17] Water, critically needed to sustain all kinds of life, is understood to be God's gift to the land—and also to people and all other living things.[18] Only YHWH/God could make it rain.

3. YHWH/God Sends Rain, Providing for Humans and Other Creatures

Several such texts also make a connection between YHWH/God's care for the earth or the land and his care both for people—who depend on its produce—and for other creatures. Thus, for instance, in Deut 11:13–15:

> If you will only heed his every commandment that I am commanding you today, loving YHWH your God, and serving him with all your heart and with all your soul—then he will

---

17. See, e.g., Job 5:10; 37:5–6; Isa 35:1–2, 6b–7; and Ezek 34:26.

18. See Hart, *Sacramental Commons*, 79–95 (discussing biblical texts relating to water and current issues such as water pollution and privatization). As to Native American traditions as to the source of water and its intended beneficiaries, see Rebecca Hiers, "Water."

give the rain for your land in its season, the early rain and the later rain, and you will gather in your grain, your wine, and your oil; and he will give grass in your fields for your [cattle], and you will eat your fill.

So also, in Deut 28:12, Moses assures his people: "YHWH will open for you his rich storehouse, the heavens, to give you the rain in your land in season." And again, in Ps 104:

> You make springs gush forth in the valleys;
> they flow between the hills,
> they give drink to every wild animal;
> the wild asses quench their thirst.
> By the streams the birds of the air have their habitation;
> they sing among the branches;
> from your lofty abode you water the mountains;
> the earth is satisfied with the fruit of your work.
> You cause the grass to grow for the cattle,
> and plants for people to use. (Ps 104:10–14a)

> The trees of YHWH are watered abundantly,
> the cedars of Lebanon that he planted.
> In them the birds build their nests;
> the stork has her home in the fir trees. (Ps 104:16–17)[19]

Several other texts express the understanding that by sending rain, YHWH/God thereby provides for the needs of domestic animals and/or wildlife, as well as for human populations.[20] These and

---

19. See also Ps 147:8–9:

> He covers the heavens with clouds, prepares rain for the earth, makes grass grow on the hills. He gives to the animals their food, And to the young ravens when they cry.

And see Pss 65:9–13 and 107:35–38. As to Ps 104, Robb writes aptly: "Psalm 104 is a beautiful psalm, extolling the marvel of creation independent of its value to humankind.... This Psalm makes reference to many of the major life-support systems: the wind currents in the air envelope; saltwater oceans, freshwater streams, and the hydrologic cycle; forests, grasslands, and croplands; mountain ranges; and the solar and lunar cycles. The Psalm celebrates habitat for all the creatures and agriculture for humankind." Robb, *Wind, Sun, Soil, Spirit*, 144.

20. See, e.g., 2 Kgs 3:15–17, 20; Isa 43:19–21; Jer 5:24; and Joel 2:22–23. Cf. Job 36:27–31; Zech 10:1; and Matt 5:44–45 (God causes rain to fall for the benefit of humankind, on both the "righteous" and the "unrighteous"). See also Gen 2:9, which tells that when YHWH/God planted the garden of Eden, he "made to grow every tree

other biblical texts show profound gratitude to YHWH/God for providing water. Another notable instance is the occasion in the wilderness when, at YHWH's command, Moses brought abundant water out of "the rock" for both the people and their cattle to drink (Num 20:8–11).

YHWH/God's caring for animals, birds, "creeping things," and sea creatures—in short, all kinds of living beings—is a central, though commonly overlooked, theme found throughout biblical tradition. Such caring on the part of YHWH/God suggests that those who love and worship this God should likewise love and care for all living things.

4. Initial Blessings: "Be Fruitful and Multiply"

Many people assume that human beings were the only creatures YHWH/God told to "be fruitful and multiply." Actually, biblical tradition declares that all kinds of creatures were so instructed as well. On the fifth day of creation, according to the first (or P) creation story, God brought forth or created sea monsters, along with "every living creature that moves, of every kind, with which the waters swarm, and every winged bird of every kind" (Gen 1:20–21). All of these, "God blessed," saying, "Be fruitful and multiply and fill the waters in the seas, and let birds multiply on the earth" (Gen 1:22). The next day, as the story is told, God created—or caused the earth to "bring forth"—land creatures of every kind, "cattle and creeping things and wild animals of the earth of every kind," and, in due course, humankind, both male and female (Gen 1:24–27).

Genesis 6:1 marks the beginning of the prologue to the flood story: "When people began to multiply on the face of the ground . . ." Because of pervasive human depravity, YHWH/God "determined to make an end of all flesh," for "the earth [was] filled with violence because of them."[21] Following the flood, after its waters

---

that is pleasant to the sight and good for food." The text does not say that this food was provided only for human beings. The story goes on to say that a river watered the garden. The river then is said to have divided into four rivers that provide water for the entire then-known world (Gen 2:10–14).

21. Gen 6:11–13. Genesis 6:5–8, which evidently derives from the older J source,

had receded, God tells Noah to bring out of the ark all the land creatures—"every living thing that is with you of all flesh—birds and animals and every creeping thing that creeps on the earth"—so that *they* might "abound on the earth, and be fruitful and multiply on the earth" (Gen 8:17). There was no need to repeat the instruction to sea creatures, to be "fruitful and multiply and fill the waters in the seas" (Gen 1:22), for the flood would not have affected their populations. Birds, on the other hand, were told to "multiply on the earth" both before and after the flood.[22]

Thus not only the forebears of later humankind but also those of all other species were authorized to "abound" or "breed abundantly" (RSV), and "be fruitful and multiply" on land and in the sea. This authorization accords with the fundamental biblical belief that all kinds of creatures that YHWH/God brought into being are "good," indeed, "very good" (Gen 1:31). By the time Ps 104 was written, it seems to have been understood that both land and sea creatures had already fulfilled their missions to multiply and fill both land and sea:

> O YHWH, how manifold are your works!
> In wisdom have you made them all;
> the earth is full of your creatures.
> Yonder is the sea, great and wide,
> creeping things innumerable are there,
> living things both small and great. (Ps 104:24–25)

In a later narrative, as the Israelites, still in the wilderness, contemplate invading the land of Canaan, YHWH/God assures them that he will cause its indigenous peoples to be driven out only

---

identifies man (or humankind) as the sole source of evil, though at the same time stating that YHWH had decided to "blot out" not only humankind but also animals, creeping things, and birds of the air, for he was "sorry" that he had "made them." The P version, which picks up at Gen 6:9, states that in God's sight, "the earth was corrupt" and "filled with violence," for "all flesh had corrupted its ways upon the earth" (Gen 6:11–13).

22. Gen 1:22; 8:17. Perhaps the narrator was uncertain whether other birds would have perished in the flood. As the story is told, Noah had with him on the ark at least one raven and one dove—possibly in addition to one or more pairs of each kind (Gen 8:6–12). As with land creatures, after the flood, God told Noah to bring birds with him from the ark so that they, too, might "abound on the earth" as well as "be fruitful and multiply" upon it (Gen 8:17).

gradually, lest "the wild animals . . . multiply against" them there (Exod 23:29-30). The implication is that while wildlife was free to reproduce in their respective wilderness habitats, they were not to do so in Canaan once the Israelites were settled there.

5. YHWH/God Saves Endangered Species from the Great Flood

Having observed that "the wickedness of man was great in the earth" and determined to "make and end of all flesh," YHWH/God instructs Noah to build a huge ship and bring on board breeding pairs of "every living thing, of all flesh," along with "every kind of food that is eaten" to preserve all these species from the impending flood (Gen 6:5-21). The passenger list on the ark (as it is commonly called)[23] included "two of every kind . . . male and female": "birds according to their kinds, and of the animals according to their kinds," and "of every creeping thing of the ground according to its kind . . . to keep them alive" (Gen 6:19-20).[24] As the story is told, all these species were endangered by the coming flood. YHWH/God himself wished to preserve all kinds of species,[25] and instructed Noah to do what was necessary to bring about that result. YHWH/God's concern and involvement are further expressed in certain noteworthy details: after Noah and his family, and "every wild animal," "all the domestic animals," "every creeping thing," and "every bird, every winged creature," "male and female of all

---

23. "Ship" is a more apt term. According to the biblical narrative, the vessel was 450 feet long (the length of one and a half football fields), 75 feet wide, and 45 feet high, with three decks. The narrator apparently realized that to get all the requisite pairs of creatures, along with their feed or fodder, on board would require a great deal of space. Commenting on the ship's size, Martin Luther exclaimed: "If it were not in Scripture, I would not believe it." Quoted in Bainton, *Here I Stand*, 296.

24. This list is repeated several times in the course of the narration. See Gen 7:14-16; 8:17, 19. Another version of the flood story, commonly attributed to J, lists seven pairs of clean animals and birds (those suitable for sacrificial offerings) and one pair of other animals and birds. Gen 7:2-9; 8:20-21.

25. The birds and animals on the ark were said to be all those "in which there was the breath of life" (Gen 7:14-15). It probably was understood that there would have been no need to preserve sea creatures on board the ark, since they would not have been adversely affected by the flood. It also seems to have been understood that the flood would not have destroyed trees or other vegetation, and that all these were or would be in good order after the floodwaters receded.

flesh" had gone on board the ark, YHWH himself shut them in (Gen 7:13–16). Then, as floodwaters peaked, "God remembered Noah and all the wild animals and all the domestic animals that were with him in the ark" and caused the waters to subside (Gen 8:1). From the narrators' perspective, YHWH/God clearly was concerned not only with the human passengers but also with all the other kinds as well. All kinds of species were precious to him; all were to be preserved from extinction. The ark can be said to have been about the world's first known wildlife sanctuary. It also could be said to symbolize recognition that humans and other living things were—and still are—"in the same boat."

6. The Everlasting Covenant between YHWH/God and Every Living Creature of All Flesh

In the immediate sequel to the flood story (Gen 9:8–17), God tells Noah *five separate times* that he was establishing his covenant not only with him and his descendants but also with every living creature.[26] In this covenant, God promises never again to send a flood to destroy the earth or all flesh (Gen 9:11, 15). One version of this covenant says that it was made with Noah, his descendants, and with all those creatures that were "with" Noah on the ark: "the birds, the domestic animals, and every animal of the earth" (Gen 9:9–10). Another version says that it was made with Noah and with "every living creature" that was with him "for all future generations" (Gen 9:12). The other versions are, if possible, even more inclusive: "between me and you and every living creature of all flesh" (Gen 9:15); "between God and every living creature of all flesh that is on the earth" (Gen 9:16); and "between me and all flesh that is on the earth" (Gen 9:17). The last two versions do not specifically mention Noah or humankind, but it was probably understood that the expression "all flesh" included human beings. A sixth version,

---

26. Gen 9:9–10, 12, 15, 16, 17. The text of the entire passage is quoted above at the beginning of pt. 1 of this book. See Bouma-Prediger, *For the Beauty*, 96–100, discussing this covenant which, as he puts it, was "established with the earth and its plethora of creatures" (99).

still more inclusively, perhaps, identifies the rainbow as "a sign of the covenant" between YHWH/God and "the earth" (Gen 9:12).[27]

The covenant thus variously described was made not only with Noah and his family and other creatures living in those days; it was said also to be a covenant which YHWH made between himself and Noah "and every living creature" that was with Noah *"for all future generations"* (Gen 9:12 [emphasis added]). Indeed, it was described as "the everlasting covenant between God and every living creature of all flesh that is upon the earth" (Gen 9:16). These biblical texts indicate that all kinds of species were meant to continue "upon the earth" for all time as co-beneficiaries of this covenant.[28]

7. YHWH/God's Continuing Care for All Creatures

Several biblical texts refer to other aspects of YHWH/God's actions in regard to nonhuman creatures. For instance, in the book of Job, YHWH declares that it was he who made Behemoth, the great land creature, providing him with food on "the mountains . . . where all the wild beasts play" and do so there and in other habitats as well (Job 40:15-23).[29] Similarly, says the psalmist, YHWH formed Leviathan, the great sea creature, to "sport in" the sea, which also "teems with things innumerable, living things both small and great" (Ps 104:25-26 RSV). It is understood that YHWH/God

---

27. In this context, "the earth" appears to mean both the earth or world itself and all living beings for which it provides habitat.

28. See former U.S. Interior Secretary Bruce Babbitt, "Between Flood and Rainbow," as to the rainbow as sign of this covenant: "We are thus instructed that this everlasting covenant was made to protect the whole of creation, not for the exclusive use and disposition of mankind, but for the purposes of the Creator." As to the significance of this covenant as to relations between humans and other creatures, see below, ch. 4C.

29. See Jacobson, "Biblical Bases," 45-46: "God cares even for the chaos, monsters—Behemoth and Leviathan . . . and in this expansive, no-holds-barred caring, God invites Job to see all of creation as part of God's family whom God births, cares for, sustains, disciplines, and admires. This part of our tradition invites us to see ourselves as intimately connected with creation, as brothers and sisters with the whole of creation—all God's children, with the world as home. All creatures and all creation are therefore our neighbors, which the Law [Torah] enjoins us to care for. It is sadly a part of the tradition we often neglect."

created and continues to care for all these creatures. Some, if not all of them, were expected to be free to "play," "sport," or otherwise enjoy their lives entirely apart from human presence or activity.

Portions of YHWH's earlier "speech" to Job indicate YHWH's care for other wild creatures. It is YHWH who enables the lion to hunt its prey and "satisfy the appetite of the young lions." And it is YHWH who "provides for the raven [her] prey, when [her] young ones cry to God, and wander about for lack of food" (Job 38:39-41).[30] It is YHWH who watches over the birthing and nurturing of mountain goats and deer, and their subsequent venturing forth as free creatures (Job 39:1-4). It is YHWH who "has let the wild ass go free" and "loosed the bonds of the swift ass, to which (he has) given the steppes for [his] home, [and] the salt land for [his] dwelling place" (Job 39:5-6)—another biblical instance of what might be called "designated wildlife habitat." And it is by YHWH's wisdom that the hawk "soars [and] spreads [his] wings" and "that the eagle mounts up and makes [his] nest on high" and "spies out [his] prey" (Job 39:26-30).

YHWH/God's *hesed* or steadfast love is not reserved for people alon, but extends to both "humans and animals": "Your steadfast love, O YHWH, extends to the heavens . . . you save humans and animals alike, O YHWH" (Ps 36:5-6).[31] Similarly, Ps 104 praises YHWH/God at some length for his care in providing for the needs of wildlife, domestic animals, and humans, alike:

> You make springs gush forth in the valleys;
> they flow between the hills,
> giving drink to every wild animal;
> the wild asses quench their thirst.
> By the streams the birds of the air have their habitation;
> they sing among the branches. . . .
> You cause the grass to grow for the cattle,
> and plants for people to use,
> to bring forth food from the earth;

---

30. Here, and elsewhere in this paragraph, the RSV's gender-specific reading is preferred to the NRSV's "its" translation. Biblical creatures are seen typically as living beings, with gender, rather than as neuter *things* or objects.

31. See also Ps 33:5: "The earth is full of the steadfast love of YHWH." And see Ps 136:25: "[YHWH/God] gives food to all flesh, for his steadfast love endures forever."

and wine to gladden the human heart,
oil to make his face shine,
and bread to strengthen man's heart.
The trees of YHWH are watered abundantly,
the cedars of Lebanon that he planted.
In them the birds build their nests;
the stork has [her] home in the fir trees.
The high mountains are for the wild goats;
the rocks are a refuge for the [rabbits].
You have made the moon to mark the seasons;
the sun knows its time for setting.
You make darkness, and it is night,
when all the wild animals of the forest come creeping out.
The young lions roar for their prey,
seeking their food from God.
When the sun rises, they withdraw
and lie down in their dens.
People go out to their work
and to their labor until the evening. . . .
Yonder is the sea, great and wide,
[which teems with] things innumerable . . . ,
living things both small and great.
There go the ships,
and Leviathan that you formed to sport in it.
These all look to you,
to give them their food in due season;
when you give to them, they gather it up;
when you open your hand, they are filled with good things.
(Ps 104:10–28)

YHWH/God's active care in providing for the needs of all creatures also is affirmed in Ps 145:

> YHWH is gracious and merciful,
> slow to anger and abounding in steadfast love.
> YHWH is good to all,
> and his compassion is over all that he has made. (Ps 145:8–9)[32]

---

32. The first part of this text has been incorporated into Christian liturgy, but the second part, "good to all" and "his compassion is over all that he made" generally is omitted.

> The eyes of all look to you,
>> and you give them their food in due season.
> You open your hand,
>> satisfying the desire of every living thing.
> YHWH is just in all his ways,
>> and kind in all his doings. (Ps 145:15–16)

Likewise, in Ps 147:9, it is said, "He gives to the animals their food, and to the young ravens when they cry."

In a text generally attributed to Second Isaiah, the prophet, speaking for YHWH/God, indicates that the water and rivers provided for the returning exiles on their way through the wilderness would also be for the benefit of the "wild animals, . . . the jackals and the ostriches," who will "honor" him for so providing (Isa 43:19–20).

In the book of Joel, YHWH/God speaks directly to the "beasts" (RSV) or "animals of the field," assuring them that he will provide their food:

> Do not fear, you animals of the field,
> for the pastures of the wilderness are green;
> the tree bears its fruit,
> the fig tree and vine give their full yield. (Joel 2:22)

At the end of the story of Jonah, YHWH/God tells Jonah that he, YHWH, had pity on Nineveh and decided to spare it not only because of all its innocent children but also because of its "much cattle" (RSV) or "many animals" (Jonah 4:11). Here as elsewhere in biblical tradition, the term translated as "cattle" generally means all kinds of domestic or farm animals. This reference to YHWH/God's concern for cattle is consistent with many other biblical texts that point to or affirm his care for the well-being of such animals.[33]

New Testament texts also refer to God's compassion and care for other creatures. The most familiar text, perhaps, is Jesus's saying about God's care for sparrows: "Are not five sparrows sold for two pennies? Yet not one of them is forgotten in God's sight" (Luke

---

33. See, e.g., Gen 7:14; 8:1; 9:10; Exod 20:10; 23:12; Lev 25:6–7; Pss 50:9–10; 104:14.

12:6).³⁴ The author of Hebrews writes still more inclusively: "And before him no creature is hidden, but all are naked and laid bare to the eyes of the one to whom we must render an account" (Heb 4:13). In two similar versions of one of his sayings, Jesus affirms that God provides food for wild birds: "Look at the birds of the air: they neither sow nor reap nor gather into barns, and yet your heavenly Father feeds them" (Matt 6:26); "Consider the ravens: they neither sow nor reap, they have neither storehouse nor barn, and yet God feeds them" (Luke 12:24).

Clearly biblical tradition affirms YHWH's or God's compassion and care for the land or earth and all the creatures that make it their home, whether human or nonhuman. The implication is that God's people should go and do likewise. The next chapter indicates that in biblical times, people recognized that other creatures enjoyed a direct and reciprocal relationship with YHWH/God. The biblical texts considered there visualize other creatures—indeed all creation—turning to YHWH/God for care and comfort and to worship him. Not only humans but all kinds of beings as well had ample cause to praise, bless, and rejoice before God.

---

34. See also Matt 10:29. And see Ps 84:3: "Even the sparrow finds a home, and the swallow a nest for herself, where she may lay her young, at your altars, O YHWH of hosts, my King and my God."

CHAPTER 3

All Creatures Call Upon, Pray To, Praise, Bless, and Rejoice before YHWH/God

THAT OTHER CREATURES RELATE directly to God is a prominent feature of biblical faith, though one commonly neglected by both biblical scholars and theologians. This chapter considers first a variety of texts where other creatures are said to "cry" or pray to YHWH/God for food or other kinds of care. The second part describes texts where other creatures are urged or expected to praise, bless, and rejoice before YHWH/God.

A. ALL CREATURES CRY OR PRAY TO YHWH/GOD

Some of the texts considered in the previous chapter refer to birds and other creatures crying or praying to God for food. Evidently it was believed that like humans, nonhuman creatures also were capable of experiencing a direct relationship with YHWH/God, calling on him for aid, in confidence that he would hear their prayers and respond. The texts already considered include the following, which are quoted briefly again here because they give explicit expression to this distinctive understanding.

One of such text is found toward the end of the book of Job where, responding to Job's laments or complaints, YHWH/God asks him:

> Who provides for the raven [her] prey,
> when [her] young ones cry to God,
> and wander about for lack of food? (Job 38:41)

The implicit answer, of course, is YHWH/God himself.

Several texts in Psalms give expression to the same understanding.

> The young lions roar for their prey,
> seeking their food from God. (Ps 104:21)

> O YHWH, . . .
> the earth is full of your creatures.
> Yonder is the sea, great and wide,
> [which teems] with . . . living things, both small and great. . . .
> These all look to you,
> to give them their food in due season. (Ps 104:24–25, 27)

> The eyes of all look to you,
> and you give them their food in due season.
> You open your hand,
> satisfying the desire of every living thing. (Ps 145:15–16)[1]

The prophet Joel declares that in his time, a period of severe drought:

> Even the wild animals cry to you
> because the watercourses are dried up,
> and fire has devoured the pastures of the wilderness. (Joel 1:20)

It will be recalled that in the story of Jonah, it is said that the king of Nineveh commanded all inhabitants, both "man and beast" (RSV), "humans and animals" alike, to fast, put on sackcloth, and "cry mightily to God" so that God might perhaps spare them from otherwise pending destruction (Jonah 3:6–9). In light of these and many other texts considered in this chapter, the idea that both "man and beast" might call on YHWH/God is not so odd as it might appear if Jonah 3:6–9 were the only such text.

---

1. See also Ps 147:9: "He gives to the animals their food, and to the young ravens when they cry."

B. ALL CREATURES PRAISE, BLESS, AND REJOICE BEFORE YHWH/GOD

Many other biblical texts also indicate that other creatures relate directly to YHWH/God by praying to him, praising, rejoicing before, or blessing him. In some cases, these creatures are expressly called upon to do so. Such texts are especially characteristic of the book of Psalms.

Psalm 69:34 summons all creation and all living creatures to praise YHWH/God: "Let heaven and earth praise him, the seas and everything that moves in them."[2] The psalmist himself will praise YHWH, and expects "all flesh" likewise to "bless his holy name forever and ever" (Ps 145:21).[3] Living creatures, trees, mountains, and "deeps" are so summoned again in Ps 148:

> Praise YHWH from the earth,
>   you sea monsters and all deeps, . . .
> Mountains and all hills,
>   fruit trees and all cedars!
> Wild animals and all cattle,
>   creeping things and flying birds! (Ps 148:7, 10)[4]

---

2. See also Ps 98:7: "Let the sea roar, and all that fills it; the world and those who live in it!," a text later repeated in 1 Chr 16:32. And see Ps 100:1: "Make a joyful noise to YHWH, all the earth!" Psalm 19:1–4 declares that the heavens and/or the firmament continually "are telling the glory of God" and proclaiming "his handiwork."

3. See Lagat, *Christian Faith*, 67: "The end of the book of Psalms [Ps 150] proclaims, 'Let everything that has breath praise the Lord.' This command to worship God is addressed not just to his human creation but to other animate life. In Ps 148 the exhortation is widened to include all creation, moon, and stars, sea creatures, mountains, trees and birds, all offer their existence to him, and so are to offer him praise."

4. See G. G., *Creatures Praysing*. This seventeenth-century author, who evidently wished to remain anonymous, begins his book by quoting Ps 148:7–10 and argues throughout for the exemplary, natural religion of animals. See, e.g.: "[We should] rightly consider that the praises of God do not necessarily imply the most exact and magnificent order and forme, such as might well beseeme the Majestie of a Deitie (both men and Angels come short in that excellent service) but the praises of God require no more in effect, then the power and ability wherewith God hath first inabled the Creature: for he accepts our imperfect prayers, and descends to our weakenesse. Thus the stocks and the stones in their silence, and in their natural properties; the beasts in their sounds and their cries, in their sense and in their motions, all serve to praise him: for God requires no more then he hath first give, the right employment of his gifts is indeed to praise him." G. G., *Creatures Praysing*, 2.

See also Heide, *My Father's World*, 149–50. More recently a church in Massachusetts

Second Isaiah[5] promises that the land itself—both wilderness and deserts—will "be glad," and "rejoice and blossom . . . and rejoice with joy and singing."

> The wilderness and the dry land shall be glad,
>   the desert shall rejoice and blossom;
> like the crocus it shall blossom abundantly,
>   and rejoice with joy and singing. (Isa 35:1)

Similarly, the psalmist invites the heavens, the earth, the sea, and all creatures of land and sea to rejoice, along with "all the trees of the field":

> Let the heavens be glad,
>   and let the earth rejoice!
> Let the sea roar,
>   and all that fills it;
> let the field exult,
>   and everything in it!
> Then shall all the trees of the field
>   sing for joy before YHWH:
>   for he is coming. (Ps 96:11–12a; repeated in 1 Chr 16:31–33)

The book of Psalms concludes in crescendo, invoking praise from all animate creatures—"everything that breathes": "Let everything that breathes praise YHWH! Praise YHWH!" (Ps 150:6).[6]

---

decided to encourage members to bring their dogs to Sunday services. The minister "got the idea from reading the Bible. She came across a Psalm that talks about 'letting all living things praise the Lord.'" Associated Press, "Church Opens Doors."

5. See Richard Hiers, *Trinity Guide to Bible*, 95–96.

6. See also Pss 66:1–2, 4; 96:1; 98:4; and 100:1, where "all the earth" evidently includes all people and all other beings as well. This faith-understanding also comes to expression in later Christian liturgy; for instance, in the hymn "All Creatures of Our God and King," attributed to St. Francis of Assisi; and the traditional doxology: "Praise God from whom all blessings flow; Praise Him all creatures here below" (Ken, "Praise God"). Apparently in order to avoid referring to God with male pronouns, some churches have recently adopted an alternative version which, however, omits reference to "all creatures": "Praise God from whom all blessings flow; Praise Christ, all people here below; Praise Holy Spirit evermore; Praise Triune God whom we adore." Here again we see a tendency in modern piety to shift from biblical faith to some kind of anthropocentric interpretation. See also "All People That on Earth Do Dwell," by William Kethe, which can begin: "All creatures that on earth do dwell, sing to the Lord with cheerful voice . . . Come ye before Him and rejoice."

That other creatures can praise, rejoice before, bless, or otherwise worship YHWH/God is affirmed in many other biblical writings as well. As in Ps 96:11–12, the prophet Isaiah (or Second Isaiah) addresses all creatures of land and sea:

> Sing to YHWH a new song,
>> his praise from the end of the earth!
> Let the sea roar and all that fills it,
>> the coastlands and their inhabitants. (Isa 42:10)

Speaking by the same prophet about his plans to bring the exiles back from Babylon, YHWH says:

> The wild animals will honor me,
>> the jackals and the ostriches;
> for I give water in the wilderness,
>> rivers in the desert. (Isa 43:20)

The story of Tobit includes a human prayer that likewise expresses this kind of faith-understanding: "Let the heavens and the whole creation bless you forever" (Tob 8:5). So also does Ps 103:22: "Bless YHWH, all his works, in all places of his dominion."

All creation as well as certain kinds of creatures are addressed in the Song of the Three Young Men (RSV), which begins,

> Bless the Lord, all you works of the Lord;
>> sing praises to him and highly exalt him forever.
> (Sg Three, v. 35)

Not only humans but also plants and other animate creatures are thus summoned:

> Bless the Lord, all things that grow in the ground;
>> sing praise to him and highly exalt him for ever.
> Bless the Lord, you whales and all [creatures that move] in the waters,
>> sing praise to him and highly exalt him forever.
> Bless the Lord, all birds of the air,
>> sing praise to him and highly exalt him forever.
> Bless the Lord, all wild animals and cattle;
>> sing praise to him and highly exalt him forever.
> Bless the Lord, all people on earth;

> sing praise to him and highly exalt him forever.
> (Sg Three vv. 54, 57–60)[7]

Perhaps it is not surprising that the last writing in the New Testament anticipates that in the eagerly awaited time to come—at the beginning of the messianic age—all creatures would join in blessing and praising God:

> Then I heard every creature in heaven and on earth and under the earth and in the sea, and all that is in them, singing, "To the one seated on the throne and to the Lamb be blessing and honor and glory and might forever and ever!" (Rev 5:13)[8]

This expectation accords with the Isaianic assurance that in the coming age, "all flesh" would worship YHWH:

> From new moon to new moon,
>   and from Sabbath to Sabbath,
> all flesh shall come to worship before me,
>   says YHWH. (Isa 66:23)

In biblical tradition, all kinds of creatures were believed to have the capacity to praise and bless their Creator, and often are represented as doing so.[9] And some, or all, would do so in the coming age, as well. As will be seen, many other biblical passages show that other creatures besides humans were expected to be among those present in that future messianic age.[10]

Chapter Two has examined a range of texts which understand that YHWH/God cares directly for all creation and for all the creatures he brought and continues to bring into being. This chapter has focused on the reciprocal movement: belief that other creatures—other than humans—could look to and call upon YHWH/

---

7. Nearly the entire text of the Prayer of Azariah or, more properly, the Song of the Three Young Men, vv. 35–65, is included in the Book of Common Prayer as *Benedicite, omni opera Domini*. Episcopal Church, *Book of Common Prayer*, 11–13.

8. See Howell, "Reflections," 249: "If we fail to care for the land and some of these creatures become extinct, how can they sing praises to God, to Christ? . . . A Ghanaian Christian view of land care necessarily requires concerted practical action."

9. See Santmire, *Celebrating Nature by Faith*, 14: God depends on a variety of the creatures he has made "to respond in their own canons of spontaneity and praise."

10. See below, ch. 11.

God to meet their needs and bless and praise him for his continuing care.[11] How humans were believed to fit into the world of relationships between YHWH/God and other creatures is considered next, in part 2 of this book.

---

11. Another implication of this text, and of the others considered in this chapter, is that God does not need humanity in order to be worshipped. See Santmire, *Celebrating Nature by Faith*, 40: "This is what the Bible shows us. God has a history with nature and values nature in itself, independent of God's relationship with the human creature. God creates a grand and beautiful world of nature for God's own purposes. It is harmonious, it is good. All its members are variously and sometimes exquisitely interrelated."

PART TWO

YHWH/God, the Creation, All Creatures, and Human Beings

And of every living thing, of all flesh, you shall bring two of every kind into the ark, to keep them alive with you; they shall be male and female. Of the birds according to their kinds, and of the animals according to their kinds, of every creeping thing of the ground according to its kind, two of every kind shall come into you, to keep them alive. Also take with you every kind of food that is eaten, and store it up; and it shall serve as food for you and for them." Noah did this; he did all that God commanded him. (Gen 6:19–22)

The wolf shall live with the lamb,
    the leopard shall lie down with the kid,
the calf and the lion and the fatling together,
    and a little child shall lead them.
The cow and the bear shall graze,
    their young shall lie down together;
    and the lion shall eat straw like the ox.
    The nursing child shall play over the hole of the asp,
    and the weaned child shall put its hand on the adder's den.
They will not hurt or destroy
    on all my holy mountain;
for the earth shall be full of the knowledge of YHWH
    as the waters cover the sea. (Isa 11:6–9)

Attention in part 1 focused on biblical understandings and affirmations as to relationships between God on one hand, and the created world (or universe) and all kinds of nonhuman living beings, on the other. Human beings appeared only in the background. Part 2 now considers a wide range of biblical texts that have to do with relationships among YHWH/God, human beings, and the rest of creation, including all other kinds of life-forms. Some of these texts are in the form of narratives, others in the form of laws, psalms, proverbs, prophecies, or parables.

Many texts indicate what humans should do or not do in relation to the creation and other creatures. Other texts consider ways in which humans and other creatures are linked together, and how humans are, in many ways, like other creatures. Several texts show considerable interest in and appreciation of nature, particularly other creatures, some of them seen as providing models for human conduct. It also will be observed that other creatures are often seen as agents of YHWH/God's purposes in his dealings with human beings. Chapter 11 considers texts that look forward to conditions of life in the future messianic age, when humankind and all nature—that is, all creation would be at peace.

CHAPTER 4

The Primordial Commandments and the P Covenant with Noah and with "Every Living Creature of All Flesh"

MOST BIBLICAL LAWS FOUND in the books of Exodus, Numbers, Leviticus, and Deuteronomy are said to have been mediated by Moses to the people of Israel during their sojourn in the Sinai Peninsula. In addition, several commands or instructions appear earlier in the book of Genesis. This chapter considers those commands and instructions set out in Genesis that had to do with the progenitors of both humans and other living beings.

A. ON BEING FRUITFUL, MULTIPLYING, FILLING AND SUBDUING THE EARTH, AND HAVING DOMINION

Near the end of the P or priestly creation story (Gen 1:1–2:4a),[1] the first man and woman were "blessed" by God and ordered (or authorized) to "be fruitful and multiply, and fill the earth and subdue it," and to have "dominion"[2] over other living creatures (Gen

---

1. As to P tradition in Gen 1–10, see generally Steck, *World and Environment*, 89–113; and Rad, *Old Testament Theology*, 232–79.

2. See Tull, *Inhabiting Eden*, 23–26. As to the meaning of "dominion," Tull pointedly observes: "If, as this [biblical] writer thought, God had given humans responsibility to rule other animals, it is difficult to imagine how this verse could possibly

1:26–28).[3] In recent years a few morally serious commentators have suggested that Judaism and Christianity are to be blamed for the contemporary environmental crisis because people throughout the world in ensuing centuries allowed themselves to be misguided by these and certain other supposedly disastrous biblical mandates.[4] This kind of complaint fails to take into account the biblical context in which the aboriginal human couple was so instructed.[5]

According to Gen 1:26–28, only this first human couple was authorized to subdue the earth and have dominion.[6] Nothing was said about their descendants having been given such authority. Moreover, as the narrative unfolds, everything in Gen 1 necessarily preceded the time of the great flood (Gen 6–9), after which the whole structure of relations among humans, other creatures, and God was altered radically. These mandates may well have been understood to apply—at most—to people living during that antediluvian era. Curiously, both critics and proponents of biblical perspectives often seem unaware that the Bible continues beyond Gen 1:28, and has considerably more to say about nature and

---

have been intended to authorize exploiting, extracting, raping, pillaging, and using up everything within reach" (25).

3. Simkins notes that there is no biblical basis for the often-repeated assertion that the second (J) creation story's account of the first man's naming other animals (Gen 2:18–20) signifies human superiority or dominance over them. Simkins, *Creator and Creation*, 183.

4. For a variety of critiques and responses by other commentators, see, e.g., Barbour, *Ethics*, 74–80; J. Cobb, *Is It Too Late*, ix–x; Cohen, "On Classical Judaism"; Cone, *Redacted Dominionism*, 26–48; Derr, "Religion's Responsibility"; Derr, *Environmental Ethics*, 21–32; Douma, *Environmental Stewardship*, 29–31; Larsen and Larsen, *While Creation Waits*; Heide, *My Father's World*, 24–29, 146–49; Nash, *Loving Nature*, 68–92; North, *Dominion Covenant*, 27–36; Passmore, *Man's Responsibility for Nature*, 3–25; Schaeffer, *Pollution*; and G. Wright, *Old Testament Ethics*, 118–29.

5. Such complaints also tend to overestimate the impact of these biblical texts on cultures where Judaism, Christianity, and their Scriptures have had little or no identifiable influence. And they underestimate the influence of other and more significant factors. See Commoner, *Closing Circle*, 1–6; Dubos, *God Within*, 160–62; Fortin, "Bible Made Me Do"; Mason, *Unnatural Order*; Miller, *Planet to Choose*, 67–74; Nash, *Loving Nature*, 75; Russell, *Earth, Humanity, and God*, 86–93; and Steck, *World and Environment*, 31–42.

6. As to modern evangelical reflections, see Lin, *Nature of Environmental Stewardship*, 52–59.

environmental issues.[7] The instructions to "subdue the earth" and "have dominion" over other creatures were not repeated after the flood to Noah's descendants—the progenitors of all subsequent humankind.

Some interpretations of Gen 1:26–28 suggest that these verses meant that humans were given (or assigned) responsibility for tending the garden and caring for the well-being of other creatures; others read these verses as legitimating exploitation of the earth's resources and other life-forms for human benefit.[8] However one interprets these texts, a great many other biblical texts call on humans to respect the earth and care positively for the well-being of other creatures. Certain biblical covenants leave no doubt that God was believed to be concerned for the well-being of all life-forms, not only for that of humans.[9]

The Genesis story relates that before the flood, humanity had already multiplied (Gen 6:1) and "filled [the earth] with violence" (Gen 6:11).[10] Perhaps the narrator understood that such violence derived, at least in part, from humans abusing their authority to subdue and dominate the created order. Tradition commonly thought to derive from J attributes YHWH/God's decision to bring

---

7. This point was emphasized by Anderson, "Creation and Ecology," in *Creation in Old Testament*, 152–71.

8. Several excellent studies address these and related issues. See, e.g., Abrecht et al., *Faith, Science*, 34–43; Anderson, *From Creation*, 111–31; Bird, "Male and Female"; Berry, *Gift of Good Land*, 268–69; Brouman and Legge, *Law Relating to Animals*, 2–6; Callicott, "Genesis and John Muir"; Gottfried, *Economics, Ecology*, 36–39; Granberg-Michaelson, *Worldly Spirituality*, 53–72; Hayden, *Lost Gospel of Earth*, 60–66, 81–102; Hall, *Imaging God*; Jacobson, "Biblical Bases," 46–48; Limburg, "Way of an Eagle"; Martin-Schramm and Stivers, *Christian Environmental Ethics*, 112–204; Nash, *Loving Nature*, 102–8; Pojman, *Global Environmental Ethics*, 97–103; Rolston, *Environmental Ethics*, 338; Steck, *World and Environment*, 102–8, 194–200; Steffen, "In Defense of Dominion"; Trible, "Ancient Priests," 74–79; G. Tucker, "Rain on a Land"; Twum-Baah, "Bible and Environment," 20–22; De Vries, *Champions of the Poor*, 113–14; and Wilkinson, *Earthkeeping in the Nineties*, 275–325. As to Jewish responses, see, e.g., Schorsch, "Learning"; and Schwartz, "Jewish Theory."

9. See below, sect. C of this chapter and ch. 11 of this book. And see generally McCoy, "Creation and Covenant."

10. Arguably, the P account at Gen 6:11–22 likewise attributes "violence" to humanity but not to other creatures, though other creatures somehow may have been corrupted by human depravity. See Anderson, *Creation in Old Testament*, 161–65.

on the flood entirely to his recognizing the full extent of human depravity:

> YHWH saw that the wickedness of humankind was great upon the earth and that every imagination of the thoughts of their hearts was only evil continually. And YHWH was sorry that he had made humankind on the earth, and it grieved him to his heart. (Gen 6:5–6)

Clearly, humankind had gotten out of hand. As a result of the flood, the human population was reduced to a small group consisting of Noah and his immediate family. It is not clear that human nature had improved to any great extent in the aftermath of the flood. Nevertheless, YHWH/God "said in his heart, 'I will never again curse the ground because of humankind, for the imagination of the human heart is evil from his youth'" (Gen 8:21). YHWH/God evidently was prepared to continue the human experiment; but neither Noah and his family nor any later generation of humankind was ever again told to "subdue" the earth or to "have dominion" over other living creatures.[11] Perhaps it was thought that humankind had shown itself unfit to be entrusted with such authority again.

Moreover, numerous biblical texts recognize that in postdiluvian times, humankind's domination over other creatures was significantly qualified or limited.[12] Furthermore, biblical tradition

---

11. Granberg-Michaelson, *Worldly Spirituality*, 64, notes that after the flood, repetition of these commands was "conspicuously omitted." The author of Ps 8:5–8, however, may represent a strand of biblical understanding to the effect that humans were to have dominion over other life-forms in the era after the flood. The character of such dominion is not indicated in this psalm. See Gray, "Critique of Dominion Theology"; and Tubbs, "Humble Dominion." In the NT, Ps 8 is read as a prophetic description of Christ's, not humankind's, rule or dominion: Eph 1:20–22; Heb 2:5–10. Psalm 91:13, which seems to echo Ps 8:6–8, is set in the context of a series of reassurances to those who put their trust in YHWH. Luke 10:19 may have been drawn in part from Ps 91:13, and Mark 6:7 (which probably is an earlier version of this saying) refers only to Jesus giving his followers "authority over the unclean spirits." There is no mention here of serpents or scorpions. Wisdom of Solomon 9:1–3 and Sir 17:2–4 merely recapitulate Gen 1.

12. In Job 40, YHWH urges that Job (and, implicitly, other humans) could never hope to subdue the great creatures Behemoth and Leviathan. See below, ch. 7B. Several other texts in Job and Psalms make clear that many creatures for whom YHWH cares were meant to remain free from human control. See, e.g., Job 38:39–41; 39:1–12,

generally maintains that YHWH/God has dominion over both history and all creation.[13] As the Genesis narrative stands, humans had been given authority to subdue the earth and hold dominion over other living things, but only during the primordial period before the flood.

After the flood, Noah and his sons were instructed to be "fruitful and multiply and fill the earth" (Gen 9:1, 7); this time, however, the instruction was given in the context of the situation immediately after a flood that had destroyed all other human life. The instruction evidently was intended simply to replenish the human population. It was not presented as an ordinance binding upon all humanity in later eras. Nor is it repeated, or even alluded to, in later biblical traditions or periods. According to Gen 9:19, the whole earth had already been "peopled" (or repeopled) by Noah's descendants, at least by the time the story was written. It can be inferred that the early Genesis narrators understood that, so far as human populations were concerned, the command to be fruitful and multiply given to Noah and his sons had been fulfilled as early as the era described in Gen 10:1–32.

Although those persons who survived the flood were told afterwards to "be fruitful and multiply [and] abound on the earth and

---

26–30; Pss 50:9–12; 104:10–13, 17–18, 20–22, 24–30; 145:13–16; and 147:8–9. See generally G. Tucker, "Rain on a Land." On the book of Job as a critique of anthropocentrism, see Hayden, *Lost Gospel of Earth*, 74–81. On Ps 104, see Steck, *World and Environment*, 78–89. "The absence of humankind's dominion as a theme in the remainder of the Old and New Testaments reflects the loss of humankind's status as dominator of the earth." And see Barlow, "Why the Christian Right," 802; Nash, *Loving Nature*, 102; Hill, *Christian Faith and Environment*, 44, as to texts indicative of human limitations and insignificance. In some texts, other creatures are said to have dominion over humans. See generally Kay, "Concepts of Nature," 309, 314–17. Biblical texts also contemplate that in the time (or times) of future judgment, other creatures would serve as agents of YHWH's dominion by inflicting retribution upon depraved humankind. See below, ch. 10B.

13. See, e.g., Judg 2:11–23; 1 Kgs 11:26–39; 2 Kgs 17:1–18; 24:18–20; Job 38:4—39:8; Pss 22:27–28; 90–91; 94; 96–99; 135:5–12; 145:13; Amos 1–3; Jonah; and all other biblical prophets. In the NT, see, e.g., 1 Pet 5:11. See generally McAfee, "Ecology and Biblical Studies," 36–38. And see above, ch. 2, and below, ch. 10. Modern translators and liturgists often prefer to avoid using words like "Lord" or "King" when referring to God, substituting power- or status-neutral terms instead. Such substitutions fail to represent the consistently biblical representation of God as the one having dominion.

multiply in it,"[14] they were not instructed or authorized to "subdue the earth" or to "have dominion" over other creatures.[15] All other descendants of those who had been so authorized had perished in the flood. At any rate, by the time the biblical narratives were being set down, it may have been assumed that humankind had done all the multiplying that was required. Genesis 10:32 sums up the account of the growth of human populations in Gen 10:1–31: "These are the families of Noah's sons, according to their genealogies, in their nations; and from these the nations spread abroad on the earth after the flood."

Moreover, as has been seen,[16] humans were not the only beings instructed to "be fruitful and multiply" in primordial times. All kinds of sea creatures and birds had been so commanded the "day" they were created (Gen 1:20–22). Sea creatures were not again ordered to "be fruitful and multiply" after the flood. The flood, of course, would not have affected seagoing species.[17] But after the flood, as the story is told, God declared that all creatures of the land and air—"all flesh—birds and animals and every creeping thing that creeps on the earth"—were to "abound" or "breed abundantly" (RSV) and "be fruitful and multiply on the earth" (Gen 8:17). Implicitly, all these postdiluvian families of air-breathing creatures were intended to enjoy life and space in the world and perpetuate their respective species—so long as the earth endured.[18] None of these texts calls upon humans or other species to keep on being fruitful and multiplying up to the brink of ecological catastrophe, whether in the form of gradual Malthusian overcrowding or sudden population collapse. From the standpoint of the biblical

---

14. Gen 9:7; cf. 9:1: "Be fruitful and multiply, and fill the earth."

15. Cf. Gen 1:28 where the primordial couple is so instructed. After the flood, however, God tells Noah and his sons: "The fear and dread of you shall rest on every animal of the earth, and on every bird of the air, on everything that creeps on the ground and on all the fish of the sea; into your hands they are delivered" (Gen 9:2).

16. See above, ch. 2B4.

17. See Gen 7:22: "Everything on dry land in whose nostrils was the breath of life died." Under these conditions, marine mammals would have survived the floodwaters without needing to board the ark.

18. That implication is made explicit in the covenant God made with all living beings in Gen 9. See below, sect. C of the present chapter.

writers who set down these instructions or commandments, they already had been fulfilled. By the time the psalmist was writing, all creatures *had been* fruitful and multiplied.[19] A later biblical author reflects on the questions as to overpopulation and the earth's carrying capacity[20] in the form of a dialogue between Ezra, also known as Salathiel, and the angel Jeremiel:

> Then I answered and said, "Could thou not have created at one time [all] those who have been and who will be, [so] that thou mightest show thy judgement the sooner?" He replied to me and said, "The creation cannot make more haste than the Creator, neither can the world hold at one time [all] those who have been created in it."[21]

B. AFTER VEGETARIANISM: RESPECTING THE LIFE OF ANIMALS KILLED FOR FOOD

Before the flood, humans, birds, and all other land creatures had been vegetarians (Gen 1:29–30). As the story is told, neither humans nor any of the creatures on board the ark ate meat of any kind.[22] After the flood, however, the era of human vegetarianism was over. The initial harmony between humans and other creatures that had obtained in the garden of Eden and on the ark came to an end. Now other creatures—the beasts of the earth, birds of the air, creeping things on the ground, and fish of the sea—had reason to fear and dread humankind (Gen 9:1–3). Some humans would become hunters[23] and fishers.[24] Nevertheless, human beings were

---

19. See, e.g., Ps. 104:24: "O YHWH, how manifold are your works!... The earth is full of your creatures." Psalm 104 and P tradition were set down during approximately the same period, in or close to the fifth century BCE. See also Sir 16:29–30.

20. See J. Cobb, *Is It Too Late*, 49–52.

21. 2 Esd (4 Ezra) 5:43–44. See also 2 Esd 5:45–49.

22. See Gen 6:21, where YHWH tells Noah: "Take with you every kind of food that is eaten, and store it up; and it shall be food for you and for [every living thing]."

23. See Gen 10:8–9; also 25:27; 27:3–4, 30–33. For recent critical reflections as to hunting, see, e.g., Regan, "Philosophical Perspectives on Hunting"; and Cohn, "Exploding the Hunting Myths."

24. Gen 9:2. Strangely little is said about fishing or eating fish in the Jewish Scriptures or Old Testament. The only explicit instances are Num 11:5; Ezek 47:10; and

to respect the "life" of every living thing they killed for food. The "life" of each creature was thought to be contained in or identified with its blood (Gen 9:4). Humans now were permitted to eat the flesh of other creatures but were not permitted to consume their blood (Gen 9:3–4). The context suggests that this prohibition may have been intended to apply to fish as well as to other life-forms. This limitation expresses a kind of reverence or respect for life, that is, the lives of all God's creatures. These other creatures might be killed and eaten as food, but their "life" must not be destroyed.[25] Evidently it was understood that an animal's life/blood somehow would be preserved by being returned to the ground. Similar provisions appear in later Israelite or Jewish laws governing the slaughter of animals for food.[26] Unlike these later laws, which were meant as guidance for Israel or the Jewish people, the Gen 9:4 prohibition against eating flesh with its life or blood, in its terms, applied to all the descendants of Noah, that is, to all humankind, whatever their nationality.[27] This understanding may have been in the minds of those early Jewish-Christian leaders who agreed that gentile converts to Christianity should not eat blood or the meat of animals that had been strangled.[28]

The story of Noah and the ark, as such, is neither law nor covenant. But it provides the context for, and is closely interwoven with, the P account of God's subsequent covenant with all living beings and their progeny. It also provides significant insight regarding the biblical appreciation and affirmation of the value of all other life-forms and sets the stage for an ongoing, positive relationship between Noah's descendants—later humankind—and these other kinds of creatures.

Tobit 6:1–5. See also Neh 13:16.

25. Clearly more is involved here than a mere "visceral prohibition against the consumption of blood." Schorsch, "Learning," 31. Compare traditional Native American practices expressing gratitude and concern for the life of animals killed for food.

26. See Lev 17:10–14; Deut 12:20–27, and below, ch. 5A2.

27. According to Gen 10:1–32, all later humankind descended from Noah.

28. Acts 15:19–20, 28–29.

C. GENESIS 9:8–17: THE P COVENANT WITH NOAH AND WITH EVERY LIVING CREATURE OF ALL FLESH

This covenant has been considered previously in part 1, where attention was focused on biblical traditions concerning relationships between YHWH/God and other-than-human creatures. Now the focus is on its implications for relationships between humans and other creatures. In the biblical narrative, this covenant follows immediately after the end of the story about the great flood. In that story, pursuant to YHWH/God's instructions, Noah saved not only his immediate family but also one or more pairs of all other air-breathing species, so that they, too, might not only survive but be fruitful and multiply afterwards.[29]

In this context, P tradition then refers *five times* to the *covenant* God made with Noah and his sons *and* with all kinds of living creatures.[30] This was the first and most explicitly inclusive of all biblical covenants. It was first in the sense that in the completed biblical narrative, it comes before all accounts of covenants made with Abraham and his descendants,[31] and it was the most inclusive because of its extension to all living beings.

The terms of these several texts regarding this covenant leave no doubt as to its inclusiveness. It was made with Noah, his sons, their descendants, and "with every living creature . . . the birds, the domestic animals, and every animal of the earth . . . as many as came out of the ark" (Gen 9:9–10). According to Gen 9:12, this covenant is between God and Noah and Noah's sons "and every living creature . . . *for all future generations*." In Gen 9:15, God speaks of the "covenant which is between me [God] and you *and every living creature of all flesh*," while Gen 9:16 refers to "*the everlasting covenant between God and every living creature of all flesh that is on*

---

29. See above, ch. 2B5, and below, ch. 9B1a.

30. The text of Gen 9:8–17 is quoted above at the beginning of pt. 1. See generally Anderson, *From Creation*, 156–64; Granberg-Michaelson, *Worldly Spirituality*, 73–90; and Martin-Schramm and Stivers, *Christian Environmental Ethics*, 177.

31. The other main biblical covenants include those described in Gen 12:1–3; 15:1–21; 17:1–14; 26:1–5; 28:13–15; Exod 19:5–6; 20:1—23:33; and 34:10–27. On biblical covenants, see generally Simkins, *Creator and Creation*, 152–72.

the earth."[32] Finally in Gen 9:17, God again points to "the covenant which I have established *between me and all flesh that is on the earth*" (emphases added throughout Gen 9).

These repetitions of this covenant and its terms clearly were intended to emphasize its inclusion not only of humans but also of "every living creature of all flesh."[33] Significantly, in these formulations, the covenant is said to be made by God with Noah *and* with *every living creature*. Not only species but individual living things were considered important.[34] This covenant implies that all life-forms and *each* living creature were meant to have their places or spaces upon the earth.[35] The time frame was not limited to the period immediately after the flood; instead, it was to continue in effect "for all future generations" (Gen 9:17).

It is striking that in each of these formulations, the covenantal language is unconditional. This covenant did not call on humans or other creatures to *do* anything in particular. Humans and other creatures were merely expected to continue in existence, from generation to generation, as the kinds of beings they had been created to be. According to the P creation narrative, God had pronounced all living beings "good," indeed, "very good" (Gen 1:20–31).[36] The terms of this covenant imply that all life-forms and all living beings were valued by God, and that the human participants in the covenant should, therefore, appreciate and affirm their value as well.

---

32. Emphasis added in these quotations from Gen 9:12–17. Compare Isa 24:5 ("the everlasting covenant") and Ps 145:13 ("everlasting kingdom").

33. Cf. Simkins, *Creator and Creation*, 154–56, characterizing the P covenant more broadly, as God's covenant with *all creation*. McDaniel reflects on contemporary implications of this P covenant in his chapter "God Who Loves Animals."

34. In Gen 9:13, the covenant is said to have been made between God and "the earth." Here it seems likely that "the earth" stands for the fuller expression "every living creature of all flesh that is on the earth" (Gen 9:16) or "all flesh that is on the earth" (Gen 9:17).

35. "The covenant (9:17) . . . suggests that the Creator's purpose is to provide living space for all organisms, so that they may share the earth together." Nash, *Loving Nature*, 101.

36. See also Wis 1:14: "For [God] created all things that they might exist, and the [creatures] of the earth are wholesome"; and Sir 39:16: "All the works of the Lord are very good." See above, ch. 1B. As to biblical creation traditions, see Barbour, *Religion*, 130–35.

Thus, this covenant could be seen as the foundation for later biblical laws mandating people's concern for animal well-being. Clearly this was not an anthropocentric covenant;[37] rather, it was made with and for the benefit of all kinds of living creatures. It does not provide any warrant for humans to exploit or destroy other species.[38] It was a long-term covenant, sealed with the sign of the rainbow, and intended to remain operative throughout all history (Gen 9:12–17). It could be inferred from this covenant that future generations of humans should be concerned with the welfare not only of their own progeny but also with the well-being of future generations of all other creatures as well.[39]

37. Several commentators have demonstrated that biblical faith generally is not anthropocentric. See, e.g., Bergant, "Is Biblical Worldview Anthropocentric"; J. Cobb, *Sustainability*, 92–93; and Barlow, "Christian Right," 802: "In short, the [biblical] environmental narrative is neither biocentric nor anthropocentric; it is theocentric." Cf. Hart, *Sacramental Commons*, 17–18, discussing "creation-centered consciousness" in contrast to other types of "consciousness," including "theocentric," which he understands to mean believing in God "in isolation from the fruits of divine creativity." Other commentators use the term "theocentric" inclusively. Cf. Santmire, *Celebrating Nature by Faith*, xiii–xv ("theocosmocentric," opposing Karl Barth's "theoanthropocentric" paradigm).

On the significant difference between theocentric and anthropocentric ethics, see generally Gustafson, *Sense of the Divine*. Compare Derr, *Environmental Ethics* (undertaking to make a strong case for anthropocentric environmental ethics), and Nash's critique of Derr's position (Derr, *Environmental Ethics*, 105–24). Anthropocentric faith occasionally informs biblical values. See, e.g., Wis 11:15; 13:14 ("worthless animals" not to be worshiped). But compare Wis 11:24—12:1 (classic statement of theocentric faith and correlative reverence for life).

38. Nothing in this covenant suggests that humans were to have dominion over other creatures. God, who initiated this covenant, was the one who had dominion. See above, ch. 2A.

39. See generally the several essays published in Partridge, *Responsibilities to Future Generations*. These essays attempt to ground such responsibility on philosophical and mainly humanistic or anthropocentric considerations. The problematics of such attempts are evident in the essay by Thompson, "Are We Obliged." Thompson answers this question in the negative and concludes: "I have to confess that I go on my selfish and polluting way with a certain amount of bad conscience—as I imagine you do. But your guilty self-indulgence may bother you a little less if you try to believe—as I do—that we are not obligated to future others." Thompson, "Are We Obliged," 202. Some decades ago, the Club of Rome observed: "The majority of the world's people are concerned with matters that affect only family or friends over a short period of time. . . . Only a few people have a global perspective that extends far into the future." Meadows et al., *Limits to Growth*, 23–25. An illustration: some years ago, the present writer attended a local League of Women Voters meeting where the director of the

A related text that probably derives from J tradition is equally emphatic in its assurance as to YHWH/God's care for humankind and other creatures alike in future times following the great flood:

> YHWH said in his heart, "I will never again curse the ground because of humankind, for the imagination of the human heart is evil from his youth; nor will I ever again destroy every living creature as I have done. As long as the earth endures, seedtime and harvest, cold and heat, summer and winter, day and night, shall not cease." (Gen 8:21–22)

YHWH/God would continue to sustain his creation and all living creatures "as long as the earth endures." Later traditions also affirm God's care for all kinds of living creatures.[40] Other biblical texts anticipate that at the end of history, in the future or messianic age, YHWH/God would make operative a new covenant under which all creatures would dwell together in peace.[41]

In the meantime, biblical faith understood that humankind and all these other creatures with whom YHWH/God had made this initial covenant were meant to share their lives before him in this good world which he had made for his own purposes. That life together would include many kinds of interactions. These are considered in the following six chapters.

---

local power plant was asked about the consequences of fueling generators with coal. His candid reply: I sure as hell don't give a damn what happens twenty years from now [because] by then I'll be dead."

40. See above, ch. 2B. Numerous biblical texts likewise represent wildlife and domestic animals calling upon YHWH or God to sustain them; and praising, blessing, or giving him thanks for doing so, or for his other mercies. See above, ch. 3.

41. See below, ch. 11.

CHAPTER 5

Animal Sacrifices

STUDIES CONCERNED WITH THE Bible and nature, particularly those concerned with biblical faith and environmental ethics, often pay little or no attention to the many texts that call for animal sacrifices.[1] Nevertheless, such texts constitute a substantial portion of biblical law and reveal significant perspectives regarding both the value of animals before God and human responsibilities for their well-being.

Biblical tradition records two seemingly conflicting attitudes or understandings in regard to animal sacrifices. On the one hand, the books of Exodus, Leviticus, Numbers, and Deuteronomy contain numerous laws calling for various types of animal sacrifices that YHWH/God was understood to desire or require. On the other hand, many biblical voices are found protesting against the entire practice of offering sacrifices, particularly animal sacrifices.

The first part of this chapter focuses on biblical laws regarding sacrifices and discusses biblical rationales for carrying them out. The second part of the chapter considers a range of biblical texts that generally oppose, devalue, and deplore the whole institution of animal sacrifice. These texts urge that God no longer requires—or

---

1. A notable exception is the excellent chapter by Rogerson, "What Was the Meaning."

never did ask for—such sacrifices, among other reasons, because all animals already belong to him.

A. SACRIFICIAL LAWS: ANIMAL SACRIFICES

At the outset, it should be observed that biblical laws regarding animal sacrifices were understood to apply only to the people of Israel and their descendants. Yet long before there were Israelites, Abel is said to have offered "firstlings of his flock" of sheep (Gen 4:4), even though he had not been commanded or instructed to do so. And Noah offered a number of "clean" animals and birds in sacrifice after the flood (Gen 8:20) but, again, without having been so commanded.[2] As the Balaam-Balak story is told, YHWH/God ignores Balak's repeated sacrificial offerings (Num 23:1—24:25), possibly because Balak was a foreigner, but more likely because it was understood that YHWH/God will do what he intends, regardless. Job, the protagonist in the book by that name, offered burnt offerings on behalf of his sons (Job 1:5). But Job was not an Israelite, either.[3] A great many biblical laws do specify a range of animal sacrifices that Israelites were instructed to offer for a variety of purposes.

Somewhat paradoxically, several of these laws also underscore the importance of animal life. Both implicitly and explicitly, such laws affirm that animals belong to and are given by God, who values them highly. Those who have cattle or farm animals received them as gifts from YHWH/God, and are called on to show their gratitude by returning some of them to the Giver of all life. That animals might be sacrificed in place of humans likewise indicates a sense of their worth, as if an animal's life was considered somehow equivalent in value to a human life. Respect or reverence for the life of sacrificed (or slaughtered) animals comes to expression

---

2. It is implied that YHWH accepted Noah's offerings when he "smelled the pleasing odor" (Gen 8:21).

3. Job is described as "a man in the land of Uz" (Job 1:1), and thus presumably was an Edomite.

explicitly in laws governing disposal of their blood, which is associated closely, in biblical thought, with the life of each animal.[4]

1. Consecration of the Firstborn: One of the Earliest Laws

The requirement that firstborn sons and firstborn domestic animals be sacrificed or consecrated to YHWH/God appears in all of the law codes except H (the Holiness Code). Several laws provide for redeeming firstborns and, in some instances, specify that firstborn sons may be redeemed by offering an animal instead.

Perhaps the earliest such law is Exod 34:19-20.[5] This sets out the rationale for offering firstborn sons and animals: "All that first opens the womb is mine," says YHWH/God.[6] This text also provides for redeeming both firstborn sons and firstborn donkeys' or asses' colts,[7] although the manner in which firstborn sons were to be redeemed is not stated. Firstborn asses' colts might be "redeemed" or spared by offering a lamb instead. The underlying thought seems to have been that because domestic animals come from and therefore belong to YHWH/God, their firstborn should be returned to him. This was to be done either in the form of a sacrificial offering in the case of a clean animal or, in the case of an unclean animal, by killing it, unless it was redeemed by offering another animal instead. Thus any sense that humans *owned* their domestic animals was limited or qualified by recognition that YHWH/God was entitled to all firstborns, as his own.

A somewhat similar law is found in the Covenant Code, Exod 22:29b-30, which required that firstborn sons, as well as firstborn oxen and sheep, be "given" to God. The story of Abraham's substitution of a ram for his firstborn son, Isaac, may have been told and

---

4. Much of the discussion in this part of the chapter is drawn from the author's article "Reverence for Life."

5. This law is considered part of the Ritual Decalogue (RD), which is considered the earliest or most ancient collection of laws to be found in the Bible.

6. It was YHWH or God, of course, who created all life-forms in the first place. Gen 1:11-27 [P]; Gen 2:6-23 [J].

7. The NRSV translators usually seem to prefer "donkey" to "ass" (RSV). The latter term is more familiar in many classical texts, and is generally used in this book rather than "donkey."

recorded in order to allow or, perhaps, to require that thereafter animals were to be sacrificed instead of firstborn sons (Gen 22:1–14).[8] The story suggests that before God, a ram was considered to have as much value as a son. The requirement to sacrifice firstborn sons and firstborn oxen and sheep alike implies that both human and these animal offspring were understood to have their common origin and value in relation to God—the One who not only created the first humans and animals, long ago, but who also continues to endow them with fertility in order to ensure the perpetuation of their respective species.

Laws deriving from the Deuteronomic reform[9] contain somewhat related provisions. According to Deut 15:19–20, all firstborn male sheep and oxen and all firstborn male animals from every householder's herds and flocks were to be sacrificed and eaten "in the presence of YHWH" at the central shrine. Exodus laws had not distinguished between blemished and unblemished animals, but the Deuteronomic version says that blemished firstborn animals should not be sacrificed to YHWH.[10] Blemished firstborns, however, might be slaughtered locally and eaten (Deut 15:21–22); but as with the secular slaughter provision in Deut 12:15–28, the animals' blood must not be consumed. Rather, the blood must be poured out on the ground (Deut 15:23), evidently in order to preserve each animal's life by returning it to its source.[11]

In contrast to earlier law codes, the Priestly Code is concerned primarily with sacrificial offerings. A number of PC laws relate to firstborns, both human and animal. Several such laws, in one way and another, exempt Israelite firstborn humans and provide alternatives to sacrificing firstborn animals. Such laws are found in PC portions of Exodus and Numbers.

---

8. Both the CC and Gen 22 probably were included in E or the Northern tradition, which was collected and written down between 950 and 850 BCE. In that tradition, the Gen 22 story may have functioned as case law (or common law), construing and modifying the sacrificial ordinance set out in Exod 22:29–30.

9. As to the Deuteronomic reform, see below, sect. A2a of this chapter.

10. Compare Deut 17:1, to the same effect.

11. See Deut 12:15–16, 20–25.

Consecration of Firstborn Israelites and Their Cattle to YHWH/God

Exodus 13:1–2 reads: "YHWH said to Moses: 'Consecrate to me all the firstborn; whatever is the first to open the womb among the Israelites, [both] of human beings and animals, is mine.'" The term "consecrate" may mean to sacrifice, or it may mean to set aside as holy. In any case, the language is species- and gender-inclusive: "all the firstborn; whatever is the first to open the womb." Exodus 13:12a likewise uses inclusive language: "You shall set apart to YHWH all that first opens the womb." Verse 12b, however, refers only to the "firstborn of your [cattle or] livestock[12] that are male." Verse 13 then provides for the redemption of firstborn sons and firstling asses. As in Exod 34:19–20, firstling asses were to be redeemed by offering a lamb; but if not redeemed, the young ass's neck was to be broken (Exod 13:13). Another PC law, however, Num 18:15–19, provides that the firstborn of *unclean* animals—which term would include asses—were to be redeemed by payment of five shekels, whereas firstborn clean animals, namely, cows, sheep, and goats, were to be designated as "holy"; that is, after they had been slaughtered, the meat was to be given to the priests and their families "as a perpetual due."

Numbers 3:11–13 and 8:16–19: Levites instead of firstborn Israelites. These verses add that YHWH took the Levites (or tribe of Levi)[13] *instead of* the firstborn among the people of Israel generally and consecrated them to be permanent assistants to the "sons of Aaron," which term, in P tradition, designates the priests.[14] It may be that this provision was modeled on the story in 1 Sam

---

12. NRSV translators prefer the term "livestock." The word "livestock" possibly connotes a sense that the animals so categorized exist only for human use. In this book, the RSV's usual translations, "cattle" or "domestic animals," are generally followed instead.

13. As to Levites, see Richard Hiers, *Trinity Guide to Bible*, 16–17, 53–54.

14. See also Num 3:41a, 45a; 18:6.

1:1—2:21.[15] These Numbers texts provide a different explanation for Israel's abandoning the practice of offering firstborn sons.[16]

Numbers 3:40–45: Firstborn cattle of the Levites instead. Numbers 3:41a and 45a add that YHWH declared to Moses that he would accept the firstborn *cattle* of the Levites "as substitutes for all the firstborn among the livestock of the Israelites." Subsequent tradition in Numbers calls for enormous numbers of sacrificial offerings but refers only once to offering firstborn cattle or "livestock" (Num 18:15–18). No other biblical tradition dating after ca. 400 BCE refers to firstborn offerings of any sort. Possibly Num 3:40–45 represents a shift in priestly circles away from the idea that God required the sacrifice of the firstborn cattle of all Israelites. Those of the Levites would be enough.

2. Other Laws Governing Animal Sacrifice and Slaughter

Apart from laws relating to offering firstborns, few provisions regarding animal sacrifices are found in the earlier law codes. The *only* other provisions in the RD are those in Exod 34:25.[17] These are repeated, with slight variations, in the CC, in Exod 23:18.[18] The only other reference to animal sacrifice in the CC is at Exod 20:24. This passage describes the altar upon which sheep and oxen were to be sacrificed as burnt and peace offerings. Earlier portions of the Deuteronomic Code (Deut 5, 20–25) do not contain any laws concerning animal sacrifices.[19] Even the relatively recent H includes only a few provisions regarding animal sacrifices: Lev 19:5–8;

---

15. That story tells how Hannah, out of gratitude to YHWH for granting her prayer for a son, "lent" this son, Samuel, to YHWH by giving him as an assistant to the priest Eli.

16. Compare Gen 22:1–14, which presents an alternative explanation.

17. "You shall not offer the blood of my sacrifice with leaven, and the sacrifice of the festival of the Passover shall not be left until morning." Both of these provisions relate to Passover observance.

18. "You shall not offer the blood of my sacrifice with anything leavened, or let the fat of my festival remain until the morning."

19. The only possible exception is Deut 21:1–9, which provides for killing a heifer in order to "purge the guilt of innocent blood," when a murder has been committed by a person unknown.

22:17–29; 23:12–20; and possibly 23:36–38. The later addition to the Deuteronomic Code, Deut 12–19, provides that sacrifices were to be offered only at the temple in Jerusalem. It includes three sets of laws regarding animal sacrifices besides those relating to firstborns: Deut 16:2–7 (the Passover sacrifice); Deut 17:1 (barring sacrifice of blemished oxen or sheep); and Deut 18:1–3 (portions of sacrificed animals constituting "the priests' due from the people" [RSV]). Most of the other biblical laws regarding sacrificial offerings are found in the Priestly Code.

a. The Deuteronomic Reform: Worship in One Place; Secular Slaughter and Respect for Sacrificial Animals' Life

Nothing in early biblical laws or narratives indicates that the Israelites were originally required to worship in a single location. Canaanites and other indigenous peoples had worshiped their gods at numerous local shrines. So had the Israelites, it seems, until the latter part of the seventh century BCE,[20] when D was amended or expanded to require that Israelites (or Judahites) offer sacrifices at only the one "place." The new provisions are summarized in the following subsection of this chapter.

I. DEUTERONOMY 12:1–13:1: SACRIFICIAL WORSHIP IN ONLY THE ONE PLACE

Deuteronomy 12:5–7 sets out a completely new requirement: the people of Israel (or Judah)[21] were now told that they might offer animal sacrifices at only "the place that YHWH your God will choose out of all your tribes as his habitation to put his name there." Seventh-century and subsequent readers in biblical times would have recognized "the place" as the Jerusalem temple.[22] This, and related

---

20. Major shrines reportedly used in earlier times included Bethel, Gilgal, Hebron, Shechem, and Shiloh. On the Deuteronomic reform program, see generally Rad, *Deuteronomy*, 87–94.

21. The Deuteronomic reform is generally dated ca. 622 BCE.

22. Israelites did not succeed in occupying Jerusalem until the time of David, some two hundred years after their settlement or conquest of the rest of the land; and

commandments, probably were part of the Deuteronomic reform of ca. 622 BCE. The reform evidently was intended to reduce rural Israelites' (or, more precisely, Judahites')[23] temptation to worship the gods associated with the old Canaanite cult shrines. As if to drive home this new understanding, the requirement that sacrifices may be presented in only the one place is repeated several times in Deut 12.[24] In earlier laws set out in CC and H, there was no requirement that Passover, the Feast of Weeks, or the Feast of Booths be observed in only "the one place."[25] According to Deut 16:1–17, however, all three of these major festivals now were to be observed there, and there only, at least so far as sacrificial offerings were concerned.[26]

A corollary to mandating worship in only the one place was the requirement that the Israelites must no longer worship at the old shrines where they and their neighbors had "served their gods, on the mountain height, on the hills, and under every leafy tree" (Deut 12:2). The Israelites were to "break down" the altars and images representing or associated with the gods worshiped at these cult shrines (Deut 12:3).[27] Worship of these other gods was forbidden not only because, according to Israelite belief, YHWH/God alone was the god who created everything and continues to give of creation's bounty to his people but also because worshipers of other gods engaged in "abominable" and cruel practices.[28] Worship of Canaanite and other foreign deities often involved depraved

---

the temple was not built until the time of Solomon, ca. 950 BCE, nearly three hundred years, according to tradition, after YHWH gave Moses "the law" on Mt. Sinai.

23. Israel, the Northern Kingdom, had been overrun by Assyria ca. 722/21 BCE. The Southern Kingdom, Judah, retained its national identity until the Babylonian conquest and the beginning of the exile, ca. 587/86 BCE. See Richard Hiers, *Nation of Immigrants*, 22–29.

24. Deut 12:5–7, 11–14, 17–19, 26–28. This "one place," the Jerusalem temple, also came to be regarded as a bird sanctuary, according to Ps 84:1–3. See Gaster, *Myth, Legend, and Custom*, 765–66.

25. See Exod 23:14–17; Lev 23:4–21, 33–34.

26. See Deut 16:2, 5–7, 10–11, 15, 16.

27. Compare Exod 34:13.

28. Deut 12:31: "Because every abominable thing that YHWH hates they have done for their gods. They would even burn their sons and their daughters in the fire to their gods."

practices—which earlier Israelites, too, sometimes had followed.[29] Thus, after the Deuteronomic reform went into effect, animal sacrifices could no longer be offered at the places that previously had served as cult shrines.

1. Deuteronomy 12:15–16, 20–25: Secular Slaughter and Reverence for Life

It appears that in earlier biblical times, whenever a domestic animal was killed for food, the animal, or part of it, was to be offered to YHWH/God, usually at one of the nearby cult shrines. Conversely, when an animal or agricultural sacrifice was made to YHWH/God, those who offered the sacrifice and others in the community were permitted or expected to share the festive meal.[30] Because the old cult shrines would now be closed pursuant to the Deuteronomic reform, new provisions in Deut 12 allowed rural Israelites to slaughter animals locally for food without religious ceremony.[31] Those who ate the flesh of such animals, however, were still not permitted to consume blood, "for the blood is the life, and you shall not eat the life with the meat" (Deut 12:23). Instead, the animal's blood must be poured "out on the ground like water" (Deut 12:24).[32] Such provisions also appear in later P narratives and laws.[33] Although animals killed for food in rural areas were no longer offered to YHWH/God, Deut 12 shows sensitivity to, and respect for, the life of such animals. Their life was to be returned to

---

29. See, e.g., Lev 18:21; Deut 18:10–12; 23:17–18; Judg 11:30–31; 1 Kgs 16:34; 2 Kgs 3:27; 16:3; 21:6; Jer 7:31; 19:4–6; 32:35; Ezek 16:20–21.

30. See, e.g., Exod 23:14–17; Lev 23:4–44; 1 Sam 9:11–13, 22–24.

31. Deuteronomy 12:27 provided that when animal offerings were presented at the central shrine, their blood was to be "poured out on the altar of YHWH," thereby returning the animals' lives directly to him. Deuteronomy 12:20–21 allowed that animals might be slaughtered locally, without religious ceremony at the central shrine, but only if the trip to Jerusalem was "too far." Deuteronomy 12:15, however, gives permission for secular slaughter "within any of your towns" without further qualification.

32. See also Deut 15:21–23 regarding treatment of the blood of blemished firstborns. *Presumably* the same procedures were to apply when wild animals were killed for food. See Deut 12:15, 22; and compare Lev 17:13–14.

33. See Gen 9:3–4; Lev 17:10–11.

the ground, out of which, ultimately, according to the old J creation narrative, all such creatures, along with humankind, originally had been formed (Gen 2:18–19).[34]

b. New Sacrificial Offerings in the Priestly Code

Long ago, the pioneering German biblical scholar Julius Wellhausen observed that several types of sacrificial offerings appear for the first time in the PC.[35] A few of these new PC laws are described in what follows. In one way and another, these laws, too, demonstrate that the biblical writers believed and affirmed that animals are valued by God, and that his people must treat them accordingly.

1. Ordination of Priests and Other Occasions

Exodus 24–40 consists largely of priestly laws and narratives regarding the tent of meeting or tabernacle, along with descriptions of its elaborate furnishings. The tent or tabernacle supposedly served as the sole place of worship during the period of Israel's sojourn in the wilderness.[36] Most of the priestly laws in Exodus regarding sacrificial offerings are found in ch. 29, which details the procedures to be followed in consecrating or ordaining Aaron's sons as priests.

Similar sacrificial ordinances for these and other occasions also are to be found in PC portions of Leviticus and Numbers.[37] These laws imply that God was pleased by such offerings and that because of these offerings, he would overlook the shortcomings of the priests and other Israelites. Whether all the numerous and varied animal sacrifices described in these chapters were actually carried out during the period of Israel's sojourn in the wilderness

---

34. See below, ch. 6A and B.

35. Wellhausen, *Prolegomenon to the History*, 1–82.

36. The tent of meeting or tabernacle and its elaborate furnishings probably represented a glorified version of what had been Solomon's temple as remembered or imagined and projected back into the wilderness period by P writers in later times.

37. See, e.g., Lev 1, 3–8; Num 7, 15, 28–29.

(a time of scarcity and bare subsistence),[38] or prior to the construction of Solomon's temple,[39] need not be determined.

II. Sacrifices to Heal or Purify

Lev 14:1–54: Curing leprosy. Various bird and animal sacrifices are described here in connection with procedures for curing leprosy. References to guilt and sin offerings in Lev 14:12–14, 21–22 suggest that persons with this disease were thought to have been so afflicted because they had sinned.[40] Leviticus 14:30–31 implies that sacrificial offerings could atone for their transgressions. Other procedures described in Lev 14:6–7, 52, indicate that it was also believed that the blood of sacrificial birds or animals could have a cleansing or therapeutic effect for humans suffering from leprosy.[41]

Numbers 19:1–22: Ashes of a red heifer. This law, purportedly given by YHWH/God to Moses and Aaron in the wilderness, instructed them to slaughter an unblemished red heifer, have the old priest Eleazar sprinkle some of her blood "towards the front of the tent of meeting," and then burn the remains to ashes. The ashes, mixed with water, then could be used to purify anyone made unclean by contact with a dead body or with a dead person's bone or a grave.[42]

---

38. See, e.g., Exod 16:1–36; Num 11:4–15.

39. See 1 Kgs 5–8. See Rogerson, "What Was the Meaning," discussing a wide range of biblical perspectives on sacrifices and suggesting that P and PC traditions as to sacrifices probably represent an idealized, rather than an actual or historical, account.

40. Cf. John 9:1–2, indicating belief in NT times that illness derived from sin.

41. Cf. Tob 6:4, 6–8 (fish heart, liver, and gall used for exorcism and healing blindness).

42. Compare Deut 21:1–9, which prescribes a ceremony for "purging the guilt of innocent blood" in circumstances where someone has been killed, but the murderer remains undetected. Elders of the nearest city were to take a young heifer to an uncultivated valley with running water, break its neck, and then wash their hands over her. Although this ceremony is not described as a sacrifice, its stated intent was to provide forgiveness for the community that might otherwise be held accountable for "the guilt of innocent blood" (21:7–9). As in the case of animals sacrificed in lieu of firstborn sons, the underlying sense may have been that before God, the life of the animal somehow was valued as much as the life of the human.

In somewhat different ways, these Lev 14 and Num 19 laws anticipate or parallel a certain modern perspective that values other life-forms because they are, or may be, potential sources of drugs or medicines beneficial to humans. Many other PC laws seem to have intended animal sacrifices primarily to serve Israelite needs by pleasing God, who, in return, was expected to be gracious to his people. Nevertheless, it is clear that priestly law regarded other living beings as valued by God and therefore worthy of reverence or respect, apart from their usefulness to humans.

III. Leviticus 16:1–34: Sacrifices and the Day of Atonement

This law ordained that a bull, a male goat, and a ram were to be sacrificed in observance of the annual Day of Atonement. Another male goat was to be "presented alive before YHWH" by being "sent away into the wilderness to Azazel" (Lev 16:7–10).[43] It was believed that these animal sacrifices would atone for all the sins of Israel (Lev 16:34), thereby permitting the Israelites to avoid experiencing any tangible expressions of YHWH/God's disfavor. This belief accords with the general priestly understanding that YHWH/God could be influenced favorably by proper sacrificial offerings. That YHWH/God would be willing to accept the lives (blood) of these animals instead of requiring the lives (blood) of sinful Israelites, again suggests that the lives of animals and of persons were regarded as somehow having equivalent value before the Giver of all life.

IV. Leviticus 17:1–9: Bloodguilt for Killing Animals Other Than as Gifts Offered to YHWH/God

Under terms of the Deuteronomic reform, Israelites (or Judahites) were permitted to slaughter animals for food in their local towns, provided they did not eat the animals' blood. The blood of the

---

43. Thus the modern term "scapegoat." Whether Azazel was thought to be a place in the wilderness or a spirit of some sort is not certain, though the latter meaning is commonly assumed. It is unclear whether the goat sent into the wilderness was expected to survive there.

animal was to be poured out onto the ground.[44] In contrast, Lev 17:1–7 commands that animals—specifically, oxen, lambs, and goats—were not to be slaughtered *unless* they were brought "to the priest at the door of the tent of meeting" (Lev 17:3–5).[45] The stated rationale in Lev 17:4 is that unless this procedure was followed, the man who killed the animal "shall be guilty of bloodshed; he has shed blood, and he shall be cut off from his people." The implication is that unless an animal is offered to YHWH/God, its slaughter violates the animal's life or its integrity as one of YHWH/God's creatures. Its blood is its life (Gen 9:3–4; Lev 17:10–14). The animal's life came from YHWH/God; when it is killed, its life should be returned to him. If this text is correctly attributed to P tradition, it could be seen as an attempt to re-sacralize the killing of animals for food, in opposition to the secularization of slaughter that had been allowed previously by the Deuteronomic reformers as reported in Deut 12:15–16, 20–25.

v. Leviticus 17:10–14: Animals' Blood and Reverence for Life

According to the P tradition, after the flood, God commanded Noah and his sons (meaning, presumably, all later humankind as well), not to "eat flesh with its life, that is, its blood" (Gen 9:4). The present Leviticus text provides a similar explanation:

> For the life of every creature—its blood is its life; therefore I have said to the people of Israel: You shall not eat the blood of any creature, for the life of every creature is its blood. (Lev 17:14)

Implicitly, the blood of animals sacrificed at YHWH/God's altar is thereby returned to him. The efficacy of the sacrifice is based on the value of the life contained in or constituted by the blood, thereby "making atonement" for an individual's sins or offenses (Lev 17:11). Additionally, when hunters kill a wild animal for food, they must "pour out its blood and cover it with earth" (Lev 17:13),

---

44. Deut 12:15–16.
45. Compare Lev 17:8–9.

thereby returning it to the ground.[46] Biblical tradition does not contemplate, much less approve, hunting or killing animals for "sport" or trophies.[47] The life (blood) of animals killed for food must be respected, either by sacrificing them on YHWH/God's altar, thereby returning their life to him, or in the case of wild animals, which were never sacrificed to YHWH, by pouring their blood onto the ground.[48] These laws were binding both on Israelites and on aliens sojourning among them (Lev 17:10, 12–13), just as Noah and his sons had been commanded, according to P tradition in Gen 9:4. A terser version of the prohibition against eating blood appeared earlier in H: "You shall not eat any thing with its blood" (Lev 19:26a). Implicitly, these provisions derive from and give expression to a sense of appreciation and regard for the lives of animals killed for food.[49]

The practice of returning the blood of an animal killed for food or sacrifice to the ground implies an understanding that the life of the animal would somehow be preserved. In any case, the life of the animal was to be respected.

---

46. See also Lev 7:26–27; compare Deut 12:15–16, 20–25. See Tull, *Inhabiting Eden*, 93: "Their blood cannot be consumed, but is either given to God on the altar or buried (Lev 17:10–14), 'as an acknowledgement that bringing death to living things is a concession of God's grace, and not a privilege of (human) whim'" (quoting Milgrom, *Leviticus 1–16*, 735).

47. Later rabbis strongly opposed wanton killing of animals, and disapproved of hunting and hunters. Kaplan, "Animals, Cruelty to." See also Albert Schweitzer, quoted by Kalugia, "Old Testament Insights," 88: "Fishing and killing of animals for food when it is needed is one thing, but to hunt, to chase wild animals in order to enjoy the sport of putting a bullet through the body of one of them is abhorrent to anyone who believes in the sacredness of life." For contemporary commentary on hunting and related wildlife issues, see, e.g., essays in Cohn, *Ethics and Wildlife*.

48. Compare Gen 2:7, 19: Like the first man, in J tradition, all "animals" and birds were made from the ground—to which all alike would return. See also Sir 40:1, 11. And see below, ch. 7A and B.

49. See also Deut 5:19–23 and Ezek 33:25. However, killing animals by causing their blood to drain out may not be the most humane method of slaughter now available. See Rolston, *Environmental Ethics*, 83–84; and Singer, *Animal Liberation*, 153–57, as to Jewish and Muslim slaughter procedures. It appears that in the course of time, the underlying principle of reverence for the life of slaughtered animals has given way to concern to avoid contamination by consuming the animals' blood, an entirely anthropocentric matter.

c. Animal Sacrifice Laws: Concluding Observation

One can only speculate as to the environmental impact of animal sacrifices actually carried out in biblical times. Generally, there seem to have been adequate pasture lands to sustain a variety of domestic animals, and also enough wilderness areas for wildlife. On the other hand, to the extent that domestic animals were raised in order to be sacrificed, crop and grazing lands supporting their production would have reduced wilderness areas that otherwise could have provided various ecological benefits, including habitat areas for wildlife.

Biblical laws requiring animal sacrifices necessarily presuppose the value of animal life. Thus an animal might, under prescribed circumstances, be sacrificed instead of a firstborn human; and the blood of certain animals could serve to purify or purge a person or community of guilt. Implicit in these provisions is an understanding that in some way, before God, animals and humans were of equal or equivalent worth. Moreover, laws in the three later codes specifically require that "the life" of sacrificial animals, identified with their blood, was to be preserved by returning that blood to YHWH/God's altar or to the ground. The fact that the earlier law codes include only a relatively small number of laws requiring animal sacrifices suggests that most other such laws may have been of relatively recent origin. Biblical sources that contended that the Mosaic laws had not included a demand for sacrifices could have been largely correct.[50]

Following the Deuteronomic reform, animal sacrifices might be offered lawfully only at the Jerusalem temple. Sacrificial offerings were suspended during the period of the exile (ca. 586–538 BCE) and the years immediately following, when the temple remained in ruins.[51] A similar suspension occurred later, after the re-

---

50. See Ps 40:6; Jer 7:21–24; and Amos 5:25, considered below in pt. B of this chapter.

51. See Hag 1:1–11. Isaiah 43:23–24 may reflect the situation during the period of the exile: the exiles had not offered sacrifices both because they were in Babylon and because the temple had been destroyed. See also Ps 137:1–6. Sacrificial offerings were resumed once the temple was restored, ca. 515 BCE. It is commonly thought that much or all of the Priestly Code, with its emphasis on sacrificial offerings, was written

built temple was desecrated in the time of Antiochus Epiphanes.[52] After the Romans destroyed the temple in 70 CE, both Jews and Christians,[53] adjusting their religious practices to its absence, discontinued animal sacrifices altogether.

B. OPPOSITION TO ANIMAL SACRIFICES

Notwithstanding the many laws calling for animal sacrifices, a wide range of biblical texts express opposition to the institution or practice of animal sacrifice. Some, though not all of these texts, date from the latter centuries of the biblical period. Such opposition is expressed particularly in certain psalms, wisdom texts, and prophetic writings, and is implicit in some of the Old Testament Apocrypha or deuterocanonical Scriptures. A number of New Testament passages imply that the time for offering animal sacrifices had come to an end or would soon do so.

1. Psalms

Reading through the Bible, the first text we find that repudiates sacrificial offerings explicitly is Ps 40: "Sacrifice and offering you do not desire; . . . Burnt offering and sin offering you have not required" (Ps 40:6). This text implies that YHWH/God never had asked for animal sacrifices in the first place.[54] YHWH/God's rejection of animal sacrifices is stated even more emphatically in Ps 50, where the psalmist is speaking for "the Mighty One, God YHWH":

> I will not accept a bull from your house,
>   or goats from your folds.
> For every wild animal of the forest is mine,

---

in the years following 515, though some PC traditions may date from earlier times.

52. See 1 Macc 1–4.

53. According to Acts 2:46, some Christians previously had worshiped there, as well. Hebrews 8:1—10:39 emphasizes the absence or irrelevance of the Jerusalem temple and the superiority of the "heavenly sanctuary." Revelation 21:10—22:5 looks for the coming of a new Jerusalem; but there would be no temple in this new city—other than "the Lord God the Almighty and the Lamb" (21:22).

54. So also Jer 7:21–24, considered below.

> [as are] the cattle on a thousand hills.
> I know all the birds of the air,
>   and all that moves in the field is mine.
> If I were hungry, I would not tell you,
>   for the world and all that is in it is mine.
> Do I eat the flesh of bulls,
>   or drink the blood of goats?
> Make thanksgiving your sacrifice to God,
>   and pay your vows to the Most High.
> Call upon me in the day of trouble;
>   I will deliver you, and you shall glorify me. (Ps 50:9–15)

YHWH/God already owns "every wild animal of the forest" and the "cattle on a thousand hills"; he knows "all the birds of the air," and "all that moves in the field" are already his—indeed, "the world and all that is in it" are his. If he were hungry, he would not say so, for he does not "eat the flesh of bulls" or "drink the blood of goats," nor does he desire to do so. Instead of animal sacrifices, his people should offer thanksgiving[55] and call upon him in times of trouble.[56]

Similarly, Ps 51 says that YHWH/God desires "a broken spirit, and a broken and contrite heart," not sacrifices or burnt offerings:

> O Lord, open my lips,
>   and my mouth will declare your praise.
> For you have no delight in sacrifice;
>   if I were to give a burnt offering, you would not be pleased.
> The sacrifice acceptable to God is a broken spirit;
>   a broken and contrite heart, O God, you will not despise.
> (Ps 51:15–17)

Likewise, Ps 69 affirms that praise and thanksgiving are what please YHWH/God, not animal sacrifices:

> I will praise the name of God with a song;
> I will magnify him with thanksgiving.
> This will please YHWH more than an ox

---

55. See also Ps 50:23: "They who bring thanksgiving as their sacrifice honor me."

56. Psalm 50:8, which appears to approve animal sacrifices, intrudes upon both the sense of vv. 7–11, and the meaning of the psalm as a whole. This verse probably was inserted later by a proponent of animal sacrifice.

or a bull with horns and hoofs. (Ps 69:30–31)

Again, Ps 107:22 invites offerings in the form of "thanksgiving sacrifices" and telling about YHWH/God's deeds "with songs of joy."

2. Wisdom Writings

The book of Proverbs nowhere commends animal sacrifices but discounts, if not positively rejects, such sacrifices. Proverbs 7:14 describes a harlot's or adulteress's "seduction speech," including her claim "I had to offer sacrifices, and today I have paid my vows."[57] The implication seems to be that sacrifices were thought to be offered by persons of doubtful character, and that offering them was a poor excuse for immoral conduct. Proverbs 15:8 suggests that YHWH/God prefers prayers to sacrificial offerings:

> The sacrifice of the wicked is an abomination to YHWH,
>   but the prayer of the upright is his delight.

Somewhat similarly, Prov 21:3 urges:

> To do righteousness and justice
>   is more acceptable to YHWH than sacrifice.

Qoheleth, or "the Preacher" in Ecclesiastes, likewise has nothing good to say about sacrifices. Instead, he implies that offering sacrifices is simply another way of "doing evil"—something done only by ignorant fools:

> Guard your steps when you go to the house of God;[58]
>   to draw near to listen is better than the sacrifice offered by fools;
> for they do not know [that they are] doing evil. (Eccl 5:1)

---

57. See Prov 7:10–27 for the full context.

58. Following the Deuteronomic reform, the "house of God" or temple was the only place where sacrifices might lawfully be offered.

3. Prophets

Several passages in the book of Isaiah declare YHWH/God's rejection of animal sacrifices. One such classic expression is found in Isa 1:11:

> "What to me is the multitude of your sacrifices?"
>   says YHWH;
> "I have had enough of burnt offerings of rams
>   and the fat of fed beasts;
> I do not delight in the blood of bulls,
>   or of lambs, or of goats."

Isaiah continued, making clear that what YHWH/God required was not "trampling" his "courts"—an allusion, perhaps, to animals brought into the temple for sacrifice—or any kind of "vain" (RSV) or "futile" offerings" but, rather, doing good, seeking justice, correcting oppression, defending orphans and widows:

> When you come to appear before me,
>   who asked this from your hand?
>   Trample my courts no more;
> bringing offerings is futile;
>   incense is an abomination to me.
> New moon and Sabbath and the calling of [assemblies]—
>   I cannot endure solemn assemblies with iniquity.[59]
> Your new moons and your appointed festivals[60]
>   my soul hates;
> they have become a burden to me,
>   I am weary of bearing them.
> When you stretch out your hands,
>   I will hide my eyes from you;
> even though you make many prayers,
>   I will not listen; your hands are full of blood.
> Wash yourselves; make yourselves clean;
>   remove the evil of your doings from before my eyes;
> cease to do evil,
>   learn to do good;

---

59. See also Amos 5:21–25.

60. Some appointed festivals were also occasions for offering sacrifices. See, e.g., Exod 23:18; 34:25; Lev 23:4–19; Deut 16:1–8.

>   seek justice,
>   rescue the oppressed,
>   defend the orphan,
>   plead for the widow.[61] (Isa 1:12–17)

A passage attributed to Second Isaiah suggests that YHWH/God never did require his people to bring offerings. They have burdened him with their sins, but he will "blot out" their transgressions for his own sake, not because of any sacrificial offerings:

> You have not brought me your sheep for burnt offerings,
>   or honored me with your sacrifices.
> I have not burdened you with offerings,
>   or wearied you with frankincense.
> You have not bought me sweet cane with money,
>   or satisfied me with the fat of your sacrifices.
> But you have burdened me with your sins;
>   you have wearied me with your iniquities.
> I, I am He who blots out your transgressions for my own sake,
>   and I will not remember your sins. (Isa 43:23–25)

One of the most vivid condemnations of animal sacrifices—and of other kinds of sacrificial offerings—is set out in Isa 66:1–4. This text is part of the concluding chapters of Isaiah that some interpreters attribute to Third Isaiah, an anonymous prophet in the school of Isaiah, who lived in the early years following the end of the exile but before the temple had been rebuilt. This text comes immediately after this same prophet's description of "the peaceable kingdom" that YHWH/God would bring about for all creation at the end of the age (Isa 65:25).[62]

Thus says YHWH:

> "Heaven is my throne
>   and the earth is my footstool;
> what is the house that you would build for me,
>   and what is my resting place?
> All these things my hand has made,

---

61. Cf. Jas 1:27: "Religion that is pure and undefiled before God and the Father is this: to visit orphans and widows in their affliction, and to keep oneself unstained from the world."

62. See below, ch. 11.

> and so all these things are mine,"
> says YHWH.
> "But this is the one to whom I will look,
> to the humble and contrite in spirit,
> who trembles at my word.
> Whoever slaughters an ox is like
> one who kills a human being;
> whoever sacrifices a lamb,
> like one who breaks a dog's neck;
> whoever who presents a grain offering,
> like one who offers swine's blood. . . .
> These have chosen their own ways,
> and in their abominations they take delight;
> I also will choose to punish them . . . ;
> they did what was evil in my sight,
> and chose what did not please me." (Isa 66:1–44)[63]

Heaven is YHWH/God's throne; earth is his footstool. He needs no temple for sacrificial offerings. Like other prophets, this Isaiah declares that what YHWH/God desires is a humble and contrite spirit. Slaughtering animals for sacrifice—and other sacrificial offerings—are "abominations," "evil" in YHWH/God's sight.

The prophet Jeremiah likewise condemned sacrificial offerings. Reporting YHWH's oracle as it had come to him, Jeremiah said or wrote:

> Hear, O earth; I am going to bring disaster on this people,
> the fruit of their schemes,
> because they have not given heed to my words;
> and as for my teaching they have rejected it.
> Of what use to me is frankincense that comes from Sheba,
> or sweet cane from a distant land?
> Your burnt offerings are not acceptable,
> nor are your sacrifices pleasing to me. (Jer 6:19–20)

---

63. The sayings or writings of Third Isaiah are generally dated ca. 520 BCE. By then, many of the exiles had returned to Jerusalem, but the temple had not yet been rebuilt. The prophet evidently was urging his contemporaries not to go forward with building or rebuilding the temple (or "house") and not to resume making sacrificial offerings there. Some interpreters, however, suggest that the prophet meant only to oppose unrealistic expectations (compare Hag 2:20–23) or improper sacrifices (compare Mal 1:6–14).

What his contemporaries should have done was to "look, and ask for the ancient paths, where the good way lies; and walk in it" (Jer 6:16). The same prophet, again speaking or writing YHWH/God's oracle, sarcastically tells his people to go ahead and keep on offering sacrifices, adding that YHWH/God *never did command animal sacrifices* all those years their fathers were in the wilderness when the law was given to Israel:

> Thus says YHWH of hosts, the God of Israel: "Add your burnt offerings to your sacrifices, and eat the flesh. [But] in the day that I brought your ancestors out of the land of Egypt, I did not speak to them or command them concerning burnt offerings and sacrifices. But this command I gave them, 'Obey my voice, and I will be your God, and you shall be my people; and walk only in the way that I command you, so that it may be well with you.' Yet they did not obey or incline their ear, but, in the stubbornness of their evil will, they walked in their own counsels, and looked backward rather than forward." (Jer 7:21–24)

Elsewhere, also, Jeremiah warns that animal sacrifices will do no good for those who offer them.[64]

Hosea, one of the earliest Israelite prophets, already had made clear what YHWH/God desired: "For I desire steadfast love and not sacrifice, the knowledge of God rather than burnt offerings" (Hos 6:6).[65] Moreover, sacrificing animals is an offense YHWH/God will not tolerate: "In Gilgal they sacrifice bulls, so their altars shall be like stone heaps on the furrows of the field" (Hos 12.11).

Amos, Hosea's contemporary, likewise warned that YHWH/God could not be bought off with sacrifices. He spoke (or wrote) sardonically about the Israelites' love of sacrificial offerings:

> "Come to Bethel[66]—and transgress;
>   to Gilgal—and multiply transgression;
> bring your sacrifices every morning,
>   your tithes every three days;

---

64. Jer 11:15; 14:12.

65. See also Hos 8:11–13.

66. Bethel and Gilgal were cultic centers in Israel where Israelites offered sacrifices before that nation was overrun by Assyria ca. 722 BCE.

> bring a thank offering of leavened bread,
> > and proclaim freewill offerings, publish them;
> > for so you love to do, O people of Israel!"
> > > says the Lord God. (Amos 4:4-5)

The most frequently cited prophetic passage in this regard is Amos 5:21-24, sometimes considered the essence or epitome of "classical" prophetism:

> I hate, I despise your festivals,
> > and I take no delight in your solemn assemblies.
> Even though you offer me your burnt offerings and grain offerings,
> > I will not accept them,
> and the [peace offerings of your fatted] animals
> > I will not look upon.
> Take away from me the noise of your songs;
> > I will not listen to the melody of your harps.
> But let justice roll down like waters,
> > And righteousness like an ever-flowing stream.

What YHWH/God demands is justice and righteousness: demands that cannot be avoided or ignored by those who preferred to attend "solemn assemblies," bring various sacrificial offerings, and sing hymns or otherwise make music instead.[67] Like Jeremiah, the prophet Amos also implied that YHWH/God had not asked for sacrifices during the time the people of Israel were in the wilderness—the period when, according to tradition, Moses received the law: "Did you bring to me sacrifices and offerings the forty years in the wilderness, O house of Israel?" (Amos 5:25). The implicit answer is no. The context, Amos 5:21-24, makes clear Amos's understanding that YHWH/God never desired sacrifices.

Like Amos, the prophet Micah urged that YHWH/God could not be bought off with animal—or even human—sacrifices:

> With what shall I come before YHWH,
> > and bow myself before God on high?
> Shall I come before him with burnt offerings,
> > with calves a year old?

---

67. See Berger, *Noise of Solemn Assemblies*, reflecting on implications of this and other biblical texts for contemporary ethics and social policy.

> Will YHWH be pleased with thousands of rams,
>   with ten thousands of rivers of oil?
> Shall I give my first-born for my transgression,
>   the fruit of my body for the sin of my soul? (Mic 6:6–7)

Instead, YHWH/God requires more fundamental responses in the form of humility before him and acts of justice and kindness in relation to others:

> He has told you, O [man], what is good;
>   and what does YHWH require of you
> but to do justice, and to love kindness,
>   and to walk humbly with your God? (Mic 6:8)

4. Old Testament Apocrypha/Deuterocanonical Scriptures

Several other biblical texts also set out the understanding that YHWH/God desires something other than sacrificial offerings from his people. Thus, for instance, in the Song or Psalm of Judith, she declares:

> For every sacrifice as a fragrant offering is a small thing,
> and the fat for all whole burnt offerings to you is a very little thing;
> but whoever fears the Lord is great forever. (Jdt 16:16)

Likewise, according to the author of Sir 34:23:

> The Most High is not pleased with the offerings of the ungodly, nor for a multitude of sacrifices does he forgive sins.[68]

The Prayer of Azariah, like earlier prophetic texts, proclaims that "a contrite heart and a humble spirit" are acceptable in lieu of animal sacrifices:

> In our day we have no ruler, or prophet, or leader,
>   no burnt offering, or sacrifice or oblation, or incense,
>   no place to make an offering before you and to find mercy.

---

68. Other verses in the same context condemn sacrificing "what has been wrongfully obtained" (RSV) or taken "from the property of the poor," but none of these verses refers explicitly to animal sacrifices.

> Yet with a contrite heart and a humble spirit may we be accepted,
>> as though it were with burnt offerings of rams and bulls,
>> or with tens of thousands of fat lambs;
> such may our sacrifice be in your sight today,
>> and may we unreservedly follow you,
>> for no shame will come to those who trust in you.
> (Sg Three vv. 15–17)

Possibly this prayer was composed in the early Maccabean period, following the desecration of the temple by Antiochus Epiphanes. Thus it was written when there was "no place to make an offering." The text thus foreshadows the abandonment of sacrificial worship by Jews and also by early Christians, following the destruction of the temple by the Romans in 70 CE.

5. New Testament

It is not clear to what extent Jesus himself or the early Christians may have joined with their Jewish contemporaries in making sacrificial offerings in the temple prior to its destruction. Neither Jesus—as reported in the Gospels—nor the early Christian community expressly opposed sacrificial offerings.

a. Jesus Traditions

On one occasion, described both in Matt 8:1–4 and Mark 1:40–44, after healing a man from leprosy, Jesus tells him to go to "the priest" and offer "what Moses commanded, as a testimony [or "proof" (RSV)] to them."[69] According to Lev 14:1–32, in order to cleanse a leper, the priest would sacrifice various birds and one or two lambs, as "guilt" or "sin" offerings. In these Gospel stories, Jesus tells the man to offer the sacrifice even though he already had been cleansed. Perhaps this was to be done so that the authorities would then signify that the man could be accepted back into the community as healed. Whether the Last Supper was a Passover meal—a

---

69. Apparently the pronoun "them" refers to priests or other religious authorities.

question on which scholars divide—all of the first three Gospels report that Jesus intended or desired to eat the Passover with his disciples in Jerusalem.[70] Curiously, none of these accounts actually mentions slaughtering or eating a Passover lamb.[71] Elsewhere Matthew's Gospel says that Jesus told his followers that the whole law would remain in effect "until heaven and earth pass away."[72] These texts suggest that Jesus may have understood that laws regarding sacrifice also would remain in effect until the end of the present age.

On the other hand, Jesus reportedly overturned "the tables of the money-changers and the seats of those who sold pigeons" in the temple[73] and, according to John's Gospel, drove out those who sold oxen, sheep, and pigeons within its precincts (John 2:13–15). He urged his hearers to be reconciled with their "brother" before offering their gifts "at the altar" (Matt 5:23–24), but there is no indication whether such gifts included sacrificial animals. According to Luke 4:16, it was Jesus's custom to go to "the synagogue" on Sabbath days; but sacrifices were offered only in the temple, and there are no reports of his having entered the temple for that purpose.

In Mark's Gospel, Jesus commends a scribe who has just stated, as a summary of the law:

> And "to love [God] with all the heart, and with all the understanding, and with all the strength," and "to love one's neighbor as oneself"—this is much more important than all whole burnt offerings and sacrifices. (Mark 12:33)

It would seem that Jesus's position as to whether his followers should offer animal sacrifices was somewhat ambivalent. It is fairly clear that he did not expect people to offer sacrifices in the coming age or kingdom of God. If his saying about the imminent

---

70. Matt 26:18–19; Mark 14:12–16; Luke 22:1–16.

71. Moreover, early Christian catacomb representations of the Last Supper consistently depict bread *and fish* as the only food on the table. See generally Richard Hiers and Kennedy, "Bread and Fish Eucharist."

72. Matt 5:18; see also Matt 23:23.

73. Matt 21:1–13; Mark 11:15; Luke 19:45–46.

destruction of the temple reflects his beliefs,[74] there would no longer be a temple in that future era.[75]

b. The Early Church

Early Christian attitudes toward sacrifices also seem to have been ambivalent, at first. The book of Acts reports that the early Christians in Jerusalem "day by day . . . spent much time together in the temple" (Acts 2:46). It is not said whether they offered sacrifices there, but some of them may have done so, particularly in the years before Christianity emerged from its earlier status as a movement or sect within Judaism. Writing to a gentile Christian congregation in Rome, Paul urged members of that congregation to offer themselves, perhaps through their life and work, as a "living" or "spiritual" sacrifice:

> I appeal to you therefore, brothers, by the mercies of God, to present your bodies as a living sacrifice, holy and acceptable to God, which is your spiritual worship. (Rom 12:1)

To the extent that early Christians came to understand that Jesus's death was somehow a sacrifice on their behalf, there was no longer any need for animal sacrifice—if there ever had been.[76] Paul further demythologized or reinterpreted the idea of animal sacrifices in Phil 4:18, where he refers to a parcel of gifts he had received in prison from friends in the church at Philippi as "a fragrant offering, a sacrifice acceptable and pleasing to God."

Whether written before or after the destruction of the temple in 70 AD/CE, the author of Hebrews summed up the meaning that sacrifices now were to have for the evolving Christian community:

> Through him, then, let us continually offer a sacrifice of praise to God, that is, the fruit of lips that confess his name. Do not neglect to do good and to share what you have, for such sacrifices are pleasing to God. (Heb 13:15–16)

---

74. Matt 24:1–2; Mark 13:1–2; Luke 21:5–6.
75. See also Heb 8:1—10:39; Rev 21:22.
76. See Heb 9:11—10:18.

The book of Revelation concludes with the hope and expectation that the time for the coming of the new or messianic age and the Messiah himself was near—indeed, would take place *soon*.[77] But then there would be no temple, and thus no place to offer sacrifices any more. Instead, there would be "the Lord God the Almighty and the Lamb":

> Then I saw a new heaven and a new earth; for the first heaven and the first earth had passed away; and the sea was no more. And I saw the holy city, the new Jerusalem, coming down out of heaven from God, prepared as a bride adorned for her husband. . . . I saw no temple in the city, for its temple is the Lord God the Almighty and the Lamb. (Rev 21:1–22)

As has been mentioned in this chapter, several biblical texts indicate that it was once thought that animal sacrifices could be made in lieu of human sacrifices, because animals and humans were believed to have similar value before God. Other biblical texts suggest that humans and other creatures were similar in significant ways that had nothing to do with sacrificial offerings. Such texts are considered in the following chapter.

---

77. Rev 22:7, 20. See also Rev 1:1; 3:11.

CHAPTER 6

Humans and Other Creatures

Much Alike in Many Ways

IN BIBLICAL TIMES, NECESSARILY, nothing was known as to the extent to which humans and other creatures share the same DNA or other biological and physiological similarities or connections. But biblical writers did recognize that humans and other creatures had much in common.[1] According to the P story, God created all kinds of earth creatures as well as the first human beings on the same (sixth) day (Gen 1:24–27). And, according to the J version, YHWH/God made "every beast of the field and every bird of the air" in order to provide the first man with suitable helpers and companions, so that he would not be alone (Gen 2:18–19). As has been noted earlier in this book, humans and other creatures alike were seen engaged in praying to and praising YHWH/God.[2] The present chapter examines biblical texts that understood that humans and other creatures alike were made from a common source; that alike

---

1. Later Christian theology moved away from biblical tradition's recognition that humans and nonhumans were not only different but in many respects similar. See Barbour, *Religion*, 205: "Only in the early centuries of the Christian church were the differences accentuated and absolutized by the introduction of the Greek idea of an immortal soul . . . I will suggest that by drawing an absolute line between humanity and other creatures, later Christianity contributed to the attitudes that encouraged environmental destruction." See also Page, "Animal Kingdom."

2. See above, ch. 3.

they received their spirit or breath from YHWH/God; that they were expected to experience a common fate; and that during their lifetimes, all were somehow "in it together," since what happened to humans also would likely happen to other living beings as well.

A. COMMON SOURCES: THE SAME GROUND AND THE SAME SPIRIT OR BREATH

According to the second or J creation story, YHWH/God formed both the first man and the first of "every animal of the field and every bird of the air" from or out of "the ground" (Gen 2:7, 18–19).[3] Similarly, addressing Job, YHWH/God tells him, "Behold, Behemoth, which I made just as I made you" (Job 40:15).[4] Moreover, Behemoth is said to have been "the first of the works of God" (Job 40:19 RSV).[5]

The J creation story adds that after YHWH/God "formed man of dust from the ground," he "breathed into his nostrils the breath

---

3. See Hiebert, "Rethinking Traditional Approaches," 30: "For J, humans at creation are in no respect elevated above the rest of creation. They are made out of the same dirt out of which God makes the animals and in which he plants the garden. They have the same physical breath that gives life to the animal world as a whole." Also Hiebert, "Human Vocation," 139. And see Masteler, *Woven Together*, 48: "Genesis 2 emphasizes the earthiness of humanity as a core part of what it means to be human. It is that part that connects human beings to all other creatures shaped from and for the Earth." And see J. Cobb, *Is It Too Late*, 66: "The fateful story of creation presents human beings as creatures like the rest, made from the dust of the Earth. We are co-creatures with fish, and birds and beasts. The fundamental duality lies between creator and creature, not between the human species and other animals." See generally C. Wright, *Old Testament Ethics*, 117–18. See also Rasmussen, *Earth Community, Earth Ethics*, 275 (emphasis in original): "The point is the *aboriginal companion character* of all creatures." God as common Source for humans and all other creatures is affirmed in the Christian hymn "Immortal, Invisible, God Only Wise," stanza 3: "To all life thou givest, to both great and small; In all life thou livest, the true life of all" (Smith, "Immortal, Invisible").

4. Here Behemoth may have meant either some large land animal like the hippopotamus, or a mythical prototype for all such animals.

5. Alternate translation: "It is the first of the great acts of God" (NRSV). Compare Gen 1:20–27, where man and woman are the last living beings created by God, with Gen 2:7–22, where the man is the first living being YHWH/God made or "formed," followed by "every animal of the field and every bird of the air," and finally followed by the first woman.

of life; and man became a living being" (Gen 2:7). Several biblical texts refer to the breath or spirit of YHWH/God that animates all living creatures, both human and otherwise. As has been seen, Job affirmed that "the life of every living thing and the breath of every human being" are in the "hand" of YHWH (Job 12:10). More explicitly, Elihu declared that God's spirit or breath keeps all alive:

> If he should take back his spirit to himself,
>   and gather to himself his breath,
> all flesh would perish together,
>   and [human beings][6] would return to dust. (Job 34:14–5)

This understanding is articulated again in Ps 104:

> O YHWH, how manifold are your works!
>   In wisdom you have made them all;
>   the earth is full of your creatures. . . .
> These all look to you . . .
> When you hide your face, they are dismayed;
>   when you take away their breath, they die and return to their dust.
> When you send forth your Spirit, they are created;
>   and you renew the face of the ground. (Ps 104: 24, 27–30)

Similarly, Qoheleth observes or professes: human beings and animals "all have the same breath" (Eccl 3:19). Some of the deuterocanonical writings express a similar understanding.

The book of Judith includes a song or psalm attributed to that remarkable woman. In it, she sings of the "great and glorious" doings of God and declares that all his creatures were given existence by his word and spirit:

> Let all your creatures serve you,
>   for you spoke, and they were made.
> You sent forth your spirit,
>   and they were created. (Jdt 16:14)

---

6. In order to avoid using the word "man" (RSV) where, in texts like this, more gender-inclusive terms would be appropriate, the NRSV often refers instead to "mortals." Where that term—implying or specifying human mortality—is either redundant (as here) or extraneous, such translations as "human beings" or "humans" are used instead in this book.

Likewise, the Wisdom of Solomon affirms the presence of God's "immortal spirit" in "all things":

> You spare all things, for they are yours,
>   O Lord, you who love the living.
> For your immortal spirit is in all things. (Wis 11:26—12:1)

B. HUMANS AND OTHER CREATURES: A COMMON FATE

In biblical perspective, humans and other creatures also share the same destiny; for instance, as the psalmist observes:

> [Humans] cannot abide in their pomp,
>   they are like the animals that perish. (Ps 49:12, 20)

When YHWH/God's spirit or breath is taken from them, both die: "When you take away their breath, they die and return to their dust" (Ps 104:29). Humans are not the only creatures that return to the dust from which they came.[7] Qoheleth likewise reflects upon this common destiny:

> For the fate of humans and the fate of animals is the same; as one dies, so dies the other. . . . Humans have no advantage over the animals; for all is vanity. All go to one place; all are from the dust, and all turn to dust again. Who knows whether the human spirit goes upward and the spirit of animals goes down to the earth? (Eccl 3:19–21)

Whether beyond that, the human spirit may go upward to some kind of new life, Qoheleth does not know. In his view, "time and chance"[8] happen to humans, fish, and birds, alike:

> For no one can anticipate the time of disaster. Like fish taken in a cruel net, and like birds caught in a snare, so [humans] are snared at a time of calamity, when it suddenly falls upon them. (Eccl 9:12)

---

7. Gen 3:19.
8. Eccl 9:11.

Similarly, the prophet Isaiah (or Second Isaiah) considers the mortality of all flesh, both human and otherwise. All flesh is like grass or flowers that wither and fade:

> All [flesh is] grass,
>   [and all its life span] is like the flower of the field.
> The grass withers, the flower fades,
>   when the breath of YHWH blows upon it;
>   surely the people [is] grass. (Isa 40:6b–7)

The sage of Sirach likewise sees that all living beings share the same destiny: they become old and then must die, one generation succeeding another. Here the comparison is to trees' leaves:

> All living beings become old like a garment,
>   for the decree from of old is,
>   "You must [surely] die!"
> Like abundant leaves on a spreading tree
>   that sheds some and puts forth others,
> so are the generations of flesh and blood:
>   one dies and another is born. (Sir 14:17–18)[9]

Just as humans made from the ground or dust of the earth are destined to return to it (Gen 3:19), this same sage affirms that all "kinds of living beings" must likewise so return:

> Then the Lord looked upon the earth,
>   and filled it with his good things.
> With all kinds of living beings he covered its surface,
>   and into it they must return. (Sir 16:29–30)

So also Sir 17:1: "The Lord created human beings out of earth, and makes them return to it again." Continuing to reflect on human mortality, Sirach observes, "Hard work was created for every one" until "the day they return to the mother of all the living" (Sir 40:1). This is the first and only reference in biblical tradition to "mother" earth. But, again, not only humans are so destined: "All that is of earth returns to earth, and what is from the waters returns to the sea" (Sir 40:11). All living things, human and other creatures alike,

---

9. See also 2 Esd 5:43–49, explaining that one generation follows another—because there would not be room on the earth if all living creatures were alive at the same time.

are mortal and share a common destiny. All must return to the dust or earth or to the sea from which they had come or been made.

C. IN THE MEANTIME: HUMANS AND OTHER LIVING THINGS ALIKE ARE SUBJECT TO DIVINE JUDGMENT

The most famous instance of humans and other creatures together confronting divine judgment, of course, is the Genesis flood story. In the J version, it appears that birds and air-breathing land creatures were to be destroyed, entirely because of *human* depravity:

> YHWH saw that the wickedness of humankind was great in the earth, and that every inclination of the thoughts of their hearts was only evil continually. And YHWH was sorry that he had made humankind on the earth, and it grieved him to his heart. So YHWH said, "I will blot out from the earth the human beings I have created—people together with animals and creeping things and birds of the air, for I am sorry that I have made them." (Gen 6:5–7)

The other version, generally attributed to P tradition, suggests that not only humans but "all flesh," and even, perhaps, "the earth" itself, had somehow become corrupt and violent:

> Now the earth was corrupt in God's sight, and the earth was filled with violence. And God saw that the earth was corrupt; for all flesh had corrupted its ways upon the earth. And God said to Noah, "I have determined to make an end of all flesh, for the earth is filled with violence because of them; now, I am going to destroy them along with the earth." (Gen 6:11–13)[10]

Consequently, as the story is told, all birds and air-breathing land creatures were destroyed in the great flood—except for Noah, his family, and enough pairs of all other creatures to propagate and perpetuate their respective species once the flood was over.[11]

---

10. It can be conjectured that the P narrative attributes depravity to "all flesh" in order to explain why God, who was believed just, would have destroyed other creatures along with wicked humankind.

11. Gen 6:19–21; 7:2–3, 8–9, 13–16. See above, ch. 2B5, and below, ch. 9B1a.

A similar pattern is repeated, though on a smaller scale, in many other biblical texts. Some such texts warn what will happen if the people of Israel or Judah fail to remain faithful to YHWH/God or to observe his commandments. Both humans and other creatures would therefore come to grief. Some other texts interpret catastrophes then or later to be experienced by both humans and animals as manifestations of divine judgment.

The Holiness Code concludes with a series of promises and warnings. Addressing his people, YHWH/God warns them: if they "walk contrary" (RSV) and "will not obey" him, he "will let loose wild animals among [them], and they shall bereave [them] of [their] children and destroy [their] [cattle]" and "make [them] few in number, [so that their] roads shall be deserted" (Lev 26:21–22). The Deuteronomic Code concludes with similar warnings as to disasters that will take place in the event YHWH/God's people refuse or neglect to "diligently observ[e] all his commandments" (Deut 28:15–68). Among the terrible things that would happen will be destruction of their cattle:

> Your ox shall be butchered before your eyes, but you shall not eat of it. Your donkey shall be stolen in front of you, and shall not be restored to you. Your sheep shall be given to your enemies, without anyone to help you. (Deut 28:31)

Several prophets likewise declared that YHWH/God would destroy not only his people but other living beings as well, all because of human depravity. Speaking on behalf of the Lord God, Jeremiah warned his contemporaries that God's "anger" and "wrath" would be "poured out on this place, on human beings and animals," and "on trees of the field and fruit of the ground"—it would "burn and not be quenched" (Jer 7:20). Already, the land itself was mourning, all the grass was withering, and animals and birds were being "swept away" because of human wickedness (Jer 12:4). Other prophets likewise spoke of YHWH's present or future condemnation and judgment that would affect both "man and beast":

> Hear the word of YHWH, O people of Israel;
> for YHWH has an indictment against the inhabitants of the land.

> There is no faithfulness or loyalty,
>> and no knowledge of God in the land.
> Swearing, lying, and murder, and stealing and adultery . . .
>> bloodshed follows bloodshed.
> Therefore the land mourns,
>> and all who live in it languish;
> together with the wild animals,
>> and the birds of the air,
>> even the fish of the sea are perishing. (Hos 4:1–3)

> I will utterly sweep away everything
>> from the face of the earth, says YHWH.
> I will sweep away [man and beast];
>> I will sweep away the birds of the air
>> and the fish of the sea.
> I will make the wicked stumble.
>> I will cut off humanity
>> from the face of the earth, says YHWH. (Zeph 1:2–3)

Here, as elsewhere in biblical tradition, it is understood that YHWH does not need humanity—or any of his other creations—in order to be God.

In the book of Ezekiel, sayings or oracles attributed to YHWH/God typically address the prophet as "son of man." Here Ezekiel reports what he has heard:

> The word of YHWH came to me: [Son of man], when a land sins against me by acting faithlessly, and I stretch out my hand against it, and break its staff of bread and send famine upon it, and cut off from it human beings and animals, . . . or if I bring a sword upon the land and say, "Let a sword pass through the land," and cut off human beings and animals from it; . . . or if I send a pestilence into that land, and pour out my wrath upon it with blood, to cut off humans and animals from it . . . (Ezek 14:12–19)[12]

Sirach observes a similar pattern affecting both humans and animals:

> To all creatures, [both] human and animal,

---

12. See also Ezek 14:21.

> but to sinners seven times more,
> come death and bloodshed and strife and sword,
> calamities and famine and ruin and plague. (Sir 40:8–9)

In these texts, judgment in the form of some kind of "natural" or man-made catastrophe was seen to follow upon acts of human faithlessness or depravity.

Prophets also sometimes explained then current environmental crises as expressions of divine judgment for people's misdeeds. Not only domestic animals but also wildlife may be adversely affected by such manifestations of divine judgment:

> The ground is cracked.
> Because there has been no rain on the land
> the farmers are dismayed;
> they cover their heads.
> Even the doe in the field forsakes her newborn fawn
> because there is no grass.
> The wild asses stand on the bare heights,
> they pant for air like jackals;
> their eyes fail
> because there is no herbage. (Jer 14:4–6)[13]

> How the animals groan!
> The herds of cattle wander about
> because there is no pasture for them;
> even the flocks of sheep are dazed.
> To you, O YHWH, I cry.
> For fire has devoured the pastures of the wilderness,
> and flames have burned all the trees of the field.
> Even the wild animals cry to you
> because the watercourses are dried up,
> and fire has devoured the pastures of the wilderness.
> (Joel 1:18–20)

> Therefore, the heavens above you have withheld the dew, and the earth has withheld its produce. And I have called for a drought on the land and the hills, on the grain, the new wine,

---

13. See also 1 Kgs 18:1–2, where YHWH/God is said to have withheld rain, causing drought and famine. Here, Ahab, to his credit, was concerned and undertook measures to "keep the horses and mules alive" (1 Kgs 18:5).

the oil, on what the soil produces, on human beings and animals, and on all their labors. (Hag 1:10–11)

Why innocent life-forms should suffer on that account is not explained. These texts may well reflect recognition, based on experience, that catastrophes—whether resulting from human agency, such as warfare, or from natural events, such as flooding, drought, or climate change—affect everyone and everything that lives.[14] Because both human affairs and nature were understood to be affected by YHWH/God's sovereignty or dominion, such events, necessarily, would have been regarded as manifestations of his power and purposes. To the extent that such events were destructive, they would have been seen as constituting instances of divine judgment. Likewise, in biblical perspective, YHWH/God was believed and affirmed to be just; acts of human injustice (which were many) necessarily would have been expected to evoke

---

14. In biblical times, human activities probably had little effect upon global warming. Climate change has been recognized as a serious—potentially catastrophic—threat to life on Earth only in recent years. The Club of Rome authors did not mention it; but they did report significant increases in global atmospheric carbon dioxide concentrations and climate warming in the Los Angeles Basin. Meadows et al., *Limits to Growth*, 79–80. Climate change and global warming were recognized as critical concerns only a few years later. See Council on Environmental Quality and Department of State, *Global 2000 Report*, 1:36–37, noting increasing concentrations of atmospheric carbon dioxide and resulting potential for global warming, its disruptive effects on world agriculture, and changes in precipitation patterns around the world. The report noted, prophetically: "A carbon dioxide-induced temperature rise is expected to be 3 to 4 times greater at the poles than in the middle latitudes. An increase of 5 to 10 degrees centigrade in polar temperatures could eventually lead to the melting of the Greenland and Antarctic ice caps and a gradual rise in sea level, forcing abandonment of many coastal cities" (1:37).

For recent commentary, see generally Robb, *Wind, Sun, Soil, Spirit*. Although climate change was not a factor in biblical times, Robb suggests that human activities that degrade the Earth and threaten life constitute sacrilege. See modern scientific studies showing correlations between global warming and atmospheric methane and carbon dioxide increases in recent decades, such as those reported by Gore, *Inconvenient Truth*. In biblical times, human technology was not yet capable of causing massive environmental catastrophes. The full extent of damage to marine life, birds, smaller shoreline and inland plants and animals, and humans resulting from the 2010 BP Deepwater Horizon oil blowout disaster may not be known for decades, and its effects may continue far into the future. See Begley, "What Spilxsl Will Kill"; J. Cobb, *Is It Too Late*, xi, 107–12; and Ntreh et al., *Essays on the Land*. Note also the now widely recognized effects of new synthetic and toxic chemicals and plastics threating the lives of humans and many kinds of land, sea, and flying creatures.

acts of divine justice in response. The book of Jonah presents a possible exception, or perhaps a corollary, to this pattern. At the end of the story, after the people of Nineveh and their animals ("cattle" [RSV]) all "turned from their evil ways," YHWH/God spared them from the catastrophic judgment previously decreed (Jonah 4:11). It was not too late for them to repent and change their ways.

This chapter has reviewed biblical texts that point to certain basic commonalities shared by humans and other creatures generally. All alike come from the ground, and all are given their breath or spirit by YHWH/God. Alike they experience a common fate: all are mortal and, in time, return to the dust or ground from which they came. And in the meantime, both alike suffer the consequences of human depravity, typically in the form of either man-made or natural disasters. Such consequences typically were understood as expressions of divine judgment. The following chapter considers texts that describe certain ways in which particular animals or other creatures are like YHWH/God—or YHWH/God like them—and texts that represent various creatures as similar to humans—or humans as similar to them, in other respects.

CHAPTER 7

Images of God, Humans, and Other Creatures

PEOPLE GROUNDED IN JUDEO-CHRISTIAN faiths may be inclined to believe that in biblical tradition, God is thought of as "wholly other" or unlike other beings, and human beings are considered so distinctive—if not unique—as to have little in common with animals or other kinds of creatures. This chapter first examines texts that indicate belief that God was sometimes thought of as having characteristics of various nonhuman creatures, and then turns to texts that show how human beings resemble other creatures in various ways in addition to those described in the preceding chapter.

A. THE IMAGE OF GOD IN HUMANS AND IN OTHER CREATURES

Critics of Judaism and Christianity sometimes assume that the biblical image of God is anthropomorphic, that is, that God was imagined (or imaged) in the form of an old and perhaps large man. This assumption seems to be based on the Genesis texts, where God is said to have created humankind in his own image.[1] Here, both male and female are said to have been created in the image of

---

1. Gen 1:26–77; 5:1–2. See also Sir 17:30. Biblical scholars are divided as to what particular similarities this language was meant to suggest. See Tull, *Inhabiting Eden*, 21–23.

God. It would be more accurate to say that in these biblical verses, humans, both male and female, were understood to be theomorphic, that is, like God in some important way.[2] A number of biblical texts do use physiological metaphors, attributing to God, for instance, heart,[3] eyes,[4] or hands.[5] On the whole, however, biblical tradition, like later Judaism, seems to have been careful not to attempt to describe God's appearance.[6]

Yet a number of biblical texts do compare YHWH/God to nonhuman creatures in various ways. YHWH/God's caring for his people is said to be like that of birds or other animals caring for their young. For instance, a psalm embedded in the book of Deuteronomy recalls YHWH/God's caring for Jacob (Israel) in such terms:

> As an eagle stirs up its nest,
>   and hovers over its young;
> as it spreads its wings, takes them up,
>   and bears them aloft on its pinions,
> YHWH alone guided him. (Deut 32:11–12a)

Likewise, in Exod 19:4, YHWH/God tells Moses to say to the people of Israel: "You have seen what I did to the Egyptians, and how I bore you on eagles' wings and brought you to myself." The prophet Isaiah uses a similar image as to YHWH/God's future care:

> Like birds hovering overhead, so YHWH of hosts
>   will protect Jerusalem;

---

2. See Bird, "Male and Female"; and Heide, *My Father's World*, 146: "This aspect of being created in God's image means humans have the aptitude to make decisions and act in a manner that keeps God's best interests in mind.... Humans were created with the capacity to act on God's behalf, with His desires in mind."

3. Gen 6:6; 8:21.

4. E.g., Deut 32:10; Amos 9:8.

5. E.g., Exod 13:14, 16; Deut 6:21; Job 12:9–10; Pss 95:4–5; 102:25; 145:16. Also, his "arm," e.g. Deut 26:8; Isa 40:10.

6. Note, for example, Ezekiel's reserve in describing what he had seen: "Such was the appearance of the likeness of the glory of YHWH" (Ezek 1:28b RSV). Although Dan 7:9 says that "the hair" of the "head" of "an Ancient of Days" was "like pure wool," there are no other descriptive terms. Isaiah 40:11 compares YHWH/God to a shepherd, but offers no description of his appearance. The rest of Isa 40 emphasizes YHWH/God's transcendence as to all forms and likenesses.

> he will protect and deliver it,
> > he will spare and rescue it. (Isa 31:5)

The prophet also compares YHWH/God to a lion: "As a lion or a young lion growls over its prey, . . . so YHWH of hosts will come down to fight upon Mount Zion and upon its hill" (Isa 31:4). Similarly, Jeremiah compares YHWH/God to a lion "coming up from the thickets of the Jordan" about to attack the land of Edom (Jer 49:19).[7]

Such images sometimes are less hopeful as to YHWH/God's relation to his own special people. In Lamentations, one of the survivors of the Babylonian siege compares YHWH/God to both a bear and a lion:

> He is a bear lying in wait for me,
> > a lion in hiding;
> he led me off my way and tore me to pieces;
> > he has made me desolate. (Lam 3:10–11)

Hosea likewise compares YHWH/God to a lion, who will attack Israel and Judah, in judgment for their offenses:

> For I will be like a lion to Ephraim,
> > and like a young lion to the house of Judah.
> I myself will tear and go away,
> > I will carry off, and no one shall rescue. (Hos 5:14)

And not only like a lion but also like a leopard and "a bear robbed of her cubs" (Hos 13:8).[8] This prophet also compares YHWH/God to a "moth" and to "dry rot" (Hos 5:12 RSV).

Humans, also, are sometimes compared with other creatures. As has been seen, humans and other creatures often are said to have similar origins, share the same breath or spirit, and experience the same fate or destiny.[9] In general, the comparisons show a positive appreciation of other creatures, and in some instances,

---

7. See also Jer 50:44, where the same image describes YHWH/God's prospective moves against Babylon. Several of these texts were noted by Drummond, *Rights of Animals*.

8. See also Amos 5:18–19, warning those who desire the "day of YHWH" that it would be "as if someone fled from a lion, and was met by a bear."

9. See above, ch. 6.

humans are seen as inferior, in some respects, to such creatures.[10] These kinds of comparisons are considered in the next section of this chapter

B. HUMANS COMPARED WITH OTHER LIVING BEINGS

Like human couples, all the pairs of creatures that were with Noah on the ark are described as "families" (Gen 8:17–19). Pairs of both "clean" and "unclean" animals taken onto the ark are described as "the male and his mate."
In the Hebrew text, *'ish* and *ishto* mean, literally, "man and his woman" or "mate" (Gen 7:2).
Compare Isa 34:15–16, declaring that in the coming age or era, no wild creature "shall be without her mate."

When Jacob gathers his sons before his death to tell "what will happen" to them "in the days to come," he compares some of his sons to various animals—actually identifying some of them *as* those animals. Thus "Judah is a lion's whelp" and like both a lion and a lioness (Gen 49:9); "Issachar is a strong [ass]" (Gen 49:14); Dan "shall be a snake by the roadside, a viper along the path" (Gen 49:17); "Naphtali is a doe let loose" (Gen 49:21); and "Benjamin is a ravenous wolf" (Gen 49:27). Similarly, in his last words of blessing for the tribes of Israel, Moses compares some of them to wild animals: Manasseh to a wild ox (Deut 33:17) and Gad to a lion (Deut.33:20); and Dan is said to *be* "a lion's whelp" (Deut 33:22). In a later narrative, Absalom is advised not to attack his father, David, and the latter's warriors, because "they are enraged, like a bear robbed of her cubs" (2 Sam 17:8).

Several psalms compare humans with other creatures. The soul's longing for God is like the hart's longing for water brooks or flowing streams (Ps 42:1). Humans are cautioned against being like some animals in certain respects: "Do not be like a horse or a mule, without understanding, whose temper must be curbed with bit and bridle" (Ps 32:9). The psalmist prays for deliverance from violent men—

---

10. Also see below, ch. 8.

> who plan evil things in their minds,
>> and stir up wars continually.
> They make their tongue sharp as a snake's,
>> and under their lips is the venom of vipers. (Ps 140:1–3)[11]

Humans also are compared to various predatory or dangerous animals, notably lions,[12] bulls,[13] and wild dogs.[14] More positively, the people of Israel are often described as YHWH/God's sheep or the sheep of his pasture.[15] The psalmist also characterizes YHWH/God's people as his dove (Ps 74:19).[16]

A number of proverbs compare individual persons to certain creatures. The sage advises husbands: "Rejoice in the wife of your youth, a lovely deer, a graceful doe" (Prov 5:18). Those who have pledged or given security for a neighbor's debt are urged to seek release from such obligations: "Save yourself like a gazelle from the hunter, like a bird from the hand of the fowler" (Prov 6:5). A man who follows a seductive adulteress to her home

> goes like an ox to the slaughter,
>> or bounds like a stag toward the trap
> until an arrow pierces its entrails.
>> He is like a bird rushing into a snare,
> not knowing that it will cost him his life. (Prov 7:22–23)

Other prudential advice likewise involves comparisons between people and animals. "Better to meet a she-bear robbed of [her] cubs than to confront a fool immersed in folly" (Prov 17:12). Foolish or depraved humans are compared with certain animal behaviors: "Like a bird that strays from its nest is [a man] who strays from [his] home" (Prov 27:8). "Like a roaring lion or a charging bear is a wicked ruler over a poor people" (Prov 28:15).[17] The prophet Jeremiah set down another such gnomic comparison:

---

11. See also Ps 58:3–5.
12. Pss 7:2; 10:8–9; 17:12; 22:13; 35:17; 57:4.
13. Ps 22:16.
14. Pss 22:16; 59:6–7, 14–15.
15. Pss 74:1; 78:52; 80:1; 95:7; 100:3; see also Isa 40:11; 53:6; and Ezek 34:1–24, 31.
16. See also 2 Esd 5:26.
17. The modern world presents many examples of such would-be dictators and

> Like the partridge hatching [a brood she] did not lay,
>> so are all who amass wealth unjustly;
> in midlife it will leave them,
>> and at their end they will prove to be fools. (Jer 17:11)

In the Song of Solomon, male and female lovers tenderly compare each other, or portions of the other's anatomy, to various creatures. For instance:

> Ah, you are beautiful my love;
>> ah, you are beautiful;
>> your eyes are doves. (Song 1:15)[18]

> O my dove, in the cleft of the rock,
>> in the covert of the cliff,
> let me see your face,
>> let me hear your voice. (Song 2:14)[19]

The man's hair is said to be wavy and "black as a raven" (Song 5:11). The woman's hair is said to be "like a flock of goats, moving down the slopes of Gilead" (Song 4:1; 6:5); her teeth "like a flock of ewes, that have come up from the washing" (Song 6:6);[20] her breasts "like two fawns, twins of a gazelle" (Song 4:5; 7:3).[21] She herself—the "fairest among women"—is like a "mare among Pharaoh's chariots" (Song 1:8–9). The man himself "is like a gazelle or a young stag" (Song 2:9, 17). The lovers also compare each other—or themselves—to flowers (crocuses, lilies, henna blossoms),[22] beautiful or stately trees (apple, palm, cedar),[23] and various spices and fruits.[24]

With apparent sympathy, Isaiah compares Moabite refugees to "fluttering birds" and "scattered nestlings" (Isa 16:2). To him "who sits above the circle of the earth," the human inhabitants are "like grasshoppers" (Isa 40:22).

---

their effects on the people upon whom they inflict their tyranny.

18. See also Song 4:1 and 5:12.
19. See also Song 6:9.
20. See also Song 4:2.
21. See also Song 7:7–8.
22. Song 1:14; 2:1–2; 5:13.
23. Song 2:3; 5:15; 7:7–8.
24. Song 4:3, 13–14; 5:13; 6:7.

The author of Sir 13:15–19 sees a number of similarities between humans and other creatures. Both tend to group together with their own kind; moreover, animal predators are to their prey as human predators are to human prey:

> Every creature loves its like,
>   and every person [his or her] neighbor.
> All living beings associate with their own kind,
>   and people stick close to those like themselves.
> What does a wolf have in common with a lamb?
>   No more has a sinner with the devout.
> What peace is there between a hyena and a dog?
>   And what peace between the rich and the poor?
> Wild asses in the wilderness are the prey of lions;
>   likewise the poor are feeding grounds for the rich.
> (Sir 13:15–19)

Again, the sage observes:

> Birds [flock] with their own kind;
>   so honesty comes home to those who practice it.
> A lion lies in wait for prey;
>   so does sin for evildoers. (Sir 27:9–10)

Another writer sees a parallel between human parents' love for their children and that of animal parents for their offspring:

> Observe how complex is a mother's love for her children, which draws everything toward an emotion felt in her inmost parts. Even unreasoning animals, as well as human beings, have a sympathy and parental love for their offspring. (4 Macc 14:13–14)[25]

As has been seen, many biblical texts represent both humans and nonhuman creatures as similar, in that both may have direct relationships with YHWH/God: calling on him for help in times of

---

25. Fourth Maccabees develops this comparison more fully in the verses that follow. See below, ch. 8. Compare 2 Pet 2:12, describing "ungodly" persons as being "like irrational animals, mere creatures of instance, born to be caught and killed." Similarly, Jude v. 10. The idea that animals are "unreasoning" or "irrational" may have derived from Greek culture and ideology. As to Enlightenment and latter-day attempts to characterize animals as "irrational" and therefore unworthy of care, see Midgley, *Animals*, 45–64.

need and praising, glorifying, blessing, or rejoicing before him.[26] Other texts also offer comparisons between humans and certain other creatures. Such comparisons are not always flattering as to the human counterparts.[27]

YHWH/God's "speeches" to Job point to the physical strength or formidable nature of certain creatures and to relative human weakness or limitation. For example, the wild ox:

> Is the wild ox willing to serve you?
>   Will he spend the night at your crib?
> Can you tie [him] in the furrow with ropes,
>   or will [he] harrow the valleys after you? (Job 39:9-10)[28]

The implicit answer to all four questions is no. The wild ox is too powerful to be tamed and harnessed. Equally or more so is Behemoth, meaning here, perhaps, the hippopotamus.[29]

> Look at Behemoth, which I made as I made you;
>   it eats grass like an ox.
> Its strength is in its loins,
>   and its power in the muscles of its belly.
> It makes its tail stiff like a cedar;
>   the sinews of its thighs are knit together.
> Its bones are tubes of bronze,
>   its limbs like bars of iron. . . .
> Even if the river is turbulent, it is not frightened;
>   it is confident though Jordan rushes against its mouth.
> Can one take it with hooks,
>   or pierce its nose with a snare? (Job 40:15-18, 23-24)

---

26. See above, ch. 3.

27. Tull, *Inhabiting Eden*, 94-95: God's "prophets and sages compare animals favorably to people (Isa 1:3; Jer 8:7) and commend learning from them (Prov 6:6-8; Job 12:7-8)."

28. The RSV translators describe the wild ox, Behemoth, and Leviathan in male terms as "he" rather than as "it." The NRSV editors evidently thought it better here, as in some other instances, to characterize some other-than-human creatures in gender-neutral or neuter language. Doing so, however, may obscure the biblical understanding that animals have gender, emotions, reasoning, intentions, and in other respects are like human persons. See, e.g., the NRSV translation of Job 40:15-18, 23-24; 41:8-10, 25-34, quoted below.

29. See DeWitt, "Behemoth and Batrachians."

And then there is the even still more formidable creature Leviathan. Whether this creature's description is "mythical" or based on encounters with crocodiles or large sea creatures, the entire forty-first chapter of Job is devoted to describing his awesome power. So far as humans are concerned, he is untouchable:

> Lay hands on it;
>> think of the battle; you will not do it again!
>
> Any hope of capturing it will be disappointed;
>> were not even the gods overwhelmed at the sight of it?
>
> No one is so fierce as to dare to stir it up.
> Who then is he that can stand before [me]. (Job 41:8–10)

Leviathan is described even more vividly in the concluding verses of the YHWH/God's speech, which also conclude the chapter:

> When it raises itself up the gods are afraid;
>> at the crashing they are beside themselves.
>
> Though the sword reaches it, it does not avail,
>> nor does the spear, the dart, or the javelin.
>
> It counts iron as straw,
>> and bronze as rotten wood.
>
> The arrow cannot make it flee;
>> slingstones, for it, are turned to chaff.
>
> [Likewise] clubs are counted as chaff;
>> it laughs at the rattle of javelins.
>
> Its underparts are like sharp potsherds;
>> it spreads itself like a threshing sledge on the mire.
>
> It makes the deep boil like a pot;
>> it makes the sea like a pot of ointment.
>
> It leaves a shining wake behind it;
>> [so that] one would think the deep white-haired.
>
> On earth it has no equal,
>> a creature without fear.
>
> It surveys everything that is lofty;
>> it is king over all that are proud. (Job 41:25–34)

YHWH/God's questions to Job give the impression that like the wild ox, both Behemoth and Leviathan are creatures that he or others might still encounter, not simply legendary creatures of yore. Obviously, such creatures as these were not considered subject to human dominion.[30] Many other biblical texts also understand that human domination over other creatures was quite limited.[31]

On the whole, biblical tradition showed little, if any, interest in demonstrating human superiority to other life-forms—an interest that takes many forms in modern times, particularly in secular academic circles.[32] That humans were perceived as similar to other creatures in several respects was not a cause for chagrin or embarrassment. Instead, humans, like other living beings, were all understood to have their rightful places in the good world God had created.[33]

For the psalmist, the highest aspiration is to make his home in YHWH's temple—a sanctuary already enjoyed by sparrows and swallows:

> How lovely is your dwelling place,
>   O YHWH of hosts!
> My soul longs, indeed it faints
>   For the courts of YHWH;
> my heart and my flesh sing for joy
>   to the living God.
> Even the sparrow finds a home,
>   and the swallow a nest for herself,

---

30. See also Bouma-Prediger, *For the Beauty*, 101–2; and McKibben, *End of Nature*, 71–77. As to Behemoth and Leviathan, McKibben writes: "The message, though not precisely an answer to Job's plaint, is that we may not judge everything from our point of view—that all nature is not ours to subdue." McKibben, *End of Nature*, 76. And see Bland and Webb, *Creation, Character, and Wisdom*, 175–76:

"Though we have become quite comfortable with a worldview that has, for at least the last two centuries, understood the world to be fundamentally knowable and malleable—parsed into elaborate taxonomies, manipulated in ever more sophisticated laboratories, and confidently subjugated to human ingenuity—the sages model a very different outlook. It is wonder which provokes Job, after seeing Behemoth and Leviathan, to repent of hubris and humble himself before the Creator of all."

31. See above, ch. 2, and below, ch. 10.

32. See Midgley, *Animals*. See also Keller, "No More Sea," 190: "Yahweh's scornful invocation of Leviathan's indomitable superiority to all human order specifically stresses the creature's absolute resistance to domestication and commodification.... When we set ourselves apart from and above nature, hoping to transcend finitude, we only set ourselves at odds with a creator not made in our image: one who in the image of a whirlwind and a whale parodies human political economy based on the conquest and exploitation of the nonhuman."

33. See above, ch. 1.

> where she may lay her young,
> at your altars, O YHWH of hosts,
> my King and my God. (Ps 84:1–4)

Comparisons between humans and other creatures are implicit in other texts and contexts. Biblical traditions include many observations or comments about the world, birds, animals, and other creatures. These observations and comments can be viewed as reflecting a kind of scientific or proto-scientific interest in the Earth's environment and its innumerable species. Some texts suggest that humans might do well to emulate the wisdom or behavior of other creatures. And several texts indicate sympathy or empathy with the plight or feelings of other creatures. Such texts are considered in the following chapter.

CHAPTER 8

Observation and Appreciation of Creation and All Living Beings

IN HIS LECTURES ON Christian ethics, the late H. Richard Niebuhr often suggested that the first move in the moral life is appreciation of the other. Appreciation means, among other things, recognizing and valuing something or someone, at least for some quality or characteristic found in the other or, more fundamentally, for being the person or being the other is. Appreciation is expressed in many biblical texts that consider the characteristics or ways of other creatures. Sometimes these texts express wonder at the marvelous abilities of such creatures, often showing admiration and respect for them. Appreciation and wonder are articulated, along with detailed observations, especially in the books of Job, Psalms, Proverbs, Song of Solomon, Ecclesiastes, the Wisdom of Solomon, Sirach, and a number of sayings attributed to Jesus in the first three Gospels. Many of these texts represent the kind of careful observations that can be characterized as an early form of inductive science.[1] Some of these, and other biblical observations, go on to represent certain animals or other creatures as models for human emulation or imitation. And several of these offer shrewd observations about human nature.

---

1. See generally Tull, *Inhabiting Eden*, 29–37; and Warren, *All Things Wise*, 34–37.

A. Observation and Appreciation of "Nature"

Three texts already considered show appreciation for the feelings and behavior of bears or mother-bears robbed of their cubs.[2] Some other texts previously examined in other connections will be touched upon again briefly here. A number of other texts that derive from and express careful observation and interest in "nature" also will be described in this chapter.[3]

1. Genesis and the Law: "Clean" and "Unclean"

Priestly tradition in Genesis is concerned to distinguish between "clean" and "unclean" animals (Gen 7:2–3, 8–9). Those who classified animals, birds, insects, and other creatures as clean or unclean must have closely observed their physical characteristics and affinities. Certain legal texts set forth the anatomical details that mark such distinctions. It is likely that the distinctions P refers to in Genesis were grounded on customs or laws represented in these texts.

Leviticus 11:1–37 and Deut 14:3–20 define the categories of clean and unclean animals, in part by reference to certain common characteristics.[4] Such characteristics include whether the animal "has divided hoofs and is cleft-footed and chews the cud" (Lev 11:3); whether water creatures have both "fins and scales" (Lev 11:9–10); whether those "winged insects that walk on all fours . . . have jointed legs above their feet with which to leap on the ground" (Lev 11:21); and whether creatures that "swarm," move about on their bellies or on all fours or have "many feet" (Lev 11:41–42). To

---

2. 2 Sam 17:8; Prov 17:12; and Hos 13:8.

3. See Dawson, *Nature and the Bible*. His core theme is that science and religion need not be in conflict, nor one putting down the other. He found that to remarkable extent, natural science's understanding of the Earth, the cosmos, plant and animal life tell similar, often parallel biblical understandings as to ways nature developed and continues to change. And that both the Bible and natural science appreciate and affirm the unity of the universe, its expansion into realms beyond our ability to measure or grasp; and, most remarkably, see the sequence of prehistoric cosmological, geological, emerging flora and biological developments events, epochs, and eras quite similarly.

4. See Richard Hiers, "Reverence for Life" (*Journal*), 164–66.

make these distinctions necessarily required careful observation of such natural phenomena.

2. The Book of Job

Job—or the author of the book of Job—can be credited as one of two leading biblical "naturalists" or "natural scientists." Or perhaps "creation scientists" would be a more apt description, for Job, like Solomon before him,[5] understood and affirmed that all existence came from and continues to come from YHWH/God as his creation.[6] Job noticed that streams dry up and disappear "in time of heat" (Job 6:15–20). He observed that papyrus and other reeds must grow in marshlands or water; elsewhere "they wither before any other plant" (Job 8:11–12). He knows that a tree, though cut down, can sprout up again from the stump (Job 14:7–9),[7] that mountains erode, and that water wears away stones and can wash away soil (Job 14:18–19). The author knows that in severe weather,

---

5. See below, pt. A4 of this chapter.

6. See Bland and Webb, *Creation, Character, and Wisdom*, 142: "Wisdom literature provides an essential perspective for our current dilemmas. Its fundamental message is that God is the creator of all, the wealthy and the poor, men and women, human faculties to see, hear, and think, and the natural resources humans use.... God is the creator of land and water, flora and fauna. God is sovereign Creator. It is out of this premise that the practice of justice flows."

7. See also Isa 11:1. Though necessarily lacking modern scientific concepts, biblical writings indicate that people in the biblical period were knowledgeable as to many aspects of nature. See Rolston, "Bible and Ecology," 17:

"The Hebrews knew how to grow vineyards and olive trees; they knew how to prepare 'wine to gladden the human heart, oil to make the face shine' (Ps. 104:15), although they did not know the bacteria of fermentation, much less had they any knowledge of unsaturated fats in the olive oil.... Abraham and Lot, and later Jacob and Esau, dispersed their flocks and their herds because 'the land could not support both of them living together.' (Gen. 13:2–13; 36:6–8)." Thus, these early biblical figures avoided enacting the "tragedy of the commons."

See generally Hardin, "Tragedy of the Commons." The prophet Ezekiel probably knew nothing about amino acids but nevertheless apparently knew something important about nutrition. The list of grains set out in Ezek 4:9 for making bread constitute a complete protein. According to panel information supplied by the manufacturers of the cereal named for this text, "Ezekiel 4:9," these grains provide not only all nine "essential amino acids" but several others as well. And it was known that "a little wine" was good for a person's health (1 Tim 5:23), but also that overindulgence has predictably deleterious consequences (Prov 23:29–35; 1 Esd 3:18–23).

"the animals go into their lairs, and remain in their dens" (Job 37:8).

And the book's author—like the best of modern scientists—knows, or comes to realize, how little he knows. Thus, in an extended discourse, he tells that YHWH asks Job, again and again, whether he has "been there" where YHWH has been, does he "know" all that YHWH does, can he do what YHWH can do? (Job 38:1—39:30). The implicit answers are all no: Job has not been, does not know, and cannot do. Major mysteries remain: as to the foundations of the earth, the bounds and depths of the sea, the expanse of the earth, morning light and darkness, the "storehouses" of snow and hail, "the way to the place where the light is distributed," the east wind, rain, thunderbolts, dewdrops, ice, hoarfrost, the constellations and other astronomical "ordinances," clouds, floods, lightnings, nature's (or creation's) provisions for wildlife, the timing of their gestation and their bearing of offspring. YHWH, not Job, nor any human, has set aside range land for the wild ass. Only YHWH can control the wild ox, make the ostrich strange and forgetful yet fearless and swift, and give strength and courage to the horse (Job 39:5–25). Summing up, YHWH asks Job:

> Is it by your wisdom that the hawk soars,
>   and spreads its wings toward the south?
> Is it at your command that the eagle mounts up
>   and makes its nest on high?
> It lives on the rock and makes its home
>   in the fastness of the rocky crag. (Job 39:26–28)

The habitat and behavior ways of Behemoth (possibly meaning the hippopotamus) likewise had been observed:

> Under the lotus plants it lies,
>   in the covert of the reeds and in the marsh.
> The lotus trees cover it for shade;
>   the willows of the wadi surround it.
> Even if the river is turbulent it is not frightened;
>   it is confident though Jordan rushes against its mouth.
>   (Job 40:21–23)

3. Psalms

The psalmist, too, knows some things about natural history: for instance, that the seas once "stood above the mountains," that later "the mountains rose" and "the valleys sank down" (Ps 104:6-8 RSV).[8] He knows how important springs of water are for animals and birds (Ps 104:10-12); which trees birds prefer for nesting (104:16-17); that high mountains provide habitat for wild goats, and rocks "a refuge" for rabbits or badgers (104:18); that wild forest animals "come creeping out" at night, while lions return to and lie down in their dens at sunrise (104:20-22); that the earth is "full" of God's creatures and that the sea teems "with living things both small and great"; and that Leviathan, like latter-day porpoises and whales, enjoys playing there (104:24-26 RSV). Several other psalms likewise show great interest in and appreciation for nature and created beings.[9]

4. "Solomonic" Wisdom Writings

Biblical tradition remembers Solomon, among other reasons, for his interest in, and knowledge about, other living things. "He would speak of trees, from the cedar that is in the Lebanon to the hyssop that grows in the wall; he would speak of animals, and birds, and reptiles, and fish" (1 Kgs 4:33).[10] Solomon might be considered the Bible's other foremost natural scientist or naturalist.[11] Much of the

---

8. This text does not clearly refer to or echo the Genesis flood story but, rather, seems to present a different cosmogony, one that involved geological evolution, possibly over a considerable period of time. Cf. Ps 90:2: "Before the mountains were brought forth, or ever you had formed the earth and the world, from everlasting to everlasting you are God." Cf. the stanza in the Christian hymn "O God Our Help in Ages Past": "Before the hills in order stood, or earth received her frame, from everlasting thou art God to endless years the same" (Watts, "Our God, Our Help").

9. See, e.g., Pss 135:6-7; 136:4-9, 25; 145:8-17; and 147:4-9, 16-18.

10. See Poole, *Christianity*, 79-82. Poole draws attention to Solomon's use of cedarwood and sponsoring naturalistic art forms such as carvings of gourds and flowers in construction of his temple.

11. There were other "naturalists" in biblical times. See Drummond, *Rights of Animals*, 85. Some 120 different kinds of animals are named in the Bible, including 37 kinds of mammals, 38 kinds of birds, and 12 types of reptiles. See Feliks, "Animals

book of Proverbs and all of Ecclesiastes, the Song of Songs (or Song of Solomon), and the Wisdom of Solomon have been attributed to him, and such interests appear prominently in these writings.

The book of Proverbs is traditionally attributed to Solomon.[12] Whether composed by Solomon or by another sage (or other sages), many of the proverbs consist of observations as to the ways of other creatures, often accompanied by implicit or explicit advice as to readers. Many of these observations constitute a form of early or proto-science.[13] Ants are viewed with special appreciation and also, as will be observed later in this chapter, as models for human prudence and practice:

> Go to the ant, you lazybones,
>   consider [her] ways, and be wise.
> Without having any chief
>   or officer or ruler,
> [she] prepares [her] food in summer,
>   and gathers [her] sustenance in harvest. (Prov 6:6–8)[14]

Several other Proverbs texts, which will be considered separately, express admiration or wonder at the ways of various creatures, sometimes also seeing them as models for human behavior.

Some texts also offer prudent advice as to sound agricultural practices. The sage recognizes the importance of oxen for successful farming:

> Where there are no oxen, there is no grain;
>   abundant crops come by the strength of the ox. (Prov 14:4)

---

in the Bible." See also Caras, "Promised Land" (as to biblical wildlife preserves in modern Israel).

12. See Prov 1:1; 10:1, and 25:1. But see Prov 30:1 and 31:1.

13. See also Prov 25:23: "The north wind brings forth rain." See Jacobson, "Biblical Bases," 50–51: "One of the basic beliefs of the sages is that observations about the world are not random or haphazard; rather, some logic underlies these observations, a logic which is discoverable if one is clever enough to figure it out. If something happens one way once, it should happen that way again, and if it doesn't, there should be some reason for it. In fact, because the world is ordered, reason itself is possible. We might observe that this line of reasoning is the original scientific thinking. We might indeed call the wisdom literature of the Hebrew scriptures the original science so long as we are careful to note that it is also poetry, art."

14. See also Prov 30:25: "The locusts have no king, yet all of them march by rank."

The farmer cannot do it all by himself. Together, the ox and the working farmer can get good results. And this Solomonic sage knows the importance of fall plowing:

> The sluggard does not plough in the autumn;
> > he will seek at harvest, and have nothing. (Prov 20:4 RSV)

Similarly, he observes:

> Anyone who tills the land will have plenty of bread,
> > but one who follows worthless pursuits will have plenty of poverty. (Prov 28:19)

YHWH/God provides the land, the seasons, and the harvest, but all to no avail unless the farmer knows enough agricultural basics and does his part by tilling or cultivating the land.

A large number of proverbs reflect close observation of human nature. For example, the sage offers this description of the phenomenon or experience of inebriation:

> Who has woe? Who has sorrow?
> > Who has strife? Who has complaining?
> Who has wounds without cause?
> > Who has redness of eyes?
> Those who linger late over wine,
> > those who keep trying mixed wines.
> Do not look at wine when it is red,
> > when it sparkles in the cup and goes down smoothly.
> At the last it bites like a serpent,
> > and stings like an adder.
> Your eyes will see strange things,
> > and your mind utter perverse things.
> You will be like one who lies down in the midst of the sea,
> > like one who lies on the top of a mast.
> "They struck me," you will say, "but I was not hurt;
> > they beat me, but I did not feel it.
> When shall I awake?
> > I will seek another drink." (Prov 23:29–35)

And he had observed a shrewd purchaser's bargaining strategy:

> "Bad, bad," says the buyer,
> > then goes away and boasts. (Prov 20:14)

The writer was familiar with other behavioral patterns. For example, as to angry speech and different ways of responding to it:

> A soft answer turns away wrath,
> > but a harsh word stirs up anger. (Prov 15:1)

> For lack of wood the fire goes out,
> > and where there is no whisperer, quarreling ceases.
> > (Prov 26:20)

And with what we might call psychology of human feelings or emotions:

> Hope deferred makes the heart sick,
> > but a desire fulfilled is a tree of life. (Prov 13:12)

> A cheerful heart is a good medicine,
> > but a downcast spirit dries up the bones. (Prov 17:22)

Many other biblical proverbs likewise recognize the complex character of human nature, a topic worthy of fuller consideration elsewhere.

Like Proverbs, Ecclesiastes is traditionally attributed to Solomon.[15] The author, commonly called Qoheleth, whether Solomon himself or some other wise and wealthy sage, describes his horticultural accomplishments: "I . . . planted vineyards for myself; I made myself gardens and parks, and planted in them all kinds of fruit trees. I made myself pools from which to water the forest of growing trees" (Eccl 2:4–6). "Solomon" evidently knew how to use irrigation to water his orchards. This sage also took note of the seasons and cycles of nature, thereby giving expression to an early version of systems analysis:

> The sun rises and the sun goes down,
> > and hurries to the place where it rises.
> The wind blows to the south,
> > and goes around to the north;
> round and round goes the wind,
> > and on its circuits the wind returns.
> All streams run to the sea,
> > but the sea is not full;

---

15. See Eccl 1:1, 16; 2:1–8, where the book's author broadly hints at this identity.

> to the place where the streams flow,
> > there they continue to flow.
> For everything there is a season,
> > and a time for every matter under heaven:
> a time to be born,
> > and a time to die;
> a time to plant,
> > and a time to pluck up what is planted. (Eccl 3:1–2)

He also knew that snakes could be charmed, and that it was prudent to have them charmed before handling or getting too close to them (Eccl 10:11).[16]

Like Job, or the author of the book of Job, Qoheleth recognizes limits to human knowledge: "Just as you do not know how the [spirit] comes to the bones in the mother's womb, so you do not know the work of God who makes everything" (Eccl 11:5). Lack of knowledge must be acknowledged but should not paralyze necessary agricultural activity. Farmers should go ahead and do the best they can on the basis of what they do know, even if future results are uncertain:

> Whoever observes the wind will not sow;
> > and whoever regards the clouds will not reap. (Eccl 11:4)

> In the morning sow your seed, and at evening do not let your hands be idle; for you do not know which will prosper, this or that, or whether both like will be good. (Eccl 11:6)

In addition, he noticed other natural phenomena and recorded them without deriving any practical lessons:

> When the clouds are full,
> > they empty rain on the earth;
> whether a tree falls to the south or to the north,
> > in the place where the tree falls, there it will lie. (Eccl 11:3)

The Song of Solomon is filled with images of nature—all seen positively as part of the good world that is to be enjoyed, partly as the setting for the lovers' expressions of affection for each other and partly for its own beauties and fragrances. Interests and

---

16. As to charming snakes, see also Ps 58:3–5.

observations here are not so much what might now be considered scientific, as aesthetic. Sun and moon, mountains and valleys, fields and "flowing streams," orchards, vineyards, and gardens are in the background. Closer by are many trees: apple, fig, pomegranate, palm, frankincense, and cedars of Lebanon. Flowers and spices lend their fragrances. Singing birds, doves, turtledoves, and ravens are named, along with both "wild" and domestic animals: lions, leopards, ewe lambs, gazelles, stags, mares, and goats. Although YHWH/God is not mentioned by name in the Song, its pages clearly express appreciation of and fondness for the created world and, especially, for the realm of living things, both flora and fauna.

In the Wisdom of Solomon, the writer—whether Solomon or someone imagining himself in Solomon's situation—shows deep interest in and appreciation of the world, its seasons and cycles, plants and animals, winds, and, like a latter-day psychologist, the "reasonings" or thoughts of human beings. Such knowledge as he has attained, he understands to be God's gift:

> For it is he who gave me unerring knowledge of what exists,
>   to know the structure of the world and the activity of the elements;
> the beginning and end and middle of times,
>   the alternations of the solstices and the changes of the seasons,
> the cycles of the year and the constellations of the stars,
>   the natures of animals and the tempers of wild animals,
> the powers of spirits and the [reasonings] of human beings,
>   the varieties of plants and the virtues of roots. (Wis 7:17–20)[17]

This sage's interest and knowledge include a remarkably wide range of what, in later times, would come to be called the natural sciences. Other biblical writings not traditionally associated with Solomon also indicate close observation of nature and living things. Often, these also express appreciation in the form of wonder, awe, or amazement at their endowments or capabilities.

---

17. Compare 1 Kgs 4:33 and Eccl 1:5–7, which credit Solomon with similar interests and understandings.

5. Proverbs 30: The Sayings of Agur

Several such texts are to be found in Prov 30. Unlike most of the book of Proverbs, this chapter is attributed to "Agur, son of Jakeh" (Prov 30:1). Like Job[18] and Qoheleth (Eccl 11:5), Agur acknowledges the limits to his understanding regarding the wondrous works of YHWH/God:

> Surely I am too stupid to be human.
> I do not have human understanding.
> I have not learned wisdom,
> nor have I knowledge of the Holy One.
> Who has ascended to heaven and come down?
> Who has gathered the wind in the hollow of the hand?
> Who has wrapped up the waters in a garment?
> Who has established all the ends of the earth?
> What is [his] name . . . ?
> Surely you know! (Prov 30:2–4)

Agur is particularly interested in observing and drawing comparisons among natural phenomena. Like the early modern scientist Carolus Linnaeus, this Agur undertook to classify natural phenomena on the basis of some common or shared trait or characteristic. Four such phenomena, he found alike in that they are simply "too wonderful" to understand:

> Three things are too wonderful for me;
> four I do not understand:
> the way of an eagle in the sky,
> the way of a snake on a rock,
> the way of a ship on the high seas,
> and the way of a man with a [maiden]. (Prov 30:18–19)

All these continue to be marvels. What are the aerodynamics of an eagle's flight? And how does a snake move so surely and swiftly without legs? Going on, Agur writes, four creatures in common are both small and yet "exceedingly wise":

> Four things on earth are small,
> but they are exceedingly wise:

---

18. See Job 40:3–5; 42:1–6.

> the ants are a people without strength,
> > yet they provide their food in the summer;
> the badgers are a people without power,
> > yet they make their homes in the rocks;
> the locusts have no king,
> > yet all of them march in rank;
> the lizard can be grasped in the hand,
> > yet it is found in kings' palaces. (Prov 30:24–28)

Both ants and badgers are here said to be "people" (Heb. *am*). The writer clearly intends to express not only wonder and awe but also respect and appreciation for what these little "people" can do.

Another set of four creatures—one of them human—have as their common trait that they are "stately in their stride":

> Three things are stately in their stride;
> > four are stately in their gait:
> the lion, which is mightiest among wild animals
> > and does not turn back before any;
> the strutting rooster, the he-goat,
> > and a king [strutting] before his people.[19] (Prov 30:29–31)

6. Sirach, the Letter of Jeremiah, and 4 Maccabees

The book of Sirach, or the Wisdom of Jesus, the Son of Sirach, also designated Ecclesiasticus, includes many appreciative references to other creatures. For instance, as to bees, the sage observes: "The bee is small among flying creatures, but [her] product is the best of sweet things" (Sir 11:3). Like other biblical writers, Sirach views all creation as good. The earth is "filled" with God's "good things." The earth's surface is covered with all kinds of living beings. And all kinds of living beings in time return to the earth.

> When the Lord created his works from the beginning,
> > and in making them, determined their boundaries,
> he arranged his works in an eternal order,
> > and their elements for all generations....

---

19. Both RSV and NRSV translators base their reading of Prov 30:31 on the Greek and other early versions, since the Hebrew text is obscure.

> Then the Lord looked upon the earth,
> and filled it with his good things.
> With all kinds of living beings he covered its surface,
> and into it they must return. (Sir 16:26–27, 29–30)

Another text in Sirach compares Wisdom[20] to a series of trees and other flora: "a cedar in Lebanon," "a cypress on the heights of Hermon," "a palm tree in Engedi," "rosebushes in Jericho," "a fair olive tree in the field," "a plane tree"; and to the fragrances of "cassia and camels' thorn," "choice myrrh," "galbanum, onycha, and stacte," and other delightful and wonderful vegetation (Sir 24:13–17). These comparisons with Wisdom clearly indicate knowledge of these several species of trees and plants, together with appreciation of and respect for them and their characteristic qualities.

Like the Solomonic sage of the book of Proverbs, Sirach not only offers wise advice but also reports keen observations as to human nature. For instance, as to people's—and other creatures'—tendency to associate with those so fortunate as to be like themselves, like "birds of a feather":

> Every creature loves its like,
> and every person the neighbor.
> All living beings associate with their own kind,
> and people stick close to those like themselves. (Sir 13:15–16)

Among other human foibles, he took note of their (or our) tendency toward excessive deference to the wealthy, matched only by indifference or hostility toward the humble or poor, for instance, the following observation:

> If the rich person slips, many come to the rescue;
> he speaks unseemly words, but they justify him.
> If the humble person slips, they even criticize him;
> he talks sense, but is not given a hearing.
> The rich person speaks and all are silent;
> they extol to the clouds what he says.
> The poor person speaks and they say, "Who is this fellow?"

---

20. Here, as in Prov 8 and several other "wisdom" writings, Wisdom is seen as a feminine person (Heb. *Hochmah*; Gk. *Sophia*), associated with YHWH/God, assisting him in carrying out his purposes.

And should he stumble, they even push him down.
(Sir 13:22–23)

Sirach also observed that humans have dual potentialities, both for good and for evil:

> What race is worthy of honor?
>   The human race.
> What race is worthy of honor?
>   Those who fear the Lord.
> What race is unworthy of honor?
>   The human race.
> What race is unworthy of honor?
>   Those who transgress the commandments. (Sir 10:19 RSV)

The Letter of Jeremiah, also known as Baruch, ch. 6, consists of an extended and imaginative polemic intended to demonstrate the futility of worshiping pagan idols. Such idols cannot even save themselves from ignominy or disaster, let alone save their adherents who foolishly call upon them. The writer appreciates and points out the superiority of wildlife: "The wild animals are better than they are, for they can flee to shelter and help themselves" (Ep Jer 6:8).

The author of 4 Maccabees observed and described in some detail how different kinds of mother birds go about nesting and protecting their young:

> For example, among birds, the ones that are tame protect their young by building on the housetops, and the others, by building in precipitous chasms and in holes and tops of trees, hatch the nestlings and ward off the intruder. If they are not able to keep the intruder away, they do what they can to help their young by flying in circles around them in the anguish of love, warning them with their own calls. (4 Macc 14:15–17)

The expression "anguish of love" indicates recognition and appreciation that such mother birds have feelings for their young—a recognition not shared by many modern commentators on animal behavior.[21] The same writer also has seen or otherwise learned how bees defend their hives:

---

21. See critique by Midgley, *Animals*.

Even bees at the time for making honeycombs defend themselves against intruders and, as though with an iron dart, sting those who approach their hive and defend it even to the death. (4 Macc 14:19)

7. Sayings of Jesus

Several New Testament texts indicate that Jesus observed and appreciated other living beings, both as wonders and as objects of God's loving care. God adorns the grass of the field or meadows with wild lilies, and such is their beauty that "even Solomon in all his glory was not clothed like one" of those lilies.[22] Jesus also recognized and gave expression to what latter-day botanists or horticulturalists still use as a standard test for identifying different plant species: "By their fruits, you shall know them." Flowers and leaves may be quite similar, but the fruit of each species is distinctive: "For each tree is known by its own fruit. Figs are not gathered from thorns, nor are grapes picked from a bramble bush" (Luke 6:44). Jesus applied this insight as a test for human behavior: "Beware of false prophets who come to you in sheep's clothing but inwardly are ravenous wolves. You will know them by their fruits" (Matt 7:15-16a). Here we see still more comparisons between humans and other living things.[23]

Jesus's parables often refer to seeds. Though probably intended to prompt appropriate responses by his hearers, these sayings indicate familiarity with natural phenomena and processes. The most extended of these is the parable of the sower in Mark 4:2-25.[24] Seeds that fall on a path (where soil is compacted) are likely to be eaten by birds; seeds fallen on rocky ground with little soil spring up quickly (perhaps because the soil is warm) but soon are scorched by the sun and, having but shallow roots, wither away. And seeds fallen among thorns are choked out as the thorns grow up (blocking light and consuming nutrients). Seeds sown on good

---

22. Matt 6:28-30; Luke 12:27-28.
23. See above, ch. 7B.
24. See also Matt 13:3-9, 18-23; and Luke 8:5-15.

soil flourish and produce good yields. Jesus also compares the kingdom of God to seed which a man scatters on the ground:

> The kingdom of God is as if someone would scatter seed upon the ground, and would sleep and rise night and day, and the seed would sprout and grow, he does not know how. The earth produces of itself, first the stalk, then the head, then the full grain in the head. But when the grain is ripe, at once he goes in with his sickle, because the harvest has come. (Mark 4:26–29)

What connection Jesus intended between the kingdom of God and the parable or similitude of the seed is debated by scholars. Passing over that question, the parable shows close observation of, and appreciation for, the wonders of nature: the mystery of growth from seed to harvest, even though the farmer "knows not how" (RSV),[25] and the wonder that the earth produces these stages of growth "of itself."

Another parable or similitude likewise compares the kingdom of God to a seed:

> And he said, "With what can we compare the kingdom of God, or what parable will we use for it? It is like a mustard seed, which, when sown upon the ground, is the smallest of all the seeds on earth; yet when it is sown it grows up and becomes the greatest of all shrubs, and puts forth large branches, so that the birds of the air can make nests in its shade." (Mark 4:30–32)[26]

A latter-day parallel might be the saying "Mighty oaks from little acorns grow." A very small seed produces a very large shrub, one large enough for birds to make nests in. Possibly the last clause was meant to echo earlier prophetic assurances that in the coming or messianic age, all kinds of birds would find shelter in great trees

---

25. Compare Eccl 11:5: "Just as you do not know how the [spirit or] breath comes to the bones in the mother's womb, so you do not know the work of God who makes everything."

26. See also Matt 13:31–32; and Luke 13:18–19.

that God himself would plant.[27] Again, we see here an expression of awe and wonder as to the ways of nature.[28]

Jesus showed his awareness that wildlife had and, implicitly, were entitled to have their own shelters in the present age, as well: "Foxes have holes, and birds of the air have nests" (Matt 8:20 = Luke 9:58). And also domestic animals. On the occasion described in Mark 7:24–30 and Matt 15:21–28, a gentile woman implored Jesus to exorcise the demon that was afflicting her daughter. Possibly because he believed his mission was first to Jewish communities, Jesus initially declined to do so: "Let the children be fed first, for it is not fair to take the children's food and throw it to the dogs." To this, the woman replied: "Sir, even the dogs under the table eat the children's crumbs." Jesus agreed and healed the daughter. Problematic as this episode may be, it is clear that Jesus, like the woman herself, recognized that dogs had their place at—if only under—the family table. Another time, comparing his own aspiration to the protective practices of a mother hen, Jesus expressed his longing to do good for the people of Jerusalem: "How often I have desired to gather your children together as a hen gathers her brood under her wings, [but] you were not willing!" (Matt 23:37 = Luke 13:34b). Here again we see empathy with, and appreciation of, other creatures' feelings, intentions, and actions

B. OTHER CREATURES AS MODELS FOR HUMAN EMULATION

A number of biblical texts suggest that other creatures can serve as models or exemplars for humans to emulate. Various anecdotes or sayings also intimate that some creatures may be wiser or more knowledgeable than their human counterparts.

Admiration for the prudent and enterprising ant expressed in Prov 6:6–8 has already been mentioned. Here the behavior of the ant is presented in contrast to that of the "lazybones" or "sluggard" (RSV), a degenerate human figure whose laziness is the subject of

---

27. See below, ch. 11.

28. See Tull, *Inhabiting Eden*, 29–37, discussing awe as a characteristic biblical response to the wonders of creation.

frequent comment in Proverbs: "Go to the ant, you lazybones; consider [her] ways and be wise."

The book of Lamentations contrasts the cruelty of human mothers during the siege of Jerusalem to the care mother jackals give their young:

> Even the jackals offer the breast
>   and nurse their young,
> but [the daughter of] my people has become cruel,
>   like the ostriches in the wilderness. (Lam 4:3)[29]

Doves likewise are seen as models for maternal care: "Mother, embrace your children; bring them up with gladness, as does a dove" (2 Esd 2:15). Parent birds are also commended for "sympathy and parental love for their offspring" in 4 Macc 14:13–17. And in the New Testament, Jesus reportedly urged his followers, who were about to go out on their urgent mission, to "be [as] wise as serpents and [as] innocent as doves" (Matt 10:16).

Humans can learn from other creatures who sometimes are represented or regarded as wiser or more knowledgeable than they. Instances appear in several different kinds of biblical writings. An example previously considered in another context is found in the story of Balaam and Balak (Num 22:21–35). Only the ass sees YHWH/God's angel blocking the way and then acts appropriately. Balaam himself had no clue as to what was happening.[30]

Job finds himself beset by certain self-righteous, so-called friends. These self-appointed worthies wish to "comfort" Job by telling him that in this life God showers blessings on the righteous, inflicts misery on the wicked, and that he, Job, should see that all his sufferings were richly deserved.[31] Job knows better, and so, he says, do "the animals" or "beasts" (RSV), "the birds of the air," and even "the plants of the earth" (or the earth itself), and "the fish of the sea." All these know better than do Job's know-it-all "friends." To them, he says:

> But ask the animals, and they will teach you;

29. Compare Job 39:13–16, commenting on ostrich parenting.
30. See Richard Hiers, *Trinity Guide to Bible*, cover art, 50–51, and 293.
31. Richard Hiers, *Trinity Guide to Bible*, 83–86.

> the birds of the air, and they will tell you;
> ask the plants of the earth, and they will teach you;
> and the fish of the sea will declare to you.
> Who among all these does not know
> that the hand of YHWH has done this?
> In his hand is the life of every living thing
> and the breath of every human being. (Job 12:7–10)[32]

A classic text in Isaiah contrasts the knowledge of ox and ass with the willful ignorance of the people of Judah and Jerusalem:

> Hear, O heavens, and listen, O earth;
> for YHWH has spoken:
> "I reared children and brought them up,
> but they have rebelled against me.
> The ox knows its owner,
> and the [ass] its master's crib;
> but Israel does not know,
> my people do not understand." (Isa 1:2–3)[33]

Similarly, the prophet Jeremiah contrasts certain kinds of birds' knowledge of nature—particularly, their sense of timing for migratory flights—with the people of Judah's ignorance or rejection of YHWH/God's laws:

> Even the stork in the heavens
> knows [her] times;
> and the turtledove, swallow, and crane
> [keep] the time of their coming;
> but my people do not know
> the ordinance of YHWH. (Jer 8:7)

---

32. Compare Job 35:10–11, where Elihu is speaking: "God . . . teaches us more than the animals of the earth, and makes us wiser than the birds of the air." Elihu's speech, of which this text is a part, evidently was composed by a later author who felt it necessary to correct or refute what Job had said, and often seems to have failed to understand what the earlier author meant to say.

33. This text is the probable basis for the extra-biblical tradition that such creatures were present when Jesus was born and "laid in a manger." See, e.g., the stanza from the Christmas carol "Good Christian Men, Rejoice": "Ox and ass before him bow, for he is in the manger, now" (Neale, "Good Christian Men, Rejoice"). This tradition may also reflect the biblical expectation that these and other kinds of animals would be present in the messianic age. See below, ch. 11.

A relatively late text sees matters quite differently. This text says, in effect, that "the beasts of the field" are more fortunate than humans because of what they do *not* know:

> Let the human race lament,
> but let the wild animals of the field be glad;
> let all [humans] who have been born lament,
> but let the [four-footed beasts] and the flocks rejoice.
> It is much better with them than with us;
> for they do not look for a judgment,
> and they do not know of any torment
> or salvation promised to them after death. (2 Esd 7:65–6)

Sirach, by way of contrast, attributes wisdom to all God's creatures:

> [The Lord himself created wisdom];
>   he saw her and took her measure;
>   he poured her out upon all his works.
> [She dwells with all flesh] according to his gift, [and he supplied her to] those who love him. (Sir 1:9–10)

The many biblical texts considered in this chapter show great interest in and appreciation of other kinds of creatures that YHWH/God brought, and continued to bring, into being. Some of these creatures were held up as examples that humans would do well to emulate. It has been said that the first "move" of the moral life is appreciation. The moral corollary or next "move" is thoughtful and effective action to protect, preserve or conserve, and promote the well-being of that which one has come to appreciate.[34]

The following chapter now turns to an examination of biblical laws and practices regarding protection, preservation, and promotion of the land or the earth and of other life-forms, particularly living beings, both human and nonhuman. Here we see both implicit and explicit instances of "environmental ethics" and the ethics of reverence or respect and active caring for nature and all living beings.

---

34. In his ethics lectures at Yale, H. Richard Niebuhr often referred to the next move of the moral life as "cultivation," a term particularly appropriate with respect to a land or agricultural ethic.

CHAPTER 9

Caring for Creation

Biblical Faith and Environmental Ethics

SEVERAL PATTERNS OR TYPES of interaction between humans and other creatures have been considered in the previous chapters of part 2. Some of these involve obligations on the part of humans to act or to refrain from acting in certain ways.[1] The last chapter focused on appreciation of other creatures, as well as plants and trees, recognition of their importance, and a sense of wonder at their ways. This chapter considers biblical texts that point to more explicit and affirmative obligations that humans have regarding the creation and other creatures. In particular: obligations to care for the land and what grows upon it, and to care for people and for other living beings.[2] Such obligations were not thought to derive

---

1. See above, especially chs. 4 and 5. See Berry, *Sex, Economy*, 96, 98: "If we read the Bible... we will discover that... our destruction of nature is not just bad stewardship, or stupid economics, or a betrayal of family responsibility; it is the most horrid blasphemy.... We have no entitlement from the Bible to exterminate or permanently destroy or hold in contempt anything on the earth or in the heavens above it or in the waters beneath it."

2. In recent years, a number of Christian denominations and other religious groups have taken positions concerning moral responsibility to care for the creation. These generally draw upon themes and values implicit in biblical tradition. See, e.g., Hill, *Christian Faith and Environment*, 155–86; Fowler, *Greening of Protestant Thought*, 13–19; and Martin-Schramm and Stivers, *Christian Environmental Ethics*, 45nn3–4. See also Brief of the National Council of the Churches of Christ in the

from, or correlate with, inherent "rights" of some sort. Nor were they derived from an anthropocentric or humanistic faith—as if only those things supposed to be good for human beings deserved attention and care. Rather, as will be seen, these obligations were understood to be grounded upon the desires and demands of God, the ultimate Source and Valuer of all that exists.[3]

A. CARING FOR THE LAND, PLANTS, AND TREES

Biblical tradition makes clear that the whole earth, both land and sea, belong to YHWH/God. The people of Israel were given their land subject to the condition that they remained faithful to him. And with that gift, came a number of responsibilities. The people of Israel were to work the land and care for it; but also to give it rest, to tend properly to fields, orchards, and vineyards, and always to remember that the gifts of the land come from YHWH/God.

1. Land Ethics

Biblical tradition does not regard land, or even the whole earth, as sacred in itself. But the whole earth is affirmed as YHWH/God's creation and is highly valued as such. People and animals are

---

U.S.A., Church World Service, and National Catholic Rural Life Conference as Amici Curiae in Support of Petitioners, before the U.S. Supreme Court in Massachusetts v. Environmental Protection Agency, 549 U.S. 497 (2007), addressing issues relating to climate change, particularly, global warming. Text available at https://scholar.google.com/scholar_case?case=18363956969502505811. This brief also provides citations and links to several other position papers, including, e.g., United States Conference of Catholic Bishops, *Global Climate Change*; Evangelical Climate Initiative, "Climate Change"; General Convention of The Episcopal Church, "Recognize Global Warming"; United Methodist Church, "Climate Change"; and Reformed Church in America, "Climate Change/Environment." See also Wilson, *Creation*, 172–73n165. And see resolution adopted by the Southern Baptist Convention, June 16, 2010, encouraging "prayer for the end of the massive oil spill in the Gulf of Mexico and for those affected by the crisis, and calling for action by the government and corporations to prevent future catastrophes." This resolution "asserted that mankind's 'dominion over the creation is not unlimited, as though we were gods and not creatures,' meaning that there is a higher standard than economic profit" (site discontinued).

3. As to the problematics of attributing "rights" to nature or created beings, see George, "Environment, Rights."

always seen as closely related to the earth. Indeed, the J creation story declares that YHWH/God formed both primordial man and "every animal of the field and every bird of the air" from "the ground" (Gen 2:7, 19). The earth is said to be "the womb" of all creatures[4] or as "the mother" of humankind, indeed, the mother of all the living. All the earth belongs to YHWH/God, and deserves care by its human inhabitants.[5] Various laws provide for giving the land periods of rest. Prophets and laws alike caution against polluting or defiling the land. And only those who remain faithful to YHWH/God may expect to dwell upon his land in the future. YHWH/God is understood as the One who gives the fruits of the land—of fields, vineyards, and orchards. Portions of these fruits were to be returned to him as expressions of thanks for having given them. Other portions were to be shared throughout the community, and also with cattle (domestic animals) and wildlife. Throughout biblical tradition, care of the land—tilling or cultivating the soil and tending vineyards and orchards—were seen as part of humankind's responsibilities to or before YHWH/God.[6]

a. *The Land Is YHWH/God's, not Israel's or Any People's*

Both creation stories (Gen 1:1—2:4a, and 2:4b–24) can readily be understood to mean that the earth and everything in it, being made by God (or YHWH), belong to him.[7] That the earth belongs to YHWH is said explicitly in the preamble to the Covenant Code: "All the earth is mine" (Exod 19:5) This theme is implicit or explicit

---

4. See 2 Esd 5:4–49.

5. Sir 40:1; 2 Esd 5:50. Something like this understanding, perhaps, is expressed in Rodgers and Hammerstein's theme song from *Oklahoma*, inferring that this wonderful ground owns us. Throughout biblical tradition, it is understood that land, the whole earth, and all creation belong to YHWH/God, not to human beings. See above, ch. 1C.

6. For thoughtful reflections on Christian ethics and contemporary land issues in Ghana, see Ntreh et al., *Essays on the Land*.

7. See above, ch. 1. Compare the perspective expressed in Woodie Guthrie's popular song "This Land Is Your Land." See Douma, *Environmental Stewardship*, 35: "The world is God's creation and therefore cannot be regarded as the possession of the *human beings* who occupy it."

in numerous biblical laws and related texts.[8] For his own purposes, YHWH/God has given his people, Israel, a temporary tenancy on the land. But he retained title to it. It remains his to do with as he chooses.

Deuteronomy 10:14. The language of this text leaves no room for doubt, either: to YHWH belong "heaven and the heaven of heavens, . . . the earth with all that is in it." In effect, the whole creation is YHWH's. Similar affirmations appear in several of the psalms.[9] The implicit corollary is that the world does not belong to humans to do with as they please. From this perspective, laying waste to an enemy's land should have been seen as a violation of YHWH/God's domain—even when such devastation was not specifically condemned.[10]

Leviticus 25:23. Here it is said that the land ultimately belongs to YHWH/God. The land referred to here is the land of promise, or Canaan. YHWH/God's ownership of land is not limited to that land, however. Other texts indicate what is already implicit in the creation narratives, that *all that that is* belongs to YHWH/God, including the land.[11] Land therefore may not be sold "in perpetuity," i.e., so as to become anyone's permanent possession.[12] The people of Israel are "strangers and guests" there.[13] People may buy and sell land—subject to laws or rights of inheritance and redemption,[14] but in the end, the land is YHWH/God's to dispose of as he chooses. This Leviticus text could be read to suggest a "land ethic," that is,

---

8. See, e.g., Exod 9:29b; Deut 10:14; Pss 24:1–2; 50:10–12; 89:11–12; 95:4–5; 96:1, 11–12. (But see Ps 115:16.) In turn, the land or earth itself is said to praise or bless YHWH. See, e.g., Pss 69:34; 100:1; Isa 49:13; Sg Three v. 52. See generally Anderson, *From Creation*, 1–18; and Santmire, *Travail of Nature*, 190–92.

9. Pss 24:1; 50:12; 89:11; 95:4–5.

10. See 2 Kgs 3:15–19, 24–25 as to "ruining" land in Moab, then Israel's enemy.

11. See, e.g., Ps 24:1 ("The earth is YHWH's"). See above, ch. 1C.

12. See Twum-Baah, "Introduction," 26–27. See also Vorster, "Ethics of Land Restitution," 685: "Land alienation on a permanent basis would have run counter to the principle of divine ownership."

13. See Hart, *Spirit of the Earth*, 51–55, 119–23. As to the status of early Israelites as sojourners, see Richard Hiers, *Nation of Immigrants*, 38–45.

14. Lev 25, 27. See Westbrook, *Property and Family*, 24–35, 53, 58–68; and Richard Hiers, "Transfer of Property."

that the land always is to be regarded as God's gift, not something to be exploited or degraded for human gain.[15]

b. Israel's Contingent Possession of the Good Land

A number of texts in Genesis say that YHWH/God promised that he would give the land of Canaan to Abram (Abraham) and his offspring or descendants without any stated qualifications.[16] One text even says that YHWH would give this land to Abram and his offspring "forever" (Gen 13:15). Nevertheless, numerous biblical texts warn that the Israelites' future possession of the promised land was contingent on their fidelity to YHWH and their observance of his covenant or commandments.

Exodus 19:5 articulates the understanding that YHWH/God intended to give the people of Israel a particular space and place on that earth—*provided* they remain faithful to him and his commandments. "Now therefore, if you obey my voice and keep my covenant, you shall be my treasured possession out of all the peoples. Indeed, the whole earth is mine, but you shall be for me a priestly kingdom and a holy nation." Other texts likewise express the contingent nature of Israel's occupancy of the promised land

---

15. See Berry, *Gift of Good Land*, 269–81; and Murphy, *Haunted by Paradise*, 106–7: "The Bible expresses particular concern for the preservation of every species of creature, strongly endorsing biological diversity. Every living creature—not just human beings—is commanded to 'be fruitful and multiply' (Gen 1:22). If God wants all creatures to multiply, then human beings should avoid causing the extinction of any species of living thing."

16. Gen 12:7; 13:14–17; 15:18–21. Later, Jacob dreams that YHWH had likewise promised to give the land on which he slept to him and his offspring (Gen 28:10–17). The extent of this land was not indicated. Such texts, read apart from others that clearly warn that Israel's possession of the land was conditioned upon their fidelity to YHWH and his covenant requirements, have prompted latter-day illusions as to absolute ownership. See Caldwell and Shrader-Frechette, *Policy for Land*, 8:

"American attitudes toward land acquisition and territorial possession have historically been reinforced, in part, by certain Biblical interpretations. Just as God 'gave' the land of Canaan to the ancient Hebrews, European colonizers believed America was given to them. Canaanites and Native Americans were not seen as having any real rights to the land. The concept of 'God-given rights' permeates American attitudes toward land and, at least in part, explains the moral indignation of land owners whose possession is threatened by a government takeover for a public purpose."

once they had settled there.¹⁷ In effect, their occupation of the land was subject to what in Anglo-American law is called a "reverter clause." The relation between landlord and tenant might also aptly describe the nature of Israel's tenancy. In any case, if the people of Israel failed to meet certain conditions, they could lose this land because YHWH/God would take it back again.¹⁸

Certain texts early in the book of Deuteronomy likewise underscore the tenuous nature of Israel's occupation of the land that had been promised to them and their forebears in the covenants of old. These texts may derive from sermons or exhortations at periodic, ancient, ceremonial gatherings when the law was read and the covenant renewed. In any case, they called on Israelites to adhere to YHWH/God's law. YHWH/God had made good on his promise to bring his people into this land. Now it was up to them to remain faithful to YHWH/God and his commandments, ordinances, and statutes.

Deuteronomy 6:3, 10-19: The peril of apostasy. Here Moses, speaking for YHWH/God, describes the land of Canaan as "a land flowing with milk and honey" (Deut 6:3). Moreover, it is a "land with fine, large cities," houses, hewn cisterns, vineyards, and olive groves (Deut 6:10-11). The land is characterized explicitly as "the good land" that YHWH/God had promised their fathers he would give them (Deut 6:18). Nevertheless, YHWH/God would destroy his people "from off the face of the earth" (RSV) if they forgot him and worshiped other gods instead (Deut 6:14-15).

Deuteronomy 8:7-20: The peril of autonomous individualism. In this exhortation, Moses draws attention to the rich resources

---

17. See, e.g., Hos 4:1—11:7; Amos 3:1-9:8a. Both prophets leave unresolved the question whether Israel would have a future. See generally Lilburne, *Sense of Place*, 5-54.

18. See McAfee, "Ecology and Biblical Studies," 37: "The entire earth, including the sociopolitical reality of the land of Israel, belongs to God, and human entitlement to the earth's resources extends only to the right of usufruct. This understanding of the relationship of divine ownership, human usufruct, and natural resources is clearly evident in Deuteronomistic theology, where the land Israel possesses is granted on condition of Israel's obedience to the Mosaic covenant; Israel's disobedience results in expulsion from the land and the return of the land to its original owner, God (cf. Deut 4:25-26; 6:10; 7:12-16; 8:6-20, etc.)."

See also C. Wright, *Old Testament Ethics*, 92-94.

with which the promised land is blessed: it is a "good land," with "flowing streams," springs and underground water, a land already planted with wheat, barley, vines, fig trees, pomegranates, olive trees, a land with honey, iron, and copper. In short, it is a land where they "will lack nothing" (Deut 8:7–9). The peril is that the people of Israel may forget YHWH/God and fail to keep his commandments, ordinances, and statutes; with the result that when they have eaten their full and become prosperous, they may indulge in the pretention that they had earned it all by their own effort and power (Deut 8:17). Those who presume to be masters of the earth are likely to lose their respect for it, along with their reverence for the God who—for a while—had entrusted it to them. And those who so forget and so presume are doomed to perish (Deut 8:18–20).

Deuteronomy 8:9 is the first and only text in the Bible regarding mineral removal or extraction: "a land whose stones are iron and from whose hills you may mine copper." The Israelites were free to use these resources, but there was no permission, much less, any injunction or commandment to use them up or degrade the environment in the process.[19]

Deuteronomy 9:4–24: The peril of moral complacency. Deuteronomy 9:4–6 cautions Israelites against believing that YHWH/God favored them in the past because they had been a righteous people, and so he would maintain them in the promised land forevermore, no matter what. On the contrary, says the text (Moses speaking on behalf of YHWH), they "are a stubborn people," with a history of

19. Compare former U.S. Interior Secretary James Watt's explanation for his decision to open eight hundred million acres of federal land for corporate exploitation: "My responsibility is to follow the Scriptures which call upon us to occupy the land until Jesus returns." Prochenau and *Washington Post* Staff Writer, "Watt Controversy." There is no such biblical text or requirement. See Robert Lekachman's comment: "At his confirmation hearing, Mr. Watt casually confided to the senators in attendance that 'I do not know how many future generations we can count on before the Lord returns.' . . . This uncertainty appeared, mysteriously, to justify opening of public lands to coal miners, oil explorers, lumbermen, resort developers, stock grazers, and other predators. Scripture, asserted Mr. Watt, endorsed his plan." Lekachman, *Greed Is Not Enough*, 51. See generally Fowler, *Greening of Protestant Thought*, 45–57. Also compare the "wise use" movement in some western U.S. states. Proponents of this movement contend that river water adjacent to agricultural property is "wasted" unless it is all used for the benefit of immediately adjacent property owners.

acting corruptly and rebelling against YHWH/God.[20] The central theme in the book of Deuteronomy is that the Israelites' conduct must change radically for the better—or else they would lose it all.

The classical prophets likewise called on their contemporaries to remain faithful to YHWH/God and his commandments—or else YHWH/God would bring judgment upon them in the form of disaster. For instance, the prophet Ezekiel addressed his contemporaries' notion that Abraham had possessed the land by his own prowess and that they themselves could count on keeping it by virtue of their numbers:

> The word of YHWH came to me: [Son of man], the inhabitants of these waste places in the land of Israel keep saying, "Abraham was only one man, yet he got possession of the land; but we are many; the land is surely given us to possess." Therefore, say to them, Thus says the Lord God: "You eat flesh with the blood, and lift up your eyes to your idols, and shed blood; shall you then possess the land? You depend on your sword, you commit abominations, and each of you defiles his neighbor's wife; shall you then possess the land?" Say this to them, "Thus says the Lord God: As I live, surely those who are in the waste places shall fall by the sword; and those who are in the open field I will give to the wild animals to be devoured; and those who are in strongholds and in caves shall die by pestilence."
> (Ezek 33:23–27)[21]

Both in Israelite tradition and in the early Christian community represented in the New Testament, it was understood that only those who remained faithful to God and had regard for his commands and purposes would retain or inherit the blessings of life in the promised land of Canaan, or in the coming messianic age or kingdom of God.[22] This understanding may give pause to

---

20. Deut 9:6–8, 12–16, 22–24, 27. Other texts in Deuteronomy also emphasize the contingent nature of Israel's occupation of or survival in the land given their forebears. See, e.g., Deut 28:15–68 and 30:15–20. See also Josh 23:14–16.

21. See also Isa 5:1–30; Jer 5:1–31; 7:1–34; Amos 5:1–20.

22. On New Testament expectations, see McAfee, "Ecology and Biblical Studies," 38–41. As to such NT beliefs about the future, see generally Richard Hiers, *Jesus and the Future*.

people who, in later times, identify with ancient Israel or wish to claim to be heirs to its land or other supposedly unqualified biblical blessings.

c. Against Pollution of the Land

In biblical times, toxic modern chemical and biological pollutants, of course, were unknown. But biblical law showed concern about other ways human actions could pollute the land.[23] Failure—by Israel, Judah, or even all humankind—to adhere to YHWH/God's "everlasting covenant" by violating his commandments and statutes pollutes the earth, wrote a late Isaianic prophet:

> The earth dries up and withers,
>   the world languishes and withers;
>   the heavens languish together with the earth.
> The earth lies polluted
>   under its inhabitants;
> for they have transgressed laws,
>   violated the statutes,
>   broken the everlasting covenant.
> Therefore a curse devours the earth,
>   and its inhabitants suffer for their guilt;
> therefor the inhabitants of the earth dwindled,
>   and few people are left. (Isa 24:4–6)

By the "everlasting covenant," the writer probably meant the covenant "between God and every living creature of all flesh" characterized in Gen 9:16 as "the everlasting covenant."[24] The prophet Jeremiah likewise chastised his contemporaries for failing to remain faithful to YHWH/God and his law, thereby defiling or polluting the land:

> I brought you into a plentiful land
>   to eat its fruits and its good things.
> But when you entered you defiled my land,
>   and made my heritage an abomination. (Jer 2:7)

---

23. See generally Schaeffer, *Pollution*.
24. See above, ch. 2B6.

> If a man divorces his wife and she goes from him
>> and becomes another man's wife, will he return to her?
> Would not such a land be greatly polluted? . . .
> You have polluted the land
>> with your whoring and wickedness. (Jer 3:1–2)

> For my eyes are on all their ways;
>> they are not hid from me,
>> nor is their iniquity concealed from my sight.
> And I will doubly repay their iniquity and their sin,
>> because they have polluted my land with the
> carcasses of their detestable idols,
>> and have filled my inheritance with their abominations.
> (Jer 16:17–18)

Biblical laws identify other related types of pollution.

Numbers 35:30–34: Cleansing the land of bloodshed. Numbers 35 distinguishes between manslaughter and murder. A murderer must be put to death, but only if more than one witness testifies as to the accused's guilt, presumably at a trial of some sort.[25] Numbers 35:33–34 seems to say that human blood shed by a murderer pollutes or defiles the land and that the only way such pollution can be removed or expiated is "by the blood of the one who shed it."[26] The stated purpose of this law was neither retribution nor deterrence but, rather, to cleanse the land.

Deuteronomy 21:22–23: Keeping the land undefiled. A criminal executed for committing a capital offense might afterwards be hung or impaled on a tree. This procedure probably was intended to deter others from committing such heinous offenses. The executed offender's body must be taken down and buried the same day, lest the land be defiled. As in Num 19:1–22, the theory may have been that contact with, or even proximity to, a dead body caused a person to become ritually unclean and that others who had contact with a person so contaminated would spread further defilement. This law may also reflect public health concerns based on experience.

---

25. Compare the trial scene in Susanna vv. 28–60.

26. Compare the procedure prescribed in Deut 21:1–9 where the murderer had not been found. See generally Gaster, *Myth, Legend, and Custom*, 69–72.

Deuteronomy 23:12–14: Sanitary arrangements. This law prohibits the people of Israel from polluting their "camp" with their excrement. When need to defecate arises, they are to go outside the camp to a designated area, taking along a digging stick or "trowel." There, they are to make a hole, use it, and cover it up with earth afterwards.[27] This law was intended to apply during the Israelite's sojourn in the wilderness and also, probably, after they had entered the land of promise. Thus they were to keep their land both ritually clean or "holy" and sanitary. Urban sanitary arrangements are nowhere mentioned.[28]

Wisdom of Solomon 2:6–9: Trashing the land. This text characterizes the creed of pleasure-seekers who would exploit the good things of creation and leave their trash everywhere behind:

> Come, therefore, let us enjoy the good things that exist,
>   and make use of the creation to the full as in youth.
> Let us take our fill of costly wine and perfumes,
>   and let no flower of spring pass us by.
> Let us crown ourselves with rosebuds
>   before they wither.
> Let none of us fail to share in our revelry
>   everywhere let us leave signs of enjoyment,
> because this is our portion, and this our lot.

Such, says the sage, was the reasoning of the "ungodly," those who "were led astray, for their wickedness blinded them" (Wis 1:16; 2:21). By way of contrast, in the NT it is said that those who participated in the miraculous or sacramental meal of bread and fish in the wilderness afterwards picked up what was left and (presumably) packed it out.[29]

---

27. As to possible implications of this law for addressing similar problems in modern Ghana, see Ntreh, "Introduction," 10–11.

28. Biblical tradition contains few other references to defecation: notably, 1 Sam 24:3 and 1 Kgs 18:27.

29. Mark 6:30–44; 8:1–9; Matt 14:13–21; 15:32–39; Luke 9:10–17; John 6:1–13.

d. Tilling the Ground

Biblical tradition sees humans as caretakers of the land. As the J creation story is told, immediately after creating the first man (*adam*) from the dust of the ground (*adamah*), YHWH/God "planted a garden in Eden, in the east; and there he put the man whom he had formed" (Gen 2:8). The J story then explains what this primordial man was supposed to do: "YHWH God took the man and put him in the garden of Eden to till it and keep it" (Gen 2:15).[30] The Hebrew verb *abad*, here translated as to "till" or cultivate, also means to *serve* (as in the Hebrew noun *ebed*, "servant" or "slave"); and the verb *shamar*, translated as to "keep," also means to "keep safe," "protect," or "preserve." Those who till the ground thereby *serve* the ground and, at the same time, serve YHWH/God (Gen 2:15; 3:23). And keeping the land would mean protecting and preserving it. The text of Gen 2:15 thus qualifies or offsets the earlier instruction—given only to the first man and woman—to *subdue* the earth (Gen 1:28). YHWH/God's instruction (or permission) to do so was not repeated when humankind started over again after the great flood. Even after the original (or aboriginal) man and woman were banished from the garden of Eden, the first task YHWH/God assigned or reassigned the man (*ha adam*) was to till, cultivate, or serve (*abad*) the ground, soil, or land (*adamah*),[31] "from which he was taken" (Gen 3:23).

The P creation story uses somewhat different language. Instead of being made from the ground, both members of the primordial couple are said to have been made "in the image of God" and to have been given "dominion . . . over all the earth" (Gen 1:26–27). Moreover, they were also charged to "subdue" the earth (Gen 1:28). Yet subsequently, as the J narrative resumes, after the man eats the forbidden fruit, YHWH/God warns him:

---

30. See also Gen 2:5. See Martin-Schramm and Stivers, *Christian Environmental Ethics*, 103, discussing Gen 2:15 as the basis for understanding "stewardship" of the land as "preserving and protecting what God has made." The authors also discuss stewardship in connection with Gen 1:26–28 and other biblical texts. Martin-Schramm and Stivers, *Christian Environmental Ethics*, 102–4.

31. See Hiebert, "Rethinking Traditional Approaches," 30; Hiebert, "Human Vocation"; and Rasmussen, *Earth Community, Earth Ethics*, 232.

> Cursed is the ground because of you;
> in toil you shall eat of it all the days of your life;
> thorns and thistles it shall bring forth for you;
> and you shall eat the plants of the field. (Gen 3:17–19)

Human dominion over the earth is qualified here by the fact that humankind is destined to return to it. As the ancient college song *Gaudeamus igitur* puts it, *nos habebit humus*, "the earth shall have us."

As the J narrative continues into the next generation, the situation goes from bad to worse. Cain, the first couple's first son, likewise was described as "a tiller of the ground" (Gen 4:2). But after murdering his brother, Cain and, implicitly, all his descendants were "cursed from the ground":[32]

> And now you are cursed from the ground, which has opened its mouth to receive your brother's blood from your hand. When you till the ground, it will no longer yield to you its strength. (Gen 4:11–12)

People would still have to till or serve the ground. But now tilling the ground would mean dealing with thorns and thistles, it would be hard work, and full yields could no longer be expected.[33] Subduing—or serving—the land would no longer be easy tasks.

Nevertheless, tilling the soil—farm work or agriculture—continued to be regarded as a high calling in later biblical tradition. Following the great flood, Noah—who, as the account unfolds, was the father of all later humankind—also was said to be "a tiller of the soil" (Gen 9:20).[34] Moreover, he was the first to plant a

---

32. According to the J genealogy in Gen 4:17–19, Cain was the ancestor of Lamech, who, if the same as the Lamech named in Gen 5:28–31, was the father of Noah. Noah was said to be the father or forefather of all later humankind.

33. Genesis 5:29 reports Lamech's hopes for his newborn son, Noah: "Out of the ground that YHWH has cursed this one shall bring us relief from our work and from the toil of our hands." Although this hope was not fulfilled, Noah played a major role in preserving humankind and all other air-breathing species. See pt. B1a of this chapter.

34. Genesis 9:20 describes Noah as "the first tiller of the soil." Both the first man in the J narrative, and Cain had been described as tillers of the soil. The narrator in Gen 9 may have meant that Noah was the first tiller of the soil after the flood. Or these stories may have originated separately.

vineyard (Gen 9:20). His offspring were to carry on this work in ensuing generations. King Uzziah was later remembered positively for practicing agriculture and for his love of the soil.[35] Likewise, King Solomon was celebrated for planting vineyards and making gardens and parks (Eccl 2:4–5). And the prophet Amos recalled that he himself had been "a dresser of fig trees" (Amos 7:14). Job, characterized as a "blameless and upright man" (Job 1:1), was also a farmer, who, it can be inferred, cared well for his land.[36] A relatively late text recalls the era of peace enjoyed under the rule of Simon during the Maccabean period:

> They tilled their land in peace;
>   the ground gave its increase,
>   and the trees of the plains their fruit. (1 Macc 14:8)
>
> He established peace in the land,
>   and Israel rejoiced with great joy.
> All the people sat under their own vines and his fig trees,
>   and there was none to make them afraid. (1 Macc 14:11–12)

According to biblical wisdom tradition, farm work was made by God himself: "Do not hate hard labor or farm work, which was created by the Most High" (Sir 7:15). This text may have been intended to recall Gen 2:15 and 3:23, where it is said that YHWH/God put the original man in the garden of Eden to till it and then, after ejecting him from the garden, commanded him to "till the ground from which he was taken." Wisdom tradition understood that caring for the soil would have its rewards: "Those who till their land will have plenty of food" (Prov 12:11; 28:19) and "Anyone who tends a fig tree will eat its fruit" (Prov 27:18).[37] Working the ground was a matter of high priority: "Get everything ready for you in the field, and after that build your house" (Prov 24:27).

---

35. "He had farmers and vinedressers in the hills and in the fertile lands, for he loved the soil" (2 Chr 26:10).

36. See Job 31:38, 40. The implication in these verses is that Job's land had *not* "cried out" against him, nor had its furrows "wept."

37. Conversely, according to Prov 20:4 and 24:30–31, those who fail to plough their fields or tend their vineyards will end up with little or nothing.

Biblical prophets anticipated that in the coming or messianic age, people would still plough fields and tend to fruit trees:

> They shall beat their swords into plowshares,
>   and their spears into pruning hooks. (Isa 2:4; Mic 4:3)

> The time is surely coming, says YHWH,
>   when the one who plows shall overtake the one who reaps,
>   and the treader of grapes the one who sows the seed.
>   (Amos 9:13a–c)

Other prophetic texts likewise look for abundant agricultural blessings in the future messianic or coming age.[38]

Clearly, tilling the soil, tending to fields, vineyards, and orchards, were noble callings assigned to God's people, whether in the present age or in the age to come. These were basic features of biblical environmental ethics. Notwithstanding spreading urbanization and rapidly developing technologies in modern times, human beings continue to depend on the soil and those who cultivate, serve, and preserve it.[39]

e. Sabbath Rest for the Land

Biblical laws provide that the land itself was to be allowed to "rest" periodically. None of the Sabbath day commandments[40] mentions the *land's* resting, but, implicitly, the land itself would rest on

---

38. See, e.g., Isa 30:23–25; Ezek 34:27, 29; 36:8–11, 29–30, 34–36; and Amos 9:13d–14. See below, ch. 11.

39. See Hiebert, "Rethinking Traditional Approaches," 29–30: "Our productive soil, without which we will not endure, is in serious peril, and we as a society must be somehow reminded of our dependence on it in order to respond to the threats to it. In this regard, I can think of no more powerful and necessary image than the creation of human life in J's creation story, which claims that we are all, whether we like it or not, farmers. Made out of arable soil, our destinies are forever and irrevocably tied to its productive health." Compare the popular notion that food comes from grocery stores. Arable land was already vanishing rapidly fifty years ago. See Meadows et al., *Limits to Growth*, 57–63. Also, Murphy, *Haunted by Paradise*, 108: "Agriculture today destroys myriad natural habitats and species. But modern agriculture is more like mining the soil than cultivating a garden."

40. Exod 20:8–11; 23:12; 34:21; Deut 5:12–15.

Sabbath days, for no one would work upon it.[41] The Sabbatical Year laws so provide in explicit terms.

Exodus 23:10–11 states that after six years of sowing the land and gathering its yield, Israelite farmers were to let the land "rest and lie fallow" on the seventh or Sabbatical Year. So far as is known, Israelite farmers did not practice crop rotation or other modern soil conservation strategies. The sense of this law is that the land itself desired or needed a rest after producing crops for six consecutive years.[42] Likewise, vineyards and olive orchards should be allowed to rest (23:11). The Jubilee Year provisions in Lev 25 also, though only implicitly, provided for the land to rest during the Fiftieth or Jubilee Year.[43] The land itself was to be respected and nurtured, not simply used, let alone exploited or degraded.

Leviticus 26:34–35, 43: The exile—an extended Sabbath for the land. Leviticus 26 probably concludes the Holiness Code. YHWH/God is still speaking, the narrator says, through Moses.[44] Leviticus 26:3–13 describes how the Israelites will prosper if they observe YHWH/God's statutes and commandments. But the writer seems to have been cognizant of the sixth-century BCE Babylonian conquest of Judah and the subsequent exile. What would become of the land of Judah when its people were deported into exile? According to Lev 26:34–35 and 43, this land would then enjoy a long Sabbath rest—in compensation for the Israelites' (or Judahites') previous failure to observe the old requirements providing that the land should rest every seventh year.[45] Here, again, we see that the land itself was to be respected and protected against overuse. If not so respected and protected, serious consequences would follow.

---

41. See below, pt. B2f of the present chapter.

42. See also Lev 25:7–12, especially v. 4: "But in the seventh year there shall be a Sabbath of complete rest for the land." See Westbrook, *Property and Family*, 37: "The land, being God's land, must keep the Sabbath, that is, the Sabbath principle is extended to cover nature as well as man."

43. See Lev 25:8–12.

44. See Lev 25:1–2.

45. Exod 23:10–11; Lev 25:1–7.

2. Abundant Gifts of the Land: For YHWH/God, People, and Other Creatures

The land was the source of all agricultural crops. This understanding is implicit in the so-called "cultic calendar" of agricultural harvest ceremonies. Appreciation and respect for the land's yields comes to expression in several biblical laws and related texts. The gifts of the land were ultimately gifts from God. These gifts were to be used appropriately and not taken for granted. It was understood that the land's bounty was to be enjoyed both by people—whether rich or poor—and by animals, whether domestic cattle or wildlife.

a. The Land of Milk and Honey

In Num 13:17–33, the promised land is described as a land "that flows with milk and honey" (Num 13:27).[46] It was also said to be a land of pomegranates and figs, and grapes so abundant or large that to carry a single cluster required two men with a pole (Num 13:23–24). These narratives probably date from relatively early J or E sources. Later accounts of life in the promised land do not recall such preternatural fertility or abundance; but several biblical and intertestamental texts do look for superabundant fruit and grain harvests in the future messianic age.[47] Because the land was already occupied by Canaanites and other peoples, the Israelites would not immediately gain entrance to or ascendancy over it. The books of Joshua and Judges subsequently undertake to describe the Israelites' "conquest" of the land and the early years of their tenuous settlement there.[48]

---

46. See also Exod 3:8, Num 14:8, and Deut 6:3. Compare Num 16:13, where two dissidents complain that Moses took them *out of* "a land flowing with milk and honey," namely, Egypt! Aldo Leopold once complained, "Conservation is getting nowhere because it is incompatible with our Abrahamic conception of land. We abuse land because we regard it as a commodity belonging to us." Leopold, *Sand County Almanac*, viii. Leopold did not cite any biblical texts in support of his contention that Abraham abused land or regarded it as a commodity. In biblical tradition, only the ungodly or depraved are represented as despoiling the creation. Wis 2:6–9.

47. See below, ch. 11.

48. See Richard Hiers, *Nation of Immigrants*, 12–21.

b. Abundant Harvests but Only on Condition of Continuing Fidelity

Deuteronomy 7:12–14: Righteousness and prosperity. If the Israelites remain faithful to YHWH/God and keep his commandments, he will cause them to multiply and also bless and multiply their fruit and produce, grain, wine, oil, and cattle. There would be no infertile male or barren female among them or among their cattle (Deut 7:14). Again, we see the understanding that it is YHWH/God who gives the increase—but only if his people keep the covenant he had made with them. Otherwise, there would be no peace or prosperity.[49]

Deuteronomy 11:8–17: Abundance and the peril of apostasy. Again, the land of promise is said to be "a land flowing with milk and honey" (Deut 11:9). Here, it is also said to be "a land of hills and valleys," watered by rain from heaven—"a land which YHWH your God cares for; the eyes of YHWH are always upon it, from the beginning of the year to the end of the year" (Deut 11:11–12 RSV). *If* the Israelites remain faithful to YHWH/God and love and serve him with all their hearts and souls, says Moses, YHWH/God will then continue to give rain in season, assuring bountiful crops of grain, wine, and oil, and providing grass in the fields for their cattle (Deut 11:13–15). But if they worship other gods, YHWH/God will "shut up the heavens," so that there will be no rain; the land will yield no fruit, and the Israelites will "perish quickly off the good land" that YHWH/God had given them (Deut 11:17). Several other biblical texts concerning agricultural conditions in later times attribute drought and crop failure to YHWH/God's disgust with his people who have forgotten him, turned to other gods, and otherwise failed to meet their covenant obligations.[50] Among the reasons the Israelites' turning to other gods is condemned is that such worship fails to acknowledge YHWH/God as the true Source of their blessings, agricultural and otherwise.[51]

---

49. See also Prov 3:9–10; Hag 1:7–11; 2:15–19; Mal 3:9–12.

50. See, e.g., 1 Kgs 17:1; 18:46; Amos 4:6–9; Hag 1:2–11; Zech 10:1–2; and Mal 3:5–12.

51. See, e.g., Jer 2:4–28; Hos 2:1–13.

Leviticus 25:18–19: The land will yield its fruit if . . . Like several other biblical traditions,[52] this H text assures the community that the land of promise will produce abundant fruit *provided* the Israelites remain faithful to YHWH/God and his laws. As generally is true in biblical perspective, it is understood that YHWH/God is the ultimate Source of all good harvests. But his people should not presume upon his favor. The implication is that good harvests and security would continue only so long as the people kept YHWH/God's covenant with them.[53]

Deuteronomy 28:1–69: Further blessings or ruin? Moses (or YHWH) here exhorts the Israelites to observe all the commandments recorded in the foregoing chapters of the Deuteronomic Code.[54] The exhortation promises future blessings, *provided* the Israelites obey YHWH/God's voice. These blessings would come in the form of abundant "fruit of the ground," cattle and other flocks (Deut 28:4, 11), and rain for the land in its seasons (Deut 28:12). But if the Israelites failed to obey YHWH/God's voice and neglected to keep all his commandments, the fruit of the ground, along with their cattle and other flocks, would be destroyed by pestilence, fiery heat, drought, and mildew; and vicious enemies would come against them.[55] Even more ominously, they would experience catastrophic droughts or climate change: "The sky over your head shall be bronze, and the earth under you iron. YHWH/God will change the rain of your land into powder, and only dust shall come upon you from the sky until you are destroyed" (Deut 28:23–24). Then, instead of having other animals as food,[56] the Israelites' bodies will "be food for every bird of the air and animal of the earth, and there shall be no one to frighten them away" (Deut

---

52. See, e.g., Deut 6:1–15; 7:12–14; 8:6–20; cf. Hag 2:15–19; Mal 3:9–12.
53. See also Lev 26:1–26. In biblical tradition, it was YHWH/God who initiated this and all other covenants.
54. The substantive provisions of that code probably concluded either with Deut 25 or 26.
55. Deut 28:15–22, 25, 30–46.
56. Compare Gen 9:2–3.

28:26).[57] Like the land, its abundant yields were YHWH/God's to give but also his to take away.

c. Responding to YHWH/God and to Persons in Need

Just as the land was YHWH/God's, so also were its products. Biblical tradition consistently views the fertility of fields, vineyards, and orchards as YHWH/God's gift to his people. In his sovereignty over creation, YHWH/God could give or withhold these gifts. Israelites were to acknowledge YHWH/God as the Giver by returning some of these products to him. The major agricultural festivals ordained in RD (Exod 34:22-24), the CC (Exod 23:14-17), H (Lev 23:1-44), and the revised Deuteronomic Code (Deut 16:1-17) were occasions for thanksgiving and celebration before YHWH/God who had provided his people with the land's abundant produce. These festivals included the Feast of Unleavened Bread (later known as Passover),[58] the Feast of Firstfruits (also known as the Feast of Weeks or Pentecost), and at the end of harvest season, the Feast of Ingathering or Feast of Booths.[59] Several biblical laws, including some relating to these periodic festivals, were grounded on recognition of YHWH/God's compassion and concern for those who were unable to supply their own needs. YHWH/God was to be acknowledged as the Giver of the earth's abundance, and his gifts were to be shared with persons in need.[60] Theocentric reverence for life, of course, included concern for human welfare.

---

57. See also Lev 26: 21-22; Deut 32:24; Jer 8:17; 19:7; Ezek 29:5; 33:27; 39:4-5, 17-20; Hos 2:12; Amos 9:3; and Wis 5:17-23, where wild beasts or "all creation" act as agents of YHWH/God's judgment. See also Rev 19:17-18. Such texts may have inspired the denouement scene in C. S. Lewis's novel *That Hideous Strength*. These and related biblical texts are considered further below in ch. 10B.

58. See also Exod 12:1-20, 43-49.

59. See generally Gaster, *Festivals of Jewish Year*, 31-104.

60. Several texts to this effect also appear in the NT. For instance, Jas 2:15-16: "If a brother or sister is ill-clad and in lack of daily food, and one of you says to them, 'Go in peace, be warmed and filled,' without giving them the things needed for the body, what does it profit?" See also, e.g., Luke 14:12-14; 16:19-31; Matt 25:31-36.

I. Offerings to YHWH

Deuteronomy 26:1-11. Once the Israelites were established in the promised land, they were to take some of the "firstfruits" or first pickings of their initial harvest, put them in a basket, take it to "the place,"[61] give it to the priest, and make the recitation set out in Deut 26:5-10b, which concludes, "So now I bring the first of the fruit of the ground that you, O YHWH, have given me." The underlying assumption, again, is that the land is YHWH/God's. The firstfruits are to be offered to him in recognition that it is he who causes the land to bring them forth.

II. Provisions for Persons in Need[62]

The law of the seventh or Sabbatical Year, found in both the Covenant Code and the Holiness Code, was intended to provide for the needs both of the human community and of cattle and wildlife.

> For six years you shall sow your land and gather in its yield; but the seventh year you shall let it rest and lie fallow, so that the poor of your people may eat; and what they leave the wild animals may eat. You shall do the same with your vineyard, and with your olive orchard. (Exod 23:10-11)

> The Sabbath of the land shall provide food for you, for yourself and for your male and female slaves and for your hired servant and the sojourner who lives with you; for your cattle and also for the beasts that are in your land all its yield shall be for food. (Lev 25:6-7 RSV)

Several other laws establish arrangements for making food available to persons in the community who were in need of assistance.

Both D and H include laws providing a "safety net" or welfare for the poor—typically widows, orphans, and sojourners or resident aliens who lacked the means to provide for themselves. Such persons were entitled to "glean" in fields, vineyards, and orchards

---

61. See above, ch. 42ai.

62. As to biblical social welfare arrangements for persons in need, see Richard Hiers, *Justice and Compassion*, 212-19.

belonging to others following the landowners' first harvests. The story of Ruth exemplifies this arrangement.[63] The poor were also entitled to continuing support under the third-year tithing law and to sharing in the two annual harvest feasts.

Deuteronomy 24:19–22: Gleaning privileges for persons in need. This law states that landowners were not to go back after forgotten sheaves, nor were they to glean grapes after the first picking or pick fruit from their olive trees a second time. The text does not explicitly name "the poor" as beneficiaries of these provisions; instead, it refers to the "the fatherless" (orphans) and widows—along with sojourners, resident aliens, or refugees (Heb. *gerim*).[64] This law and its counterparts in H accord with the understanding that the land and all that it provides are, ultimately, YHWH/God's and that YHWH/God wants these to be used for his own purposes, which here focus on the needs of those otherwise unable to support themselves. Implicit also, perhaps, is concern that the gifts of the land should not be wasted.

Leviticus 19:9–10 and 23:22: Leaving part of the harvest for the poor. These laws applied to the conduct of landowners and also, implicitly, to that of their families and their servants or hired hands. Reapers were not to harvest grainfields all the way to the edges or borders; and they were not to go back a second time to pick or cut what they had missed or left to ripen the first time around. Likewise, grape-pickers were to leave some grapes on the vines and were not to pick up grapes that had fallen to the ground. The grain and grapes that were left were for the poor and sojourners, people who did not own land or were otherwise unable to support themselves.[65] Leviticus 23:22 presents still another version of the gleaning law limiting landowners' harvesting rights and providing for the needs of the poor and the sojourner.[66]

63. See Ruth 2, where, as a sojourner and widow, Ruth gleans in order to provide both for herself and for her widowed mother-in-law with whom she was living.

64. As to *gerim*—sojourners, refugees, resident aliens—and biblical traditions regarding foreigners, see Richard Hiers, *Nation of Immigrants*.

65. See generally Hart, *Spirit of the Earth*, 77–81.

66. Compare Lev 19:9–11 and Deut 24:19–20. Under such laws, the poor had a *right* to engage in such gleaning. Cf. Prov 29:7: "The righteous know the rights of the poor." Such rights, however, were not seen as intrinsic, inherent, or "natural." Rather,

When you reap the harvest of your land, you shall not reap to the very edges of your field, or gather the gleanings of your harvest; you shall leave them for the poor and for the alien: I am YHWH your God.

This provision follows a series of laws governing celebration of the Feast of Weeks (Lev 23:15-21) but in its terms appears to apply to all harvests. Though not mentioned, it may have been assumed that wildlife also would benefit from such laws.[67]

Deuteronomy 14:22-29; 26:12-15: The third-year tithe. Deuteronomy 14:22-27 required Israelites to tithe, that is, to set aside one-tenth of their harvests each year. They were to eat this offering before YHWH at "the place" every year. But if the way was too long, they might turn the tithe into money, take the money to "the place," and buy food there to "eat in the presence of YHWH," sharing this food with the local Levite.[68] Deuteronomy 14:28-29, however, mandates that every third year the harvest tithe was to be kept at the local towns and that this tithe was to be shared not only with the local Levite but also with the sojourner, the fatherless, and the widow. These food bank arrangements evidently were intended to provide for such persons' needs throughout each three-year period.[69]

The stipulated prayer or oath, which was to be uttered "before YHWH" (Deut 26:13), consists partly of a profession that one has properly kept the third-year harvest tithing law by giving the tithe to the poor and partly of a petition to YHWH/God to "look down ... from heaven" and continue to bless Israel and "the ground" that

---

they derived from YHWH's law, which expressed his caring, here for persons in need.

67. Compare provisions for the Sabbatical Year in Exod 23:10-11 and Lev 25:2-7.

68. See above, ch. 52a, as to the Deuteronomic reform. To facilitate that reform, Deut 18:1-18 provided that local Levites who wished to move to Jerusalem were free to do so and there enjoy the same status and perquisites as those Levites (priests) who had previously officiated at the temple. Since local shrines had been closed, Levites who remained outside of Jerusalem were now unemployed and in need of assistance.

69. The story about Joseph's seven-year food bank in Egypt (Gen 41) may have provided precedent for this provision. Implicit in that story is the understanding that the land of Egypt was also YHWH/God's land; and as the story is told, the seven years of plenty provided food not only for Egypt but also for "all the world" in the following years of famine (Gen 41:57).

he had given them (Deut 26:13–15). Here, once more, this ground is characterized as "a land flowing with milk and honey" (Deut 26:15). From the context, it would seem that this prayer was to be addressed to YHWH/God in each town, rather than at the one "place." Both the third-year tithe and the accompanying prescribed oath or prayer recognize YHWH/God as the One who gives both the land and its produce.

Deuteronomy 16:9–17: The annual cycle of festivals and offerings. The cultic calendar laws in Deut 16 require that property owners share their harvests not only with their own families and servants but also with Levites, sojourners (aliens), orphans ("the fatherless"), and widows when, together, they "rejoiced in," that is, celebrated the Feast of Weeks (Deut 16:11) and the Feast of Booths (Deut 16:13–14). There were no food stamps, Aid to Families with Dependent Children, or other social welfare provisions in those days. But property owners were not the only ones entitled to benefit from the gifts of the land—which, ultimately, had come from YHWH/God to begin with.

The biblical land ethic is grounded upon recognition that the land and all the good gifts that it brings forth come from YHWH/God. The ethical corollary is that the gifts of the land are to be used for the benefit and enjoyment of all his creatures, human and otherwise. The biblical land ethic also relates to trees.

3. Care for Trees and Vegetation

According to the P narrative, all kinds of vegetation, including trees and plants, were among the things God had created at the beginning and found or pronounced "good" (Gen 1:11–12). In the J creation story, YHWH/God himself planted the garden of Eden and caused to grow there not only the two special trees, the tree of life and the tree of knowing good and evil, but also "every tree that is pleasant to the sight and good for food" (Gen 2:9). Humankind was created in the first place "to till the ground and keep it" (Gen 2:25).[70] In those early times, it was said that YHWH/God himself

---

70. Again, after their ejection from the garden of Eden the forebears of humankind

walked in this garden filled with trees (Gen 3:8). Some later texts show special appreciation for fig trees.[71] Ezekiel 47:12 anticipates that in the messianic age, "all kinds of trees for food" will grow along the banks of the river in Jerusalem. Other texts affirm also that trees were planted, valued, or cared for by YHWH/God. Some recognize their importance as wildlife habitat.[72] Not only animate beings but trees, too, are among YHWH's creations that are sometimes called upon to praise him.[73] Implicitly and, in some instances, explicitly, YHWH/God's people were expected to value and care for trees too.

a. New Orchards

Leviticus 19:23–25 suggests that when the Israelites came into their eventual homeland, they were expected to plant "all kinds of trees for food." The law specifies that fruit from these newly-planted trees should not be eaten during the first three years of the trees' life.[74] Perhaps it was believed that such young trees needed all their energy in order to establish initial growth. Though not expressly mentioned, it may have been expected that fruit left on the trees would provide food for wildlife. The fruit of the fourth year was to be set aside as "holy," that is, as an "offering of praise" to YHWH/God. How it was to be offered is not clear: perhaps it would be taken to a local sanctuary and either placed on an altar or,

---

were given one task to perform: to till the ground from which they were taken (Gen 3:23).

71. See, e.g., Prov 27:18; Zech 3:10; Mic 4:4; compare Luke 13:6–9. Attention sometimes is drawn to Jesus's so-called "cursing" a fig tree (Matt 21:18–19; Mark 11:12–14, 20–21). See, e.g., Rolston, *Environmental Ethics*, 94 and 359n3. Comparing the two Gospel accounts reveals certain legendary accretions. In Mark 11:12–14, which probably represents the earlier version, Jesus does not curse the tree. Rather, he expressed his hope that the kingdom of God would come soon. Then fruit would always be in season. See Richard Hiers, "Not the Season," and below ch. 11A.

72. See Job 40:21–22; Ps 104:16–17; Ezek 17:22–24; compare Matt 13:31–32; Luke 13:18–19.

73. See, e.g., Ps 96:12 ("all the trees of the field"); Ps 148:9 ("fruit trees and all cedars"); and Prayer of Azariah, Sg Three v. 54 ("all that grows in the ground").

74. This is the second instance of "forbidden fruit" in biblical tradition. The first, of course, was the fruit of the "tree of the knowledge of good and evil" (Gen 2:16–17).

as with certain other offerings, distributed to the poor and needy. In any event, the fourth-year provision expresses thanks or praise to YHWH/God for providing trees' fertility and fruition.

b. Of Trees and War

According to Deut 20:19–20, when the Israelites besieged a city for a long time, they were not to "destroy its trees by wielding an ax against them." The first stated rationale is that the trees might later provide them food. But then YHWH/God (or Moses) asks, rhetorically, "Are trees in the field human beings that they should come under siege from you?" Only trees known not to produce food could be cut down.[75] Others were not to be destroyed wantonly but could be cut down only for the purpose of building siege works. This law evidently was understood to apply in warfare against cities, whether within the promised land or en route to it. Deuteronomy 20:19–20 suggests that all trees were understood to be part of God's good creation and should ordinarily be left alone to live and grow.[76] Destroying enemies' fruit or olive trees or orchards at any time would violate the spirit, if not also the letter, of this law.[77]

c. Trees and Asherim

The Deuteronomic reform program called for destruction of the shrines where Canaanites, other peoples, and, in earlier times, Israelites themselves, had worshiped foreign gods "on the mountain heights, on the hills, and under every leafy tree" (Deut 12:1–2).[78] Asherim were wooden posts or poles representing Asherah, a female deity in Canaanite religion.[79] Deuteronomy 12:3 says that

---

75. See also 4 Macc 2:14: "The fruit trees of the enemy are not [to be] cut down."

76. See Rad, *Deuteronomy*, 133.

77. Radical Zionists in modern Israel have been known to cut down Palestinian settlers' fig and olive trees.

78. See above, ch. 4A2. Compare Ackerman, *Under Every Green Tree*, commending Canaanite religious practices for their recognition of female deities and sexuality.

79. See Rad, *Deuteronomy*, 115; G. Wright, *Biblical Archeology*, 6–7.

Asherim were to be destroyed; however, Deut 12:2–3 says nothing about destroying the leafy or green trees associated with the old cult shrines.[80] Biblical faith acknowledged only one god, namely, YHWH. Trees were trees, not gods or goddesses. Again, it seems, trees as such were to be respected and protected as part of YHWH/God's good creation. As will be seen, trees were expected to flourish as part of the good world that would obtain in the future messianic age.[81]

B. CARE FOR OTHER ANIMATE CREATURES: THE ETHICS OF REVERENCE FOR LIFE

A variety of biblical texts indicate that YHWH/God's people should be concerned with the well-being of other creatures. YHWH/God had made them and cares for them, and his people should care for care for them as well. Texts indicating such concern are to be found in narratives, laws, and also in several other biblical writings.

1. Biblical Narratives

The biblical creation stories, as previously observed, make clear that YHWH/God created all that is, including all kinds of living things, and found them all good (Gen 1:20–21, 24–25). The obvious implication is that people should so regard them and also be concerned about their well-being.[82] The most explicit narrative in

---

80. Compare Deut 16:21, which prohibits planting trees as Asherim by the altar at the one place. Of course, if trees were regarded as Asherim in Deut 12:1–3, they, too, would have been subject to destruction as such.

81. See below, ch. 11.

82. See Wilson, *Creation*, 10: "Our leaders, including those of the great religions, have done little to protect the living world in the midst of its sharp decline. They have ignored the command of the Abrahamic God on the fourth day of the world's birth to 'let the waters teem with countless living creatures, and let the birds fly over the land across the vault of heaven.'" The biblical texts considered in this chapter, as well as in the present book as a whole, suggest that people who wish to be faithful to the biblical God would do well to protect and preserve all kinds of living beings and species. And to oppose mistreatment of animals or other life-forms as too often practiced in contemporary culture, such as abusive neglect or mishandling of animals in laboratory experiments, zoos or circuses, factory farms, transportation,

this connection is the account of God's calling on Noah's to undertake the preservation of all living species—at any rate, all those that breathe air. Later narratives also illustrate God's concern for the well-being of many, perhaps all, kinds of living beings.

a. Preserving Biodiversity: Noah, the Ark, and the Animals

The story of Noah, the ark, and the animals has been considered previously in connection with YHWH/God's compassionate care for all creatures.[83] Here the focus is on the human role in implementing such care. Before the great flood, according to P tradition, God instructed Noah to build a huge ship[84] and to bring on board "of the birds according to their kinds, and of the animals according to their kinds, of every creeping thing of the ground according to its kind, two of every kind . . . [in order] to keep them alive."[85] This was to be done so that all these species might be spared and later emerge from the ark, in order "that they may abound upon

---

and slaughterhouses, and such activities as hunting and fishing simply for "sport," killing animals in order to obtain substances believed to enhance sexual potency, and promoting animal fights. As Wilson observes, religious leaders generally tend to be silent as to such matters.

83. See above, ch. 2B5.

84. The vessel was said to be 450 feet long, 75 feet wide, and 45 feet high, with three decks (Gen 6:15-16). A "cubit" probably measured what we would call eighteen inches.

85. Gen 6:20. See also Gen 7:14-15. See comment by former Interior Secretary Bruce Babbitt, "Between Flood and Rainbow": "God did not specify that Noah should limit [passengers on] the ark to two charismatic species, two good for hunting, two species that might provide some cure down the road, and two that might draw crowds at the city zoo. He specifies *the whole creation*."

See also Friedman, "We're in the Age": "Our generation has entered a phase that no previous generation has ever experienced: the Noah phase. With more and more species threatened with extinction by The Flood that is today's global economic juggernaut, we may be the first generation in human history that literally has to act like Noah—to save the last pairs of a wide range of species. . . . Unlike Noah, though, we're the ones causing The Flood, as more and more forests, fisheries, rivers and fertile soils are gobbled up for development." And see Council on Environmental Quality and Department of State, *Global 2000 Report*, 1:37: "An estimate prepared for the Global 2000 Study suggests that between half a million and two million species—15 to 20 percent of all species on earth—could be extinguished by 2000, mainly because of pollution. Extinction on this scale is without precedent in human history."

the earth, and be fruitful and multiply on the earth" (Gen 8:17).[86] In effect, Noah's ark project was undertaken in order to preserve biological diversity.[87]

After the flood, Noah offers YHWH/God sacrifices "of every clean animal and of every clean bird" (Gen 8:20). In the earlier J account,[88] YHWH/God had instructed Noah to take seven pairs of all clean animals and seven pairs of birds "to keep their kind alive on the face of all the earth" in the era that would follow the flood (Gen 7:1–3). Thus, these species would not be threatened with extinction when Noah later sacrificed some of each. The clear implication is that YHWH/God intended all species of animate life to be respected and preserved for all time.

YHWH/God then declares that he will never again curse the ground or destroy every living creature because of humankind (Gen 8:21). Here, the J tradition takes the form of a promise that parallels the P covenant that follows. This J promise (or covenant) is unqualified: YHWH will never again destroy every living creature, and so long as earth remains, the cycles of nature will continue (Gen 8:22).[89] The P narrative that follows then reports God's resolution never again to destroy "all flesh" or the earth by floodwaters (Gen 9:11, 15). The implication is that *all* species are precious in YHWH/God's sight and should be so also to humans.

---

86. Rolston refers to Noah's ark project as the first "Endangered Species Act." Rolston, *Environmental Ethics*, 94, 338. Critics who consider texts such as Gen 1:26–28 dispositive as to the biblical viewpoint in regard to human relations with other creatures typically ignore the Noah's ark story. See, e.g., Singer, *Animal Liberation*, 93–95. Such critics generally make no mention of the P covenant with every living creature (Gen 9:8–17) either. See above, chs. 3B6 and 4C.

87. Gore, *Earth in the Balance*, 244–45. See also Lev.19:19b–c as to preserving separate genetic strains: "You shall not let your cattle breed with a different kind; you shall not sow your field with two kinds of seed."

88. On major themes in J tradition, see Steck, *World and Environment*, 64–78.

89. This text is referred to as the basis for the later prophetic affirmation that YHWH's "covenant of peace" would never "be removed" (Isa 54:9–20).

b. Other Biblical Narratives

A variety of later biblical narratives likewise describe people's attitudes and actions in regard to the treatment of animals. These can be considered in sequence as the stories are found, beginning in the book of Genesis. Here it is said that as Jacob nears the time of death, he gathers his sons around him in order to speak his last words to them. He condemns two sons for their fierce anger and cruel wrath, "for in their anger they killed men, and at their whim they hamstrung oxen" (Gen 49:6–7). Both kinds of action were understood to have been wrongful.

Following their exodus from Egypt, but before the people of Israel have yet reached the land of Canaan, they complain to Moses: "Why have you brought the assembly of YHWH into this wilderness for us and our [cattle] to die here?" (Num 20:4). Moses and Aaron then consult with YHWH, who tells them what to do in order to provide water for "the congregation and their [cattle]" (Num 20:8–11). Later in Numbers, both Balaam's faithful she-ass and YHWH's angel chastise Balaam for having beaten the ass, prompting Balaam to confess, "I have sinned" (Num 22:22–34). Saul, as a youth, was sent to look for his father's lost asses (1 Sam 9:3). And David, as a youngster, cared for his father's sheep (1 Sam 16:11; 17:14–15).

Later, as king of both Judah and Israel, David is confronted by the prophet Nathan in regard to his having raped Bathsheba and murdered her husband. Nathan tells David that a rich man took a poor man's one, precious, pet lamb[90] and slaughtered and cooked it in order to serve it up to a visiting guest. David, in effect, sitting as chief judge, exclaims: The rich man deserves to die "because he did this thing, and because he had no pity" (2 Sam 12:5–6). Readers or listeners in biblical times would have understood that David's indignation was justified, since the rich man had failed to show pity or compassion for either the poor man or the poor man's pet lamb.

---

90. The description of the poor man and his pet lamb obviously shows compassion for both: "The poor man had nothing but one little lamb, which he had bought. He brought it up, and it grew up with him and with his children; it used to eat of his meager fare, and drink from his cup, and lie in his bosom, and it was like a daughter to him" (2 Sam 12:3).

Even Israel's apostate King Ahab was concerned to save his country's horses and mules from a severe drought (1 Kgs 18:5).[91] Explicit concern as to care for other creatures comes to expression in various biblical laws. Such laws are considered in the following subsection.

2. Humane Treatment Legislation

Several laws found in one or more of the biblical codes require what is now commonly called humane treatment of animals.[92] Implicit in many such laws is the understanding that animals, even those sacrificed to God and those killed for food, were to be treated with respect or consideration.[93] A number of these laws express what Albert Schweitzer called "the ethics of reverence for life." Such laws might also suggest standards for evaluating contemporary agricultural and animal husbandry practices, such as factory farming.[94]

---

91. A number of instances of cruelty to animals are reported in biblical narratives. Among these: accounts of the ancient *herem* practice, whereby indigenous people of Canaan and their cattle were supposed to have been destroyed (Deut 20:10–18; Josh 6:21; but see Josh 8:1–2, 27; and 11:10–14, saying that cattle were spared); Joshua's and later David's orders to hamstring captured horses (Josh 11:6–9; 2 Sam 8:3–4); Samson's gratuitously killing a lion (Judg 14:5–6) and tying torches to the tails of three hundred foxes in order to burn up neighboring Philistines' grainfields, vineyards, and olive groves (Judg 15:4–5); Saul's slaying a yoke of oxen to symbolize his message (1 Sam 11:5–9); and Daniel's poisoning a large lizard to prove it was not a god (Bel v. 27). In other instances, there was, arguably, some justification, such as Eleazar's killing a military elephant in battle (1 Macc 6:43–46); Jesus's sending demons into a herd of swine, causing their death (Matt 8:28–30; Mark 5:1–20; Luke 8:26–39); and Paul's shaking a poisonous snake off into a fire (Acts. 28:1–6). Several of these accounts are legendary, and none is presented as an example for people to follow in the future.

92. Many of the relevant texts were noted well over a century ago by Drummond, *Rights of Animals*, 15–21. For discussion of Christian perspectives on treatment of animals in modern times, see Hollands, "Animal Kingdom." For a survey of contemporary issues apart from biblical perspectives, see Francione, "Animal Rights"; Francione, "Animals, Property"; and Francione, *Animals, Property and Law*. Francione demonstrates that Anglo-American law is largely anthropocentric, according legal status or interests only to human beings, and treating animals primarily as property. See also Cohn, *Ethics and Wildlife*.

93. See Tull, *Inhabiting Eden*, 93: Under biblical law, killing animals for food "is a concession of God's grace, and not a privilege" (quoting Ellen Davis, "Becoming Human: Biblical Interpretation and Ecological Responsibility").

94. See Gene Baur, *Farm Sanctuary*, as to commonplace animal abuses in modern

a. Newborn Bull Calves, Lambs, Kids, and Their Mothers

Laws found in both the CC and H show special sensitivity to animal mothers and their offspring. Exodus 22:30 provided that a new firstborn bull calf or lamb must be allowed to remain with its mother seven days before being sacrificed. Leviticus 22:26–27 goes beyond that provision and requires that *all* young bull calves, lambs, and also kids remain with their mothers seven days prior to being offered to YHWH.[95] Neither text articulates a rationale for these requirements. It may be inferred, however, that both reflect sensitivity to the special relationship between animal mothers and their newborn offspring. These laws also may be based on concern for the health of the nursing animal mothers.

Leviticus 22:28 adds another new law that likewise seems grounded in concern or respect for the relationship between mother animals and their young. Mother cows, sheep, or goats and their young—whatever their age[96]—were not to be killed on the same day. Sensitivity to the relationship between a young animal and its mother also may have informed the ancient prohibition against boiling a kid in its own mother's milk.

b. On Not Boiling a Kid in Its Mother's Milk

Laws prohibiting cooking ("boiling") a kid (or young goat) in its own mother's milk are found in the two earliest codes, RD and CC, and then again in the revised portion of D. In each case, the law is phrased in identical terms: "You shall not boil a kid in its mother's milk" (Exod 34:26b; Exod 23:19b; Deut 14:21b). None of these texts provides further explanation or rationale regarding this prohibition.

This prohibition, which was to become the basis for the segregation of meat and milk cuisine in later traditionalist or Orthodox

---

American agriculture and meat production.

95. The Holiness Code contains no provisions for sacrificing firstborns, whether animal or human.

96. No age limits are indicated. Leviticus 22:27 says that the young animal *may* be offered as a burnt offering on the eighth day, but that practice was not mandated. The lambs to be presented as burnt offerings in Lev 23:12, 18–19 were to be a year old.

Judaism, may have been based initially on humane sensibilities. It may have been felt too cruel to cook a little kid in its own mother's milk. Similar sensibilities expressed in other provisions of biblical law tend to corroborate this interpretation. For instance, as has been mentioned, a new firstborn male calf or lamb was to remain with his mother a full week before being sacrificed (Exod 22:29b-30). Other texts in the Covenant Code (Exod 23:4-5, 10-12) explicitly express concern for the interests of various animals. Several Deuteronomic texts also show compassion or concern for the well-being of animals.[97] Such concern may have prompted the prohibition against boiling a kid in its mother's milk. This prohibition may also have been intended to prevent Israelites from emulating or participating in alien religious practices.[98]

c. Affirmative Duties to Care for Lost or Distressed Domestic Animals

Both the CC and D include laws that *require* people to assist animals that are at risk in certain situations. Both sets of laws express this affirmative duty by using prohibitive language, by saying, in effect: "You shall refrain from" leaving a distressed animal without helping it.

Exodus 23:4-5. This text says that just because one person hates another, that person should not take his or her hatred out on the other person's domestic animal. So, if someone comes upon an enemy's ox or ass that is lost or strayed, one should take the animal back to the enemy's home. Or if an enemy's ass has fallen or foundered under its burden, one should help it get up again. Here "enemy" seems to be a personal, rather than a national, enemy, although the principle might apply equally in both kinds of situations.

---

97. See, e.g., Deut 22:1-4, 6-7; 25:4. See also Isa 40:11, quoted below.

98. See Gaster, *Myth, Legend, and Custom*, 250-51. Gaster also considered sources or parallels in other cultures (251-63). See Rad, *Deuteronomy*, 102 (citing a Ugaritic milk spell). A law or practice may serve more than one purpose or function. For example, the law of levirate marriage (Deut 25:5-10) provides both for perpetuating the name of the deceased and for his widow's welfare. See Richard Hiers, *Women's Rights and Bible*, 42, 46-47, 58, 72-76.

Deuteronomy 22:1–4. Exodus 23:4–5 had to do with obligations to return an *enemy's* lost or strayed ox or ass, or to help raise an enemy's fallen ass back onto its feet. A similar law in Deut 22:1–4 refers to a *brother's* animals. In this context, the term "brother" may have been a gender-inclusive term that, in addition to relatives, also applied to friends and neighbors. The lost or strayed animals named here are oxen, sheep, and asses. Both oxen and asses were to be helped if foundered under their burdens. Together, these laws (Exod 23:4–5 and Deut 22:1–4) express a sense of compassion for domestic animals that calls for aiding and assisting those in distress, whether they belong to friends or to enemies.[99]

d. Conservation: Birds and Their Young

Deuteronomy 22:6–7 stipulates that when Israelites come upon a bird's nest where a mother bird is sitting upon her young, they may not take both the mother and the young. They may take the young birds but must let the mother go.[100] The text does not say whether the young are to be taken as food or as pets, nor does it distinguish between clean and unclean birds.[101] Presumably, only the former were permitted to be eaten.[102] The concern or sensitivity regarding the relationship between a mother animal and her young found in earlier passages may also be present in this text.[103] In any event, this law was likely prompted by conservation interests. That is, it probably was recognized that to take both the mother and her young could have the effect of endangering the survival of the species. It could be assumed that the mother bird played a key role in species survival because she could then live to hatch and raise many more

---

99. See also Deut 22:6–7; 25:4. And see 4 Macc 2:14.

100. The text also refers to eggs but does not say whether they may be taken. It may have been assumed that the eggs could be taken.

101. Compare Deut 14:11–20.

102. See Deut 14:11–18; cf. Lev 11:13–19.

103. See Rad, *Deuteronomy*, 141: "The ordinance . . . can probably be attributed only to humane motives and hardly to considerations of utility." See Lin, *Nature of Environmenal Stewardship*, 59, reflecting on the relevance of this text for Christian ethics,

broods of young.[104] Noah's ark was the classic biblical example of human engagement in wildlife conservation, and this passage likewise seems to recognize the importance of species conservation.

e. On Not Muzzling Oxen Treading Grain

Deuteronomy 25:4. According to this law, an ox that has been harnessed to thresh or "tread out" grain is not to be muzzled. Instead, he is to be free to eat of the grain as he works. Evidently the underlying idea is that it would be cruel to deny the ox food when he is working in and surrounded by it.[105] Several other biblical texts also show consideration for oxen, as well as for cattle generally.[106] Deuteronomy 22:10 may also reflect concern for the humane treatment of domestic animals: "You shall not plow with an ox and [an ass] yoked together." Pairing animals of such different sizes and weights could have been regarded as harmful to one or both of them.[107]

---

104. See Berry, *Gift of Good Land*, 273: "This, obviously, is a perfect paradigm of ecological and agricultural discipline.... The inflexible rule is that the source must be preserved. You may take the young, but you must save the breeding stock."

105. Compare Paul, in 1 Cor 9:8-11, who interprets the text allegorically to mean that a missionary is worthy of the benefits of his office. See also 1 Tim 5:18. These texts may represent a shift from theocentric to anthropocentric faith. See Ferre, *Hellfire and Lightning Rods*, 179: "The holistic sense of mutual connection to the animals with whom we live and work demands that we woo rather than rape. There is a differentiation between the farmer and his oxen, but the proper organic relation involves mutuality, not mere exploitation."

106. See Gen 8:1; Exod 22:30; 23:4; Lev 22:26-28; Num 20:8, 11, 19; Deut 22:1-4; Ps 50:10; Isa 66:3-4; and Jonah 4:11. In Gen 49:5-7, Jacob condemns his sons Simeon and Levi for their wanton cruelty in hamstringing oxen.

107. Thus Schorsch, "Learning," 31. Such biblical laws evidently had some influence on American jurisprudence. See *Stephens v. State* (*Southern Reporter* 3 [Miss. 1878] 458-59), quoted in Wise, "Legal Thinghood," 542:

> The common law recognized no rights in . . . animals, and punished no cruelty to them, except in so far as it affected the rights of individuals to such property. Such statutes [as those before the court] remedy this defect, and exhibit the spirit of that divine law which is so mindful of dumb brutes as to teach and command, not to muzzle the ox when he treadeth out the corn; not to plow with an ox and an ass together; not to take the bird that sitteth on its young or its eggs; and not to seethe a kid in its mother's milk. To disregard the rights and feelings of equals, is unjust and ungenerous, but to willfully or wantonly injure or oppress the weak

f. Sabbath Days and Years of Rest for the Benefit of Cattle and Wildlife

That the Sabbath was to be a day of rest for domestic animals as well as for Israelites is stipulated in both the CC and D versions of the Ten Commandments. An additional law to the same effect also appears elsewhere in the CC. The CC and H also provide for animal welfare in laws concerning the seventh or Sabbatical *Year* of rest.

1. The Sabbath Day of Rest

Exodus 20:10. The Sabbath law, part of the Decalogue or Ten Commandments,[108] provides that neither humans ("you, your son or your daughter, your male, or female slave . . . or the resident alien") nor cattle[109] are to do any work on the Sabbath. Here, as elsewhere in biblical discourse, the term "cattle" probably includes a variety of domestic animals. Sabbath observance serves to honor YHWH— the One who made all creation in six days and then rested on the Sabbath or seventh day (Exod 20:11); it also is a day of rest, for the well-being of both "man and beast," a day of rest based on YHWH/God's care and compassion.

Exodus 23:12. This law, likewise found in the CC, so states in explicit terms: "Six days you shall do your work, but on the seventh day you shall rest; so that your ox and your [ass] may have relief, and your homeborn slave and the resident alien may be refreshed." The Sabbath was to be a day of rest for humans and animals alike. Presumably this law applied only to "work" animals, such as oxen

---

and helpless, is mean and cowardly. Human beings have at least some means of protecting themselves against the inhumanity of man . . . but dumb brutes have none. . . . Animals whose lives are devoted to our use and pleasure, and which are capable, perhaps, of feeling as great physical pain or pleasure as ourselves, deserve, for these considerations alone, kindly treatment.

108. Slightly different versions of the Ten Commandments appear in Exod 20:1–17 and Deut 5:6–21. See also Exod 34:11–28, the only version actually identified in its text as "the Ten Commandments" (Exod 34:28).

109. The NRSV generally prefers the translation "livestock." This book follows the RSV translation, "cattle."

and asses, which are here named specifically. Others, such as sheep and goats, it may be assumed, were free to go about their browsing and other customary activities on the Sabbath as on other days.

Deuteronomy 5:12–15. This version of the Sabbath law is much like that in Exod 20:8–11. Here, however, it is said that no work is to be done by the Israelite community or their oxen, asses, or any of their other cattle so that both the Israelites and their male and female slaves might "rest." The Deuteronomic law could be read to mean that the cattle were to rest in order that the Israelites and their servants or slaves might be relieved of working with or otherwise tending the cattle. In that case, the Deuteronomic version would represent a slight shift from a theocentric to a more anthropocentric rationale.

A similar shift from theocentric to anthropocentric faith and ethics may be seen in another difference between two of these versions of the Sabbath law. In Exod 20:11, the Sabbath is to be observed because YHWH/God rested on and blessed the seventh day; in Deut 5:15, reference, instead, is to the experience of Israelites as servants in Egypt. Here the rationale seems to be that the Israelites should remember what it was like to be servants (or slaves) in Egypt, and therefore ought to show kindness to their own servants by allowing them to rest on the Sabbath day. This rationale, unlike that articulated in Exod 23:12, does not specifically indicate concern for the well-being of work animals.

II. The Sabbath Year of Rest

Exodus 23:10–11. This law requires that after every six years of sowing and harvesting, the *land* must be allowed to rest and lie fallow.[110] The stated rationale is to provide for the needs of the poor. During this seventh year, the land was expected to continue producing some yield.[111] In addition, this law clearly was intended to

---

110. See above, pt. A1 of this chapter.

111. Compare 2 Kgs 19:29–31, which refers to a two-year period when, after the Assyrians withdrew from Jerusalem, the people of Judah would "eat what grows of itself."

provide forage for wildlife: what the poor left, the "wild animals" might eat. Similar provisions appear in Lev 25:2–7.

Leviticus 25:2–7. As just noted, the CC provided that the seventh year should be a year of rest for the land, and that the poor and wild beasts might freely eat of its produce that year (Exod 23:10–11). Likewise, according to this H law, the land should not be worked during the seventh year and should be allowed to "rest." Landowners, and presumably their families and other workers, servants or slaves, were to rest too. Fields were not to be sown nor vineyards tended; whatever grew was not to be reaped, nor were grapes to be gathered (Lev 25:4–5). What grew the seventh year would provide food not only for people but also for "cattle" (domestic animals) and wildlife alike (Lev 25:7).[112] As in the case of YHWH's telling Noah to provide food for the animals on the ark,[113] YHWH instructs Israel (through Moses) to make provisions for both cattle and wildlife—here by allowing them to graze freely throughout the seventh year on what otherwise would have been cultivated fields and tended vineyards and orchards.

According to Lev 25:8–12, the fiftieth year—the Year of Jubilee—would also be a time of rest for the land.[114] There would be no sowing, reaping, or gathering. Perhaps this, too, was meant to be a time when, as in the Sabbatical Year, both cattle and wildlife might freely enjoy the yield of fields, vineyards, and orchards (Lev 25:6–7).

3. Other Biblical Traditions

Wisdom writings likewise call for consideration in the care of domestic animals. This theme is stated most explicitly in Prov 12:10: "The righteous know the needs of their animals, but the mercy of

---

112. As to YHWH's providing food for wildlife, see also Job 38:39–41; 39:5–8; Pss 104:10–14; 145:15–16.

113. Gen 6: 21–22.

114. See Ferre, *Hellfire and Lightning Rods*, 179, commenting on Lev 25:1–5: "Even the cropland itself is not mere property, to be used to the maximum without regard or restraint. The rights of the Sabbath rest are extended also to the fields by the Leviticus commandment."

the wicked is cruel." Prudential considerations also called for giving farm animals good care:

> Know well the condition of your flocks,
>   and give attention to your herds; . . .
> the lambs will provide your clothing,
>   and the goats the price of a field;
> there will be enough goats' milk for your food,
>   for the food of your household
>   and nourishment for your servant girls. (Prov 27:23–27)

Similarly, the sage of Sirach advises: "Do you have cattle? Look after them; if they are profitable to you keep them" (Sir 7:22).

Although the following text very likely was meant to symbolize the hope or expectation that YHWH/God would care for his people in the future, it also shows the kind of compassionate concern for lambs and mother sheep that would have been appreciated by contemporary herdsmen:

> He will feed his flock like a shepherd,
>   he will gather the lambs in his arms,
>   he will carry them in his bosom,
>   and gently lead those that are with young. (Isa 40:11 RSV)

A late biblical writing, 4 Maccabees, undertakes to relate "law" to "reason" with respect to both trees and distressed cattle:

> Do not consider it paradoxical when reason, through the law, can prevail even over enmity. The fruit trees of the enemy are not [to be] cut down, but one preserves the property of enemies from marauders and helps raise up [the beasts that have] fallen. (4 Macc 2:14).

Such reason evidently is informed by the conviction that trees and animals are created by God and valued by him and are therefore to be protected from harm. The law referred to here, very likely, is that found in Deut 20:19–20 and Exod 23:4–5.

In the New Testament, two variant texts represent Jesus's response when challenged for healing a man on the Sabbath. In one, he replies, "Suppose one you has only one sheep and it falls into a pit on the Sabbath, will you not lay hold of it and lift it out?" (Matt

12:11). In the other version, he says, "If one of you has [an ass] or an ox that has fallen into a well, will you not immediately pull it out [even] on a Sabbath day?" (Luke 14:5).[115] In both versions, Jesus assumes that his hearers would rescue the animals from harm, and clearly approves of their doing so. Likewise, Jesus assumes that a man whose sheep has strayed will go and search for it, and, again, approves his doing so (Matt 18:12–13; Luke 15:4–6).[116] In another saying found in Luke, Jesus likewise asks, "Does not each of you on the Sabbath untie his ox or his [ass] from the manger, and lead it away to water?" (Luke 13:15). These sayings all have to do with healing or caring for persons; but, significantly, Jesus does not argue that persons are important, while animals are not.[117] Instead, he evidently wanted his hearers to understand that the well-being of both people and animals was important,[118] and both more important than Sabbath observance.

This chapter has reviewed biblical texts that describe or require human activities undertaken on behalf of a wide range of living beings, including humans. Here attention has been focused on human beings as moral agents. Many other biblical texts describe or anticipate normative actions by other-than-human creatures. In

115. Another ancient manuscript tradition refers here to "a son" rather than "an ass" or "donkey."

116. See Murphy, *Haunted by Paradise*, 108–9: "The Bible often [represents] Jesus as a shepherd, who exercises rational dominion over his flocks solely for the good of the sheep. A good shepherd cares for the welfare of every sheep and of every cow. Prov 12:10, 1 Tim 5:18."

117. Singer notes what he considers an important exception: "Jesus himself showed indifference to the fate of nonhumans when he induced two thousand swine to hurl themselves into the sea—an act which was, apparently, quite unnecessary, since Jesus was able to cast out demons without inflicting them on any other creature." Singer, *Animal Liberation*, 199, citing Mark 5:1–13. Most modern interpreters doubt the historicity of this account, partly because they themselves do not believe in demons; but mainly because it would have been quite unusual for Jewish farmers or herdsmen to raise pigs, the quintessential "unclean" animal. Interpreters tend to regard to story as a legend intended to demonstrate Jesus's spiritual or miraculous powers. It may also reflect early Jewish-Christian animus against gentiles, who could have raised pigs.

118. See also Mark 7:24–30, where Jesus clearly approves the Greek or Syrio-Phoenician woman's rejoinder, that "the dogs under the table" were allowed to "eat the children's crumbs. Drummond thoughtfully discusses many of the NT texts noted above. Drummond, *Rights of Animals*, 23–35.

effect, these other creatures themselves are seen as moral agents, carrying out YHWH's purposes in relation to human beings. Such texts are considered in the following chapter.

CHAPTER 10

Other Creatures as YHWH/God's Agents in His Dealings with Humans

IN BIBLICAL TRADITION, ANIMALS and other nonhuman creatures frequently serve to carry out YHWH/God's purposes with respect to human beings. In some instances, these creatures are sent or commissioned to rescue or aid people in need of help. In others, such creatures act on YHWH/God's behalf to punish humans who have committed injustice or other wrongs.[1] In both kinds of situations, these creatures are portrayed as moral agents, acting on behalf of YHWH/God's purposes and in response to his instructions.

A. CREATURES HELPING HUMANS

Many biblical texts point to ways in which other creatures are or have been helpful to humans. In the second creation story, it is said that YHWH/God formed "every beast of the field and every bird of the air" in hopes of making the first man "a helper fit for him" (Gen 2:18–21). Other creatures are seen as beneficial, not only as sources of food or as working farm animals but as sources of understanding in regard to the human condition. Such creatures'

---

1. In some texts considered in this chapter, other creatures are said to have dominion over humans. See generally Kay, "Concepts of Nature," 314–17. Also above, ch. 7B, and below, pt. B of the present chapter.

actions and characteristics were recognized as further evidences of divine power, wisdom, and grace or compassion.

As the flood story is told in Genesis, after the rains have stopped, Noah sends a female dove from the ark in order to determine whether the waters have yet receded. At first, the dove returns to the ark, signifying that water still covered the earth. A week later, after he sends her out again, she returns with "a freshly plucked olive leaf" (Gen 8:10-11). Another week later, Noah sends her out again and she does not come back, and thereby demonstrates that it is now safe for him, his family, and all the other creatures to leave the ark and begin life again upon dry land. Implicitly the dove thus served and benefited all future generations of human and nonhuman terrestrial creatures alike.

Some biblical accounts depict other creatures as agents of YHWH/God, acting to make effective his concern for the people of Israel. The earliest instances of such agency occur in the stories about various plagues directed against Egypt because of Pharaoh's refusal to let the people of Israel go. Here the creatures acting at YHWH/God's behest include swarms of frogs, gnats, and flies (Exod 8:1-24), followed by a horde of locusts (Exod 10:1-15). The psalmist subsequently recalls the role played by these frogs, flies, gnats, and locusts in carrying out YHWH/God's sovereign purposes (Ps 105:30-31, 34-35).

Somewhat later in the Exodus narrative, YHWH/God promises his people, now escaped from Egypt, but still in the wilderness, that he will send hornets before them to drive out the indigenous peoples—Hittites, Canaanites, and Hivites—from the land he plans to give them (Exod 23:28). Deuteronomy 7:20 and Josh 24:12 likewise refer to hornets in this connection.

Biblical stories also describe how certain animals served or helped particular persons on various occasions, most notably, perhaps, the stories of Balaam and his ass, and Elijah and the ravens. The story of Jonah and the great fish tells how various creatures (and "natural" elements) aided not only this prophet himself but also the entire population of a foreign city—and their cattle. In the OT Apocrypha, the Letter of Jeremiah presents a somewhat different way in which certain creatures, including bats, birds, and cats, can serve the faithful, and 3 Maccabees tells how elephants rescued a stadium full of pious Jews from certain death. In the New Testament, one of Jesus's parables features dogs attending to the needs of a human being.

Balaam, a professional execrator, was en route to carry out his mission in Moab.[2] Balaam did not see the angel who, with menacing sword, suddenly blocked their way; but the ass did and, promptly sizing up the situation, wisely balked. Although Balaam beat her, the ass continued to balk and finally lay down underneath him. As a result of the ass's perception and prudence, Balaam's life was spared (Num 22:32–33). Thus Balaam was able to continue his journey, which eventuated in his pronouncing blessings upon Israel (Num 23:7—24:19). A New Testament text, though regarding Balaam somewhat unfavorably, likewise credits the ass for her good deed: "A dumb ass spoke with a human voice and restrained the prophet's madness" (2 Pet 2:16 RSV).

In the Elijah narrative, the prophet is in hiding, evidently trying to stay out of the way of King Ahab of Israel and his foreign wife Jezebel, who were devotees of the god Ba'al and the goddess Asherah. Elijah, faithful to YHWH/God, camped by a brook. "The ravens brought him bread and meat in the morning, and bread and meat in the evening; and he drank from the [brook]" (1 Kgs 17:6).[3] Thus Elijah survived and was enabled to carry on his remarkable prophetic career.[4]

Though probably not meant to be taken literally, the story (or parable) of Jonah presents some further instances of YHWH/God's calling upon or directing other creatures (and other components of

---

2. See Richard Hiers, *Trinity Guide to Bible*, 293.

3. Mark's account of Jesus temptation in "the wilderness" *may* suggest a similar situation. Mark writes, "[Jesus] was in the wilderness forty days, tempted by Satan; and he was with the wild beasts; and the angels waited on him" (Mark 1:13). Mark may have meant that the "wild beasts," like the angels, "waited on" Jesus. Or it may be that Mark considered Jesus's being "with the wild beasts" as foreshadowing the messianic age, when humans and wildlife would live together in peace. See below, ch. 11. On another occasion in the Elijah narrative (1 Kgs 19:4–8), an angel provided the prophet with food while he was in "the wilderness" forty days and forty nights, as ravens had provided for him in 1 Kgs 17:6.

4. See 1 Kgs 17:8—21:29; 2 Kgs 1:1—2:12.

nature) to accomplish his purposes. As the story is told, Jonah, for reasons later clarified, tries to avoid going to Nineveh, "that great city," as YHWH/God had instructed him to do and instead boards a ship headed in the opposite direction.[5] YHWH/God then causes a strong wind and heavy seas to threaten the ship with disaster. Reluctantly, and only after praying to YHWH and determining that doing so really was necessary, the pagan sailors throw Jonah overboard. Now a great fish, expressly acting as YHWH's agent, rescues Jonah from drowning and subsequently delivers him safely to shore:

> And YHWH appointed a great fish to swallow up Jonah; and Jonah was in the belly of the fish three days and three nights. (Jonah 1:17 RSV)
>
> Then YHWH spoke to the fish and it spewed Jonah out upon the dry land. (Jonah 2:10)

Impressed (if not convinced) by these experiences, Jonah finally goes to Nineveh as instructed. Here, in response to Jonah's grudging and ominous proclamation, "Forty days more, and Nineveh shall be overthrown," that "great city's" king, people, *and animals* put on sackcloth and cry to God and are spared the destruction otherwise in store for them (Jonah 3:1–10).[6] Jonah, who hates Nineveh, is very displeased.

YHWH/God then "appoints" a large plant to give Jonah shade as he sits outside the city. Jonah is waiting to see what would become of Nineveh—evidently hoping YHWH/God would change his mind and destroy it after all (Jonah 4:5–6). But then YHWH/God "appoints" a worm to attack the plant so that it withers, allowing the sun again to beat down upon Jonah's head. The scenario is presented as part of YHWH/God's attempt to help Jonah realize that YHWH/God is—and he, Jonah, also should be—concerned about Nineveh, "that great city, in which there are more than a hundred and twenty thousand persons who do not know their right

---

5. See Richard Hiers, *Trinity Guide to Bible*, 114–16.

6. Cf. Gen 8:1: "But God remembered Noah and all the beasts and all the cattle that were with him in the ark."

hand from their left,[7] *and also many animals*" (Jonah 4:11). Here, YHWH/God explains to Jonah that he pitied and spared Nineveh not only because of its hundred and twenty thousand young children (and also that city's adult population) but also for the sake of these "many animals" or "much cattle."

In the course of the narrative, YHWH/God appoints not only "a great fish" in order to move Jonah forward on his mission but also a plant and a worm in an attempt to enlighten him as to divine grace, mercy, and steadfast love.[8] The evident moral to the story is that YHWH/God's compassion extends to both humans—including foreigners[9]—and other creatures. The implication is that Jonah—and other people likewise—should show such compassion. At the same time, as the story unfolds, it is clear that the "great fish," was portrayed as directly instrumental in effectuating YHWH/God's determination to spare the people of Nineveh. It was also instrumental in bringing about the deliverance of that great city's "much cattle" or "many animals." Here, as in the story of Noah, the ark, and the dove, action by an animal (respectively, the "great fish" and the dove), helped preserve other creatures besides humans.[10]

The deuterocanonical (or apocryphal) Letter of Jeremiah consists entirely of a polemic against the worship of idols or images of other gods. Its thesis is that because such idols cannot look out even for themselves, it is foolish for people to pray to them or otherwise hope or expect them to help their worshipers. In this connection, various creatures serve to illustrate the point: "Bats, swallows, and birds light on their bodies and heads; and so do cats."[11] These creatures realize what the idol worshipers fail to grasp: namely, that

---

7. This description appears to refer to young children. Isaiah 7:14–16 and 8:3–4 point out other characteristics of young children.

8. Jonah 1:17; 2:10; 4:1–11.

9. See Richard Hiers, *Nation of Immigrants*, 69–78.

10. In modern times, observers have reported instances where creatures intentionally undertake to help one another. See, e.g., Schweitzer, "Ethics of Reverence." See also N. Cobb, "Black Labrador Fights" (an alligator to save ducks); and Herriott, *Dog Stories*, 418–23. Biologists recognize symbiosis as a basic feature of interactions between and among different species of living organisms. See also Polt, *50 Odd Couples*, as to animal friendships.

11. Letter of Jeremiah (Ep Jer) v. 22.

these so-called gods are totally impotent.[12] The writer's point is that those who honor the true God should follow their excellent example.

A story in 3 Maccabees features a herd of elephants, initially ordered by a wicked, if muddled, foreign king to trample to death the gathered pious Jews. But then the elephants turn around and trample their gentile enemies, thereby delivering these Jews from those who had maliciously plotted against them. There is no evidence that this episode ever occurred in history; however, the story very likely was intended to encourage Jews to remain faithful to their traditions in times of persecution. Here, again, we see the belief or idea that YHWH/God might use nonhuman creatures in order to accomplish his own purposes.

Jesus's story or parable about the rich man and Lazarus (Luke 16:19–31) tells that "even the dogs would come and lick" the poor man's sores, in order, it seems, to give comfort or healing.[13] The dogs' attention to poor Lazarus is seen in notable contrast to the indifference of the rich man, who did nothing at all to help the needy man who was lying at his gate.

But other creatures are not always or necessarily seen as good to or for human beings. Many other texts have to do with YHWH/God's using other creatures as agents of his judgment *against* people, sometimes even against the people of Israel, for their respective offenses.

---

12. Compare with Isa 1:2, where the prophet laments Israel's failure to "know" or acknowledge YHWH as their God."

13. Dogs (and cats) are often said to give comforting attention to people who are ill, for instance, in nursing homes that keep such animals for this purpose. See Peters, "Pets Have a Place": "All pet owners and most in the medical community now acknowledge the healing power of animals. Some doctors even write prescriptions giving hospital patients access to the pets they left at home." See also Herriot, *Lord God Made Them*, 228, commenting on a client's dog staying close to his master's sickbed: "'This was something that I had seen on many occasions with disabled people, that their pets stayed close by them as if conscious of their role as comforter and friend." See also *The Week*, March 4, 2022, 12, for an untitled article on a pig comforting a man.

B. OTHER CREATURES AS AGENTS OF YHWH/GOD'S JUDGMENT

A considerable number of texts, generally ignored by Bible commentators, describe YHWH/God's involving a variety of creatures in acts of divine judgment against humans. Such acts often are directed against individual wrongdoers, against other nations or peoples, and, frequently, against the people of Israel themselves. Several such texts refer to the role of creatures in times past. Others prophesy or anticipate that various creatures will act to punish or destroy Israel or other nations in the future. In many instances, these future acts of judgment appear to have been expected to occur in the final stages of the present age, in preparation for the new or messianic age to come.

1. Acts of Judgment against Individuals

Proverbs 30:17 warns that ravens and vultures will wreak vengeance upon children who mock their fathers or scorn to obey their mothers. Qoheleth observes that serpents bite those who break through walls, perhaps as acts of vandalism, if not in order to steal from within (Eccl 10:8b). A few narratives tell about animals acting as agents of YHWH/God's judgment against individuals. Lions kill two prophets who disobey certain instructions.[14] The most familiar account of this sort is the story in 1 Kgs 21–22. Here, pursuant to YHWH's word through the prophet Elijah, dogs lick up Ahab's blood and kill and devour his infamous wife, Jezebel.[15] In 2 Kgs 2:23–25, it is said that some bears attacked and mauled a number of small boys who had insulted the prophet Elisha, in accordance with that prophet's having cursed them "in the name of YHWH."

Writing in more general terms about "the creation" as agent of YHWH/God's sovereignty, one biblical sage concludes:

> For the creation, serving you who made it,

---

14. 1 Kgs 13:11–2 8. Cf. 1 Kgs 20:35–36. These may be variant versions of the same story, and neither is entirely complete or coherent; but it is clear in each case that the lion represented divine punishment for wrongdoing.

15. 1 Kgs 21:1–24; 22:29–38.

exerts itself to punish the unrighteous,
and in kindness relaxes
on behalf of those who trust in you. (Wis 16:24)

Sirach, another wisdom writer, observes that it is fitting for humans to be humble rather than proud, given the fact that, to use a modern expression, humans are part of, but not necessarily at the top of, the food chain:

For when one is dead,
he inherits maggots,
and wild animals and worms. (Sir 10:11)

This text is placed in the context of an extended reflection on human insolence, arrogance, and pride (Sir 10:6-18). The Hebrew text of Sir 7:17 is to the same effect: "Humble yourself to the utmost, for the expectation of [humans] is worms." Worms likewise figure as agents of divine judgment in the Greek version of Sir 7:17: "the ungodly" would be punished—presumably in Gehenna or hell—by "fire and worms."[16]

Another text in the Old Testament Apocrypha describes the miserable demise of the hated Antiochus Epiphanes: "And so the ungodly man's body swarmed with worms, and while he was still living in anguish and pain, his flesh rotted away" (2 Macc 9:9).[17] The account of Herod's wretched death given in Acts 12:23 possibly echoes this account: "[Herod] was eaten by worms and died."

Most texts in which various creatures are seen acting as agents of YHWH/God's judgment involve his judgment against nations: both foreign nations and also, particularly, Israel and Judah. Some relate to events in past or present times. Many refer to future times of judgment.

---

16. Compare Matt 18:8-9 and Mark 9:43-48, which anticipate that the wicked will experience eternal punishment by fire in Gehenna or hell. Mark 9:48 can be read to mean that the wicked will also experience eternal torment by "their worm." This text echoes Isa 66:24. See also Jdt 16:17.

17. Second Maccabees 9:5-28 provides the larger context.

2. Acts of Judgment against Nations or Peoples in Past and Present Times

The book of Numbers tells that YHWH/God, displeased by the Israelites' continual complaints in the wilderness, "sent fiery serpents among the people, and they bit the people, so that many Israelites died" (Num 21:5-6). The prophet Joel sees various kinds of locusts as agents sent by YHWH against Judah or the Jewish people to destroy their crops, perhaps as a foretaste of "the day of YHWH" which he believed was "near" (Joel 1:15).[18] This imagery may refer either to invading armies or to actual locusts.[19] The prophet Malachi likewise implies that YHWH/God allowed locusts (or other devouring insects) to destroy his people's crops because of their wrongdoings (Mal 3:5-11). Similarly, Amos tells his contemporaries that God had contemplated bringing locusts to devour their harvests, implicitly as punishment for their many offenses (Amos 7: 1-2).[20]

The Wisdom of Solomon includes several texts that refer to punishment by various creatures. One text adds haggadic or legendary details to the accounts of the plagues sent upon Egypt:

> In return for their foolish and wicked thoughts,
>   which led them astray to worship
>   irrational serpents and worthless animals,
> you sent upon them a multitude of irrational creatures
>   to punish them,
> that they might learn that one is punished
>   by the very things by which one sins. (Wis 1:15-16)[21]

The Israelites themselves were "troubled" in the wilderness by wild beasts and serpents "as a warning," lest they fail to follow the newly given law:

18. Joel 1:4; 2:25.

19. Compare Isa 7:18-19, where "the fly" and "the bee" apparently refer to invading Egyptian and Assyrian armies.

20. See, e.g., what might be called the "bill of particulars" set out in Amos 6:1-7, 12-13, and elsewhere in the book of Amos.

21. The same theme is picked up again in Wis 12:23-27 and 15:18—16:1. Chapter 16:1 reads: "Therefore they were deservedly punished through such creatures, and were tormented by a multitude of animals." See also Wis 16:8-9 and 17:9-10, 19.

> For when the terrible rage of wild animals
>   came upon your people
> and they were being destroyed
>   by the bites of writhing serpents,
> your wrath did not continue to the end;
>   they were troubled for a little while as a warning,
> and received a symbol of deliverance
>   to remind them of your laws' command. (Wis 16:5–6)[22]

Animals act as agents of divine judgment in later times as well. The imaginative story about elephants trampling the gentile enemies of the Jews in 3 Maccabees[23] implicitly interprets their doing so as divine judgment against these enemies because of their depravity and evil designs (3 Macc 6:21).

3. YHWH/God's Agents in Future Time or Times of Judgment against Nations or Peoples

Several prophetic texts anticipate that divine judgment will be inflicted upon other nations or their leaders who have oppressed the peoples of Israel or Judah. Such texts seem to refer to the final days of the present age, just before or at the time when YHWH/God will act decisively to restore the fortunes of his people. For instance, Isa 15:9b, "an oracle concerning Moab," declares: "a lion for those of Moab that escape, for the remnant of the land." A saying in Ezekiel is directed prospectively against the Pharaoh of Egypt: "To the animals of the earth and to the birds of the air I have given you as food" (Ezek 29:5a). Another of Ezekiel's often vivid visions refers more broadly to "the mighty" and "the princes of the earth" and the gruesome fate in store for them:

> As for you, [son of man], thus says the Lord God: "Speak to the birds of every kind and to all the wild animals, [and say to them:] Assemble and come, gather from all around to the sacrificial feast that I am preparing for you, a great sacrificial feast on the mountains of Israel, and you shall eat flesh and

---

22. See also Wis 16:10–12. These texts reinterpret or elaborate upon the account in Num 21:5–6.

23. See above, sect. A of this chapter.

drink blood. You shall eat the flesh of the mighty, and drink the blood of the princes of the earth [—of rams, of lambs, and of goats, of bulls, all of them fatlings of Bashan].[24] You shall eat fat until you are filled, and drink blood till you are drunk, at the sacrificial feast that I am preparing for you. And you shall be filled at my table with [horses and] charioteers, with warriors and all kinds of soldiers, says the Lord God." (Ezek 39:17–20)

The Song of Judith anticipates that worms will act as divine agents, inflicting misery upon enemies of the Jewish people at the coming "day of judgment":

> Woe to the nations that rise up
>   against my people!
> The Lord Almighty will take vengeance on them
>   in the day of judgment;
> he will send fire and worms into their flesh;
>   they shall weep in pain forever. (Jdt 16:17)

The Wisdom of Solomon tells that "all creation" will join to fight against the enemies of the Lord in the future time when the righteous will be vindicated (Wis 5:15–20). These texts visualize other creatures or even "all creation" as agents of divine judgment against those nations or peoples who had oppressed the people of Israel and Judah or the Jewish people.

However, many other texts that refer to such creatures as agents of YHWH/God's judgment visualize them as acting against his own people for having failed to obey his commandments or otherwise meet his expectations and requirements.

As far back as the wilderness era, the Israelites were warned what might happen. Thus, for instance, Lev 26:21–22, cautioned, if they "walk contrary" (RSV) to YHWH "and will not obey" him, YHWH/God would "let loose the wild animals" among them, robbing them of their children, destroying their cattle, and reducing them to "few in number." Likewise, Deut 28:26 warned what would happen to his people if (or when) they failed to "diligently observe

---

24. The bracketed words appear to have been added by a later scribe or interpreter. In the larger context, Ezekiel is saying that instead of people sacrificing animals, animals would devour "the mighty" humans, "the princes of the earth."

all his commandments and decrees" (Deut 28:15). Their dead bodies would become "food for every bird of the air and animal of the earth; and there shall be no one to frighten them away." As to those who forget YHWH and worship other gods, he would send "the teeth of beasts against them, with venom of things crawling in the dust" (Deut 32:24b).

Several prophets proclaimed that YHWH/God's judgment would be directed against his own people, Israel and Judah, for their various offenses. Such judgment might take the form of marauding and destructive wild beasts. For instance, Isa 56:9: "All you [beasts of the field], all you wild animals of the forest, come to devour!" Likewise, Hosea warned his fellow Israelites, speaking on behalf of YHWH: "I will lay waste her vines and her fig trees . . . , and the wild animals shall devour them" (Hos 2:12).[25] The book of Jeremiah includes several texts in which YHWH/God declares that he intends to punish—or destroy—his people because of their wrongdoing through the agency of wild animals or birds.

> Therefore, a lion from the forest shall kill them,
>   a wolf from the desert shall destroy them.
> A leopard is watching against their cities;
>   everyone who goes out of them shall be torn in pieces—
> because their transgressions are many,
>   their apostasies are great. (Jer 5:6)[26]

Again, Jeremiah proclaims YHWH/God's message against the people of Judah:

> For the people of Judah have done evil in my sight, says YHWH; they have set up their abominations[27] in the house that is called by my name, defiling it. . . . The corpses of this people will be food for the birds of the air, and for the animals

---

25. The exact reference in these texts is uncertain.

26. See also Jer 2:15 and 4:7 (where lions may symbolically represent Assyria). But see Jer 12:9c: "Go, assemble all the wild animals; bring them to devour." Here "wild animals" clearly means "wild animals." See also Ezek 39:17-20, quoted above.

27. In such contexts, "abominations" refer to images representing other gods, which, from the standpoint of biblical faith, are not gods at all but, rather, "abominations."

of the earth; and no one will frighten them away. (Jer 7:30, 33)[28]

Serpents or snakes also will be agents of YHWH/God's judgment against his people:

> "See, I am letting snakes loose,
>   adders that cannot be charmed,
>   and they shall bite you,"
>   says YHWH. (Jer 8:17)[29]

Nearly all, if not all, his people deserve severe judgment, says Jeremiah:

> Then YHWH said to me, "Though Moses and Samuel stood before me, yet my heart would not turn toward this people. Send them out of my sight, and let them go! . . . I will appoint over them four kinds of destroyers," says YHWH: "the sword to kill, the dogs to drag away, and the birds of the air and the wild animals of the earth to devour and destroy." (Jer 15:1–3)

Ezekiel likewise visualizes wild animals as agents of YHWH/God's impending judgment against his people Israel or Judah:

> The word of YHWH came to me: [Son of man], . . . say to [the inhabitants of Israel]: Thus says the Lord God: You eat flesh with the blood and lift up your eyes to your idols and shed blood. . . . You depend on your sword, you commit abominations, and each of you defiles his neighbor's wife. . . . Say this to them: Thus says the Lord God: As I live, surely those who are in the waste places shall fall by the sword; and those who are in the open field I will give to the wild animals to be devoured; and those who are in strongholds and in caves shall die by pestilence. (Ezek 33:23–27)

Another text in Ezekiel declares that his people have sinned so egregiously that if YHWH/God caused wild beasts to ravage the land in judgment, and three other outstandingly righteous men

---

28. Likewise, in Jer 16:4 and 19:7, YHWH declares that the people of Jerusalem and Judah will die by the sword and that their dead bodies will be food for the birds of the air and the beasts of the earth. See also Jer 34:20.

29. Compare Num 21:5–6 and Amos 9:3, where snakes also appear as agents of divine judgment against people.

(Noah, Daniel, and Job) were among its inhabitants, those three alone would be spared (Ezek 14:12-16). Ezekiel looks to the time of impending doom when the Lord God will send "wild animals" and other "acts of judgment" against Jerusalem (Ezek 14:21).

The prophet Amos warns that even if any of the people of Israel should try to escape his judgment by hiding at the bottom of the sea, it would be to no avail:

> And though they hide from my sight
>   at the bottom of the sea, there I will command the sea-serpent,
>   and it shall bite them. (Amos 9:3b)[30]

The seer-author of Revelation likewise visualized "wild animals of the earth" as agents of divine judgment at the end of history: "I looked and there was a pale green horse! Its rider's name was Death, and Hades followed with him; they were given authority over a fourth of the earth, to kill with sword, famine, and pestilence, and by the wild animals of the earth" (Rev 6:8). The same seer declared that an eagle would, like a prophet, proclaim "woe to the inhabitants of the earth" (Rev 8:13), after which huge locusts or locust-like creatures would come to torture the wicked (Rev 9:1-6). Finally, the seer describes a vision in which "all the birds that fly in midheaven" are summoned to devour the flesh of those deemed wicked or unworthy:

> Then I saw an angel standing in the sun, and with a loud voice he called to all the birds that fly in mid-heaven, "Come, gather for the great supper of God, to eat the flesh of kings, the flesh of captains, the flesh of mighty men, the flesh of horses and their riders, and the flesh of all men, both free and slave, both small and great." . . . And the rest were killed by the sword of the rider on the horse, the sword that issues from his mouth; and all the birds were gorged with their flesh. (Rev 19:17-18, 21)[31]

---

30. Compare Jonah 2:10: "Then YHWH spoke to the fish and it spewed Jonah out upon the dry land." In early Christian catacomb art, Jonah's great "fish" is usually represented as a large sea serpent.

31. This vision parallels and probably derives, at least in part, from Ezek 39:17-20.

However one might evaluate this scenario, it is consistent with the many earlier biblical texts that express the belief and expectation that YHWH/God would use other creatures as agents of his judgment against human beings who had violated the terms of their existence. These texts significantly qualify the aptness of the often-repeated proposition that the Bible teaches that humans were meant to have dominion over all other creatures.

CHAPTER 11

Conditions of Life in the New or Messianic Age

MOST BIBLICAL TRADITION FOCUSES on the past or present time. The past is remembered for the major events in or through which YHWH/God acted in creating all that is and, in particular, in dealing with his people, Israel. Laws, narratives, psalms, and wisdom writings all transmitted a rich understanding both of the meaning of life and of right and righteous ways of living in this world. As has been seen, YHWH/God's continuing activity as Sovereign over creation and over history was understood to be taking place in then present or "real" time.

Future times also figure large in the biblical perspective. The prophets focused not only on what was happening in their own lifetimes but also on the future, for then the reign or dominion of YHWH/God would at last bring about those conditions of life he intended for the world and all living beings to enjoy. Both the creation (or "nature") and history then would be redeemed from the vicissitudes and animosities that had operated in the past and present to diminish and corrupt the good life that had originally been intended for all.[1] Most biblical texts anticipate that the new

---

1. See generally Phan, "Eschatology and Ecology." And see Rogerson, "What Was the Meaning," 17: "In the Old Testament the guiding narratives are those that speak of an original conflict-free creation (including no conflict among animals, or between animals and humans), and which look for its restoration."

Another commentator looks for future fulfillment in consequence of the

or messianic age would be brought about in or on this world, which, however, would be greatly, if not radically, transformed.[2] In the meantime, biblical tradition calls for respect and active caring for this beautiful, amazing, and fragile Earth, the only place where humans and all other living things—our fellow travelers on what

---

transformation of human consciousness: "When humans recognize the presence of the Creator in creation, and relate to other people and other creatures as an integrated life community, and when they leave selected pristine places as they were created and use carefully other places and goods essential for meeting their needs, then they will inhabit a good place. Earth will become their shared sacred space and will be able to take care of them. The sacramental commons will nurture humankind and all life, as the Creator intended, while they walk with all life in the presence of the Spirit and life as creation's caring and creative consciousness." Hart, *Sacramental Commons*, 76 (see also 233).

2. So also most of the texts cited in this chapter. See also Ps 93:1: "[YHWH] has established the world; it never shall be moved." Some texts look for "new heavens" and a "new earth" (Ps 102:25–2 8; Isa 66:22; 2 Pet 3:10–13; Rev 21:1–4) as the place or places of final or eschatological fulfillment. Some NT texts refer to heaven as the place of future, eschatological bliss: John 14:2–4; Phil 3:20; and 1 Thess 4:16–17.

A few modern proponents of future, heavenly salvation in the form of "space age" technology urge construction of multiple space colonies. These would consist of enclosed, pressurized plexiglass cylinders orbiting the Earth at the "Libration" or "Lagrange" points. Their inhabitants supposedly would thereby escape pollution, overpopulation, conflict, and most other problems on planet Earth. See Braun, "Spiritual Survival," in his essay "Responsible Scientific Investigation." Embracing and commending Princeton Professor Gerald K. O'Neill's proposal, Braun wrote: "I think the concept of multiple space colonies can relieve us of a lot of problems here on earth. . . . Time and again we see the spectacle of a charismatic leader arousing millions for some political, racial, economic, religious, or nationalistic cause which subsequently is pursued and defended in bloody wars. In the age of space habitats this permanent danger source could be removed from the earth." Braun, "Responsible Scientific Investigation," 127.

Ehrenfeld characterizes such proposals as a "grand delusion," and their proponents as "fatuously optimistic about the future of life in barren space." Ehrenfeld, *Arrogance of Humanism*, 120–23. See also Stendahl's critique of the Braun-O'Neill proposal in Hess, *Nature of Humane Society*, 150–55. Biblical faith anticipates that in the age to come, along with everything else, human hearts would need to be radically transformed. See, e.g., Isa 11:9; Jer 31:31–34; Ezek 11:19–20; 36:26–27; Matt 5:3–9; and Gal 6:15. Billionaires enjoying joyrides by rocketing briefly into space likewise seem to assume that Earth's resources are limitless and that probable adverse environmental consequences do not matter. Current NASA plans for sending people to the moon on billion-dollar space vehicles do not apparently consider the environmental impact of rocket launches, cost of supplying any lunar colonies, and damage likely to result from by additional debris adrift in space.

Barbara Ward has described as this rocket ship Earth, hurtling through the universe at tremendous speed—can ever hope to live.[3]

This chapter reviews two related features of the future good life as anticipated by biblical prophets. The first section looks at the transformation of nature, particularly, plants, agriculture, and trees that would flourish in the messianic or coming age. The second section examines texts that refer to the presence of animals, birds, and other creatures in that future era.

A. PLANTS, HARVESTS, AND TREES

Several prophets assured their contemporaries that in the coming age—typically identified by the expression "in that day"[4]—YHWH/God would provide plentiful blessings for his people, indeed, for "all peoples." Fields, vineyards, and orchards would yield abundant harvests, vines and trees would bear ample fruit, and other trees would provide shade and shelter for all. It is noteworthy that, just as nearly all biblical tradition reflects a positive evaluation of the present world and of life in it, so likewise, various prophets visualized the coming age as a material, albeit transformed, world where life would flourish even more fully than it had in the past.

---

3. See Tull, *Inhabiting Eden*, 151: "There isn't another world like this within reach of human travel. No more frontiers can open up. The moon and Mars, everywhere else we could possibly escape to, we could have to artificially make our own reality, and it wouldn't be like this one, full of daisies we never planted. We can't discard this one. We have to mend it. It is not indestructible, but under favorable conditions it is, like all creatures including ourselves, resilient." Tull continues: "One of the Christian enemies of the environmental movement is the hope for escape from this world because, as the 'Countdown' song goes, 'Somewhere in outer space God has prepared a place for all those who trust him and obey'": the hope that it doesn't matter what we do to this earth, since we will be gone. Ronald Reagan's controversial Secretary of the Interior from 1981 to 1983, James Watt, has frequently been quoted as saying during his term that the earth is 'merely a temporary way station on the way to the road to eternal life.'" Tull, *Inhabiting Eden*, 156.

4. Such biblical terms as "in that day" often also refer to the pending time of judgment against nations or peoples. In many such texts, this time of judgment was expected to precede the beginning of the new or messianic age. See Richard Hiers, "Day of the Lord."

Isaiah 25:6[5] looks for such a time in terms of feasting on "fat" or rich and tasty food and drinking fine wine:

> On this mountain YHWH of hosts
> will make for all peoples
> a feast of rich food filled with marrow,
> of well-aged wine strained clear.[6]

Another text in Isaiah offers assurance that in the time to come, "the wilderness" would become "a fruitful field, and the fruitful field . . . a forest" (Isa 32:15).[7] Isaiah 35, which may be part of Second Isaiah, evidently referred to the expected return of Jewish exiles from Babylon; but that expectation had clearly messianic overtones. Then, desert plants would "blossom abundantly":

> The wilderness and the dry land shall be glad,
> the desert shall rejoice and blossom;
> like the crocus it shall blossom abundantly,
> and rejoice with joy and singing. (Isa 35:1a–c)[8]

Ezekiel sets forth an oracle of "the Lord God" envisioning a huge tree that would provide shade and shelter for "all kinds of beasts" and "all kinds of birds" in the future age or era:

> Thus says the Lord God: "I myself will take a sprig from the lofty top of the cedar, and will set it out; I will break off from the topmost of its young twigs a tender one, and I myself will plant it upon a high and lofty mountain; on the mountain height of Israel will I plant it, that it may bring forth boughs and bear fruit, and become a noble cedar; and under it will dwell all kinds of beasts; in the shade of its branches birds of every sort will nest. And all the trees of the field shall know that I YHWH bring low the high tree, and make high the low

---

5. Isa 25:6 is sometimes considered part of the Isaiah Apocalypse or Fourth Isaiah, and usually dated after the exile.

6. See also Hos 2:21–23. As to intertestamental, Talmudic, and early Christian beliefs in this connection, see Richard Hiers, *Jesus and the Future*, 72–86.

7. Isa 32:19, which refers to destruction of forest and city, probably belongs with Isa 32:9–14, which warned of more immediate desolation in historical time.

8. See Isa 35:10 as to additional messianic overtones: "And the ransomed of YHWH shall return . . . ; everlasting joy shall be upon their heads; they shall obtain joy and gladness, and sorrow and sighing shall flee away." See also Ezek 34:26–30.

tree, dry up the green tree, and make the dry tree flourish."
(Ezek 17:22–24 RSV)

Here it is said that YHWH/God's sovereignty or dominion would be not only experienced but also *known* by "all the trees of the field."

Another text in Ezekiel reports a vision in which the prophet sees a river where "every living creature which swarms[9] will live," which will be full of fish of "a great many kinds." This river would be bordered on either side by "all kinds of trees for food" bearing fresh fruit all year long and also providing their leaves "for healing."

> "As I came back, I saw on the bank of the river a great many trees on the one side and on the other. He said to me, ". . . Wherever the river goes, every living creature that swarms will live, and there will be very many fish; once these waters reach there. It will become fresh; and everything will live where the river goes. People will stand fishing beside the sea from Engedi to Eneglaim; it will be a place for the spreading of nets; its fish will be of a great many kinds, like the fish of the Great Sea. . . . On the banks, on both sides of the river, there will grow all kinds of trees for food. Their leaves will not wither nor their fruit fail, but they will bear fresh fruit every month, because the water for them flows from the sanctuary. Their fruit will be for food, and their leaves for healing." (Ezek 47:7–12)

That leaves and other plant materials might provide medicinal remedies, a fact long recognized by many native peoples, has only recently begun to be investigated by Western pharmaceutical companies. This text suggests that in the messianic age, people will still catch and eat fish.[10] It also takes a positive view of the prospect that there would be "very many fish" of "a great many kinds" and evidently expects that fish would always be plentiful. Modern-day overfishing and water pollution crises were not contemplated or anticipated.

The prophets Joel and Amos present the most vivid images of agricultural abundance in the messianic age. According to Joel:

---

9. Lev 11:29–33, 41–47 identifies "swarming" creatures and prohibits eating them.
10. See generally Richard Hiers and Kennedy, "Bread and Fish Eucharist."

> In that day
> the mountains shall drip sweet wine,
> > the hills shall flow with milk,
> and all the stream beds of Judah
> > shall flow with water. (Joel 3:18a–b)

Presumably grapes would still have to be picked and processed into wine, and cattle would still need to be milked, but evidently these activities would not be so burdensome as to require mention. Amos 9:13–15, sometimes attributed to a later prophet, likewise portrays the superabundant blessings of life in the coming age:

> "The time is surely coming," says YHWH,
> > "when the one who plows shall overtake the one who reaps,
> > and the treader of grapes the one who sows the seed;
> the mountains shall drip sweet wine,
> > and all the hills shall flow with it.
> I will restore the fortunes of my people Israel,
> > and they shall rebuild the ruined cities and inhabit them;
> they shall plant vineyards and drink their wine,
> > and they shall make gardens and eat their fruit.
> I will plant them upon their land,
> > and they shall never again be plucked up
> out of the land that I have given them,"
> says YHWH your God. (Amos 9:13–15)

Such texts suggest that the "curse" put upon "the ground" in ancient times would then be lifted or removed.[11] Those persons who would be so favored as to dwell in that future messianic era are visualized in an agricultural setting by other prophets as well:

> And they shall beat their swords into plowshares,
> > and their spears into pruning hooks;
> nation shall not lift up sword against nation,
> > neither shall they learn war any more;

---

11. See Gen 3:17–19: "Because you have listened to the voice of your wife, and eaten of the tree about which I commanded you, 'You shall not eat of it,' cursed be the ground because of you; in toil you shall eat of it all the days of your life; thorns and thistles it shall bring forth for you; and you shall eat plants of the field. By the sweat of your face you shall eat bread until you return to the ground." See also Gen 4:11–12: "And now you are cursed from the ground. . . . When you till the ground, it will no longer yield to you its strength."

> but they shall all sit under their own vine and under their
> own fig tree, for the mouth of YHWH of hosts has spoken.
> (Mic 4:3b–4)

A later biblical prophet visualized the future similarly: "On that day, says YHWH of hosts, every one of you shall invite each other to come under your vine and fig tree" (Zech 3:10). Jesus himself expected to find figs on a fig tree, even though "it was not the season for figs," possibly because he believed that the kingdom of God had come or soon would come near. Then all kinds of fruit would always be in season.[12] People would still have to work the ground with plows and prune their vines and orchards with pruning hooks, but they would enjoy the fruits of their labors in peace.[13]

Early in Genesis, the first man and the first woman lived in the garden of Eden, surrounded by all kinds of fruitful trees. The tree of life was also in the garden, but the man and woman never ate its fruit. The last "book" in the New Testament is the book of Revelation. The seer/author of this book promises that in the new age, particularly in the new Jerusalem, the righteous—those whose names were "written in the Lamb's book of life" (Rev 21:27)—would at last enjoy this tree's twelve kinds of fruit every month. This tree (or those trees) of life would line both sides of the river. The seer describes the scene to which he was conducted by one of the seven angels:

> Then he showed me the river of the water of life, bright as crystal, flowing from the throne of God and of the Lamb through the middle of the street of the city. On either side of the river is the tree of life with its twelve kinds of fruit, producing its fruit

---

12. Mark 11:12–14. See, e.g., Ezek 47:7–12, quoted above. See generally Richard Hiers, "Not the Season." Also Ntreh, "Introduction," 9: "In ancient Israel sitting under one's own oak trees and/or vineyard and drinking the product of one's own vine are seen as the ultimate blessings humans can obtain from God (cf. 1 Kgs 4:25, Mic 4:4, Zech 3:10). How can we receive the blessings of God when we destroy the sources of those blessings, that is the earth, the land?"

13. See also Isa 2:4b–c: "And they shall beat their swords into plowshares, and their spears into pruning hooks; nation shall not lift up sword against nation, neither shall they learn war any more." See also Jer 31:5: "Again you shall plant vineyards on the mountains of Samaria; the planters shall plant, and shall enjoy the fruit."

each month; and the leaves of the tree are for the healing of the nations. (Rev 22:1–2)[14]

Implicitly, eating this fruit would assure the partakers of eternal life.[15] The righteous would have access to these trees; all other persons would be barred (Rev 22:14–15, 18–19). This text seems to represent an elaboration upon the vision set out in Ezek 47:6–12. According to Ezekiel, in the coming age all kinds of fruit-bearing trees would grow on both sides of the river; in Revelation, perhaps only one kind of tree would be there, the tree of life,[16] but it would bear twelve different kinds of fruit.[17] In both Ezekiel and Revelation, the trees were expected to bear fresh fruit every month, and their leaves would be "for healing." Here, again, is the hope that preternatural fertility and abundance would characterize the new age. The Revelation text does not say whether its writer believed that other creatures would share the blessings of life in this new era.

B. PEOPLE, ANIMALS, AND OTHER CREATURES

In the book of Genesis, YHWH/God's primordial covenant with "every living creature of all flesh that is upon the earth" was said to be "the everlasting covenant," effective "for all future generations" (Gen 9:8–17).[18] Consistent with this promise or expectation, many biblical writings anticipate that all kinds of creatures will enjoy the

---

14. See also Rev 2:7b: "To everyone who conquers, I will give permission to eat from the tree of life that is in the paradise of God."

15. See also Rev 21:3–4.

16. Since "the tree" grew on "either side of the river," the seer evidently visualized more than one such tree. The expression "the tree" probably was used generically, referring to the type of tree. In an earlier vision, the book of Revelation proclaims that a third of the earth, a third of its trees, and a third of all green grass would be burnt up as part of the coming time of judgment (Rev 8:7).

17. Compare 2 Esd 2:12–18: "The tree of life shall give them fragrant perfume...; I have consecrated and prepared for you twelve trees loaded with various fruits."

18. Baruch likewise implies that YHWH/God intended other creatures to inhabit the earth for all time: "The one who prepared the earth for all time filled it with four-footed creatures" (Bar 3:32b).

new or transformed conditions of life in the coming or messianic age.

The prophet Hosea declared that in this coming age, YHWH/God would make a covenant of peace with his people and with all kinds of creatures of field, air, and ground:

> I will make for them a covenant on that day
>   with the wild animals [or beasts of the field],
>   the birds of the air,
>   and the creeping things of the ground;
> and I will abolish the bow, the sword,
>   and war from the land;
> and I will make you lie down in safety. (Hos 2:18)[19]

"Wild animals," "birds of the air," and "creeping things of the ground" included all types of creatures that had been with Noah on the ark.[20] YHWH/God had meant for them all to "be fruitful and multiply" afterwards.[21] As will be seen, other biblical texts also expect that in the messianic age humans and all other creatures will live together in peace and harmony.

A number of texts even suggest that in times to come, YHWH/God will drive out human populations, leaving places once occupied by people as habitat for other creatures. Some of these texts refer to the fate in store for surrounding nations. Other texts refer to that of Israel or Judah—YHWH/God's own special people. Both kinds of texts, in effect, designate places where people formerly dwelled as future wildlife refuges or habitat.

---

19. Compare Lev 26:6 (where the Israelites are told that if they obey YHWH/God's commandments, he "will remove dangerous animals from the land"), Ezek 34:25 (where the Lord God says that he will "banish wild beasts from the land"), and Job 5:22–23 (where as part of the good life, Job is told that he "shall not fear the wild animals of the earth" because "the wild animals shall be at peace" with him). See Towner, "Future of Nature," discussing several relevant biblical texts. Also see Wiley and Wiley, "Will Animals Be Redeemed?," reviewing modern theories but few biblical texts. And see McAfee, "Ecology and Biblical Studies," 38–41, describing recent observations by several biblical scholars concerning texts in both the OT and NT that anticipate "the redemption of nature as well as humans."

20. Gen 6:19–20; 7:14; 8:17.

21. Gen 8:17; see also Gen 1:22.

Several prophets proclaim that neighboring lands—lands belonging to sometime enemy nations—will be given to and occupied by various kinds of wildlife. For instance, as to Babylon:

> Wild animals will lie down there,
>   and its houses will be full of howling creatures;
> there ostriches will live
>   and there [satyrs][22] will dance.
> Hyenas will cry in its towers,
>   and jackals in its pleasant places. (Isa 13:21–22)[23]

Likewise, the prophet Jeremiah declared:

> Therefore wild animals shall live with hyenas in Babylon,
>   and ostriches shall inhabit her;
> she shall never again be peopled,
>   or inhabited for all generations. (Jer 50:39)[24]

What had been the land of Edom will become home for many, if not all, kinds of creatures: hawks, hedgehogs, owls, ravens, jackals, ostriches, wildcats, hyenas, satyrs, night hags,[25] other kinds of owls, and buzzards (Isa 34:11–15).

Seek and read from the book of YHWH.[26]

---

22. Or "goat-demons" (NRSV). The context indicates that satyrs probably were thought of as wild goats or other wild creatures, not—as commentators sometimes suggest—sinister supernatural beings of some sort. There are few evil beings in the Old Testament. Exceptions include Asmodeus, the demon-lover who (or which) is part of the story in the book of Tobit, and the "evil spirit from the Lord" that prompted Saul to throw a spear at David (1 Sam 19:9). The being who tempted the man and woman in the garden of Eden was the serpent—one of the good creatures YHWH/God had made (Gen 1:25, 31; 3:1). Satan appears in the book of Job as an overzealous prosecuting attorney in God's heavenly council, not as an evil being. Satan or the devil appear several places in the New Testament, most notably, perhaps, in the story of Jesus's temptation early in the Synoptic Gospels.

23. See also Isa 14:23, "And I will make it a possession of the hedgehog . . . says YHWH of hosts."

24. See also Jer 51:37: "And Babylon shall become a heap of ruins, a den of jackals, an object of horror and hissing, without inhabitant."

25. Or Lilith (Isa 34:14, NRSV). Again, the context suggests some kind of wildlife, such as bats or nighthawks, not supernatural beings. Later Judaism characterized Lilith as a female demon.

26. The "book of YHWH" may refer to Genesis, particularly the creation and flood stories, both of which list inclusively all kinds of living creatures. See Gen

> Not one of these shall be missing;
>> none shall be without [her] mate. . . .
> [YHWH] has cast the lot for them,
>> his hand has portioned it out to them with the line;
> they shall possess it forever,
>> from generation to generation they shall live in it.
>> (Isa 34:16–17)[27]

Birds of prey and "all the animals of the earth" will enjoy the bounty of Egyptian harvests (Isa 18:6). Flocks of animals will dwell amid the deserted cities of Syria; there "no one will make [the flocks] afraid" (Isa 17:1–2). Hazor, in Syria, will "become lair of jackals, an everlasting waste" (Jer 49:33). Nineveh, the capitol of Assyria, likewise will become a "dry waste," serving as another wildlife refuge:

> Herds shall lie down in it,
>> every wild animal;
> the desert owl and the screech owl
>> shall lodge in its capitals;
> the owl shall hoot at the window,
>> the raven croak on the threshold. (Zeph 2:14)

Some texts also anticipate a similar fate in store for Jerusalem, if not all the land of Israel or Judah:

> For the palace will be forsaken,
>> the populous city deserted;
> the hill and the watchtower
>> will become dens forever,
> the joy of wild asses,
>> a pasture for flocks. (Isa 32:14)

> I will make Jerusalem a heap of ruins,
>> a lair of jackals,
> and I will make the cities of Judah a desolation,
>> without inhabitant. (Jer 9:11)

1:20–25; 6:19–20; 7:2–3, 8–9, 13–16; 8:17–19; and 9:8–17.

27. See also Mal 1:3: "I have hated Esau; I have made his hill country a desolation and his heritage a desert for jackals." Biblical tradition considered Esau the forefather of the Edomites. Thus, as here, Esau often means Edom.

Other texts, however, offer assurances that YHWH/God will provide bountifully for both his people and other creatures in the messianic age.

> He will give rain for the seed with which you sow the ground,
>   and grain, the produce of the ground,
>   which will be rich and plenteous.
> On that day your cattle will graze in broad pastures;
>   and the oxen and [asses] that till the ground
>   will eat silage. (Isa 30:23–24)[28]
>
> Do not fear, you animals of the field,
>   for the pastures of the wilderness are green;
> the tree bears its fruit,
>   the fig tree and vine give their full yield. (Joel 2:22)

As has been noted previously, Ezek 17:22–23 describes a mighty and fruitful tree that will provide habitat for all kinds of beasts and birds in the messianic age:

> Thus says the Lord God: "I myself will take a sprig from the lofty top of the cedar, and will set it out; I will break off from the topmost of its young twigs a tender one, and I myself will plant it upon a high and lofty mountain; on the mountain height of Israel I will plant it, that it may bring forth boughs and bear fruit, and become a noble cedar; and under it will dwell all kinds of beasts; in the shade of its branches birds of every sort will nest." (Ezek 17:22–23 RSV)[29]

Cedar berries would be "fruit" or food for birds, and perhaps for some of the "beasts," though probably not suitable for human consumption. As has been seen, Ezekiel also expected that "swarming" creatures and water creatures will be present in the messianic age, at least in or near Jerusalem: "Wherever the river goes, every living

---

28. See also Isa 32:20, which suggests that in this future age, humans will no longer confine or harness domestic animals: "Happy you will be who . . . let the ox and the [ass] range freely." Compare Isa 30:24, quoted here, which says that these animals, though well provided for in the messianic age, will still serve to help "till the ground."

29. Other texts also picture great trees providing food or shelter for wildlife: Ps 104:16–17; Ezel 31:1–9, 13; Dan 4:10–12; Matt 13:31–32; Luke 13:18–19. Some of these texts may have had other symbolic meanings.

creature that swarms will live, and there will be very many fish" (Ezek 47:9).

A psalm embedded in the Prayer of Azariah calls on all creatures—including whales and all creatures that live in water, "birds of the air," and "all wild animals and cattle—to "bless the Lord," "sing praise to praise him and highly exalt him forever" (Sg Three, vv. 57–59). Likewise, the psalmist was assured that the time would come when "all flesh" will "bless [YHWH's] holy name forever and ever" (Ps 145:21). In order to do so forever, it would seem that all these creatures were expected to be among those participating in the fulfilled life of the messianic age.

Many other texts also suggest that both people and other creatures will enjoy life in the messianic age. The Messiah himself was expected to arrive in Jerusalem riding an ass's colt:

> Rejoice greatly, O daughter of Zion!
> Shout aloud, O daughter of Jerusalem!
> Lo, your king comes to you;
> triumphant and victorious is he,
> humble and riding on [an ass],
> on a colt, the foal of [an ass]. (Zech 9:9)[30]

According to Jeremiah, in the coming age, YHWH/God will "sow the house of Israel and the house of Judah with [both] the seed of humans and the seed of animals" (Jer 31:27). Here "animals" probably refers to domestic or farm animals. Similarly, Ezekiel declared, speaking for YHWH/God: "And I will multiply human beings and animals upon you. They shall increase and be fruitful" (Ezek 36:11). Several other texts likewise look for the inclusion of all kinds of creatures in the messianic age.

The writer of Isa 40:5, looking forward to the coming exiles' return from Babylon and the beginning of the messianic age, declares: "And the glory of YHWH shall be revealed, and *all flesh* shall see it together" (RSV, emphasis added).[31] In a similar vein, the book of Isaiah concludes with the reassuring promise:

30. Compare Gen 49:10–12; Matt 21:1–9; Mark 11:1–10; Luke 19:28–40; and John 12:12–16.

31. Compare NRSV: "all people." In this context, as in many other biblical passages, "all flesh" probably refers to all kinds of living creatures. See, e.g., Gen 7:15–16:

> "For as the new heavens and the new earth,
>   which I will make,
> shall remain before me," says YHWH;
>   "so shall your descendants and your name remain.
> From new moon to new moon,
>   and from Sabbath to Sabbath,
> all flesh shall come to worship before me,"
>   says YHWH. (Isa 66:22–23)[32]

The classic text depicting peace and harmony throughout all creation in the messianic age, of course, is Isa 11:6–9, commonly referred to as portraying "the peaceable kingdom."

> The wolf shall live with the lamb,
>   the leopard shall lie down with the kid,
> the calf and the lion and the fatling together,
>   and a little child shall lead them.
> The cow and the bear shall graze;
>   their young shall lie down together;
>   and the lion shall eat straw like the ox.
> The nursing child shall play
>   over the hole of the asp,
> and the weaned child shall put its
>   hand on the adder's den.
> They will not hurt or destroy
>   on all my holy mountain;
> for the earth shall be full of the knowledge of YHWH
>   as the waters cover the sea.[33] (Isa 11:6–9)

"They went into the ark with Noah, two and two of all flesh in which there was the breath of life. And those that entered, male and female of all flesh, went in as God had commanded him; and YHWH shut him in." See also Gen 7:21–22; 8:15–19; and 9:15–17, where "all flesh" also clearly refers to all kinds of living creatures, human and nonhuman alike.

32. Compare Ps 150:6: "Let everything that breathes praise YHWH!" See above, ch. 3.

33. Like many other texts that look forward to the coming or messianic age, this text makes no reference to a messiah. Some texts do look for a messiah, typically a descendant of King David. One late biblical text describes the young David in terms that may have been intended to anticipate conditions of life in the peaceable kingdom: "He played with lions as though they were young goats, and with bears as though they were lambs of the flock" (Sir 47:3).

Not only will there be peace between humans and formerly dangerous wildlife; peace and goodwill will be restored between erstwhile predators and their former prey. Implicitly, the animal kingdom will return to the vegetarian era that obtained until after the time of the flood.[34] This hope or promise is reiterated later in the book of Isaiah, by a prophet sometimes referred to as Third Isaiah:

> "The wolf and the lamb shall feed together,
>   the lion shall eat straw like the ox;
>   [and dust shall be the serpent's food.]
> They shall not hurt or destroy on all my holy mountain,"
>   says YHWH. (Isa 65:25)[35]

Some New Testament texts also intimate that many, or even all, kinds of creatures will be included in the coming or messianic age. All three Synoptic Gospels record Jesus's parable of the mustard seed, which, drawing on imagery in Ezek 17:22–24, associates the coming kingdom of God with such a seed's miraculous growth into a great shrub or tree where "the birds of the air" could "come and make nests in its branches."

> The kingdom of heaven is like a mustard seed that someone took and sowed in his field; it is the smallest of all the seeds, but when it has grown it is the greatest of shrubs and becomes

---

34. See Gen 1:29–30: "God said, 'See, I have given you every plant yielding seed that is upon the face of all the earth, and every tree with seed in its fruit; you shall have them for food. And to every beast of the earth, and to every bird of the air, and to everything that creeps on the earth, everything that has the breath of life, I have given every green plant for food.' And it was so."

35. Commenting on this text, and also on the vegetarian world that preceded the great flood, Rogerson observes: "The importance for biblical readers of a violence-free world lay not in the *fact* of its supposed existence, but in the way in which it witnessed to a possible form of existence that was also a radical criticism of the actual world of human experience. The story of the original creation and the hope for its restoration were judgments upon the present state of the world, and imperatives for action to achieve as much of the vision as was humanly possible." Rogerson, "What Was the Meaning," 12–13.

See also Ferre, *Hellfire and Lightning Rods*, 180, commenting on Isa 11:6–9: "Beyond domination and injustice, lies the messianic promise of a society, under God, in harmony with itself and with the universe."

a tree, so that the birds of the air come and make nests in its branches. (Matt 13:31–32)[36]

As has been seen, many Old Testament texts also expressed the expectation that birds of many, perhaps all species, will enjoy life in the coming age.[37]

Mark 16:15 tells that the risen Jesus instructed "the eleven" disciples: "Go into all the world and preach the good news to the whole creation."[38] And the author of Col 1:23, possibly Paul, declared that by his time, "the gospel" already had "been proclaimed to every creature under heaven." This preaching evidently was intended to prepare hearers for entrance into the coming age or kingdom of God. These texts imply that "the whole creation" or "every creature under heaven" were all meant to take part in that coming age. These texts probably inspired St. Francis of Assisi to preach to birds and other creatures—as he is said to have done, at least according to popular legend. Elsewhere, Paul wrote that "the whole creation has been groaning in labor pains until now," and that when the new age comes, "the creation itself will be set free from its bondage to decay and will obtain the freedom of the glory of the children of God" (Rom 8:21–22).[39] The implication is that in the new age, all creation, including humans and all other creatures, will be as "the children of God."

The book of Revelation includes many visions of the future. Some of these have to do with dramatic and catastrophic occurrences at the end of the present age.[40] In one of these, twenty-four

---

36. See also Mark 4:30–32; Luke 13:18–19.

37. See, e.g., Isa 12:21; 34:11, 15–16; Ezek 17:23; Hos 2:18; and Zeph 2:14.

38. This "longer ending to Mark," as biblical scholars call it, also intimates that in the new age, or just before it dawns, "those who believe" will be able to "pick up snakes" (Mark 16:18). This prospect may have derived from Isa 11:8, where it is said that in the messianic age, young children will play over or near the dens of poisonous snakes.

39. See also Col 1:20.

40. Dawson sees these and many other biblical texts as poetic reflections on both historical events and proto scientific sidereal expectations. Dawson, *Nature and the Bible*, 68: "Such pictures point not only to eclipses and meteorite showers, but to cosmic possibilities now present in the minds of astronomers; to the decay of the solar energy, and to the necessity of a renewal of our world, and to the chances of changes implied in the cometary and meteoritic matter which haunts our system."

elders and "four living creatures" are visualized singing a never-ending hymn of praise:

> Holy, holy, holy,
>   the Lord God Almighty,
>   who was and is and is to come!
>
> You are worthy, our Lord and God,
>   to receive glory and honor and power,
> for you created all things,
>   and by your will they existed and were created. (Rev 4:8, 11)[41]

Here, again, God is remembered and praised for having created everything that has ever existed. By implication, all that has ever been has been good. As it was in the beginning.[42]

Again, looking into the future, and, in accordance with the prospect and promise of Isa 66:22–23 and the import of some of these NT texts, the seer-author of Revelation declares:

> Then I heard every creature in heaven and on earth and under the earth and in the sea, and all that is in them, singing, "To the one seated on the throne and to the Lamb be blessing and honor and glory and might forever and ever." (Rev 5:13)[43]

Revelation 5:13 represents a vision of conditions in the new age, or world to come, where "every creature in heaven and on earth and under the earth and in the sea" will be present, rejoicing and praising their Creator and Redeemer.

This vision is consistent with the many other biblical texts mentioned in this chapter that anticipate that all kinds of creatures will be included in the coming age or new world. There, at last, the conditions of life YHWH/God intended for all creation from the beginning will be established forever. In the meantime, while the present age endures, these other creatures are companions in their

---

41. Compare Isa 6:3: "Holy, holy, holy is the Lord of hosts; the whole earth is full of his glory."

42. See Gen 1:1–31, culminating in the inclusive affirmation: "God saw everything that he had made, and indeed, it was very good." See above, ch. 1A, 1B.

43. Words echoed in Handel's *Messiah*. As to other ecological features of the book of Revelation, see Rossing, "River of Life."

common journeys through life in this world. Their lives and well-being are important to God, and also to those humans who worship him and affirm the goodness of the creation that God brought into being and, in his mercy, continues to sustain.

CHAPTER 12

Summary and Concluding Reflections

THIS BOOK HAS IDENTIFIED and considered several hundred biblical texts and then grouped or organized them on the basis of their respective themes or concerns. The summary that follows necessarily cannot do justice to all the particular features of biblical tradition examined in the preceding pages. It may be helpful, however, to review some of its central or recurrent understandings and motifs. This chapter then concludes with some theological and ethical reflections by insightful commentators. These underscore the point that biblical affirmations and understandings as to nature call into question all versions of contemporary secular and religious anthropocentrism. In common, these anthropocentric ideologies hold that nature has meaning and value only to the extent that it is or may be useful to human beings. Biblical faith and understanding have been shown to be fundamentally theocentric.

A. SUMMARY

The Bible consistently affirms that God created all that exists: everything that lives, the whole world, and the entire cosmos. Implicitly, all that is is good, for it is God who made it. That all that God made is good is also stated explicitly and emphatically. Moreover, all things that exist, including all kinds of creatures—both great and small—belong to God.[1]

This foundational faith-understanding has clear implications for environmental ethics based upon it. People who wish to live in accordance with biblical faith will therefore regard the creation with awe and respect, as God's handiwork, and appreciate its goodness and the goodness of all forms of life. Since God is the ultimate owner of all nature, humans have no license to claim any of it, land, sea, air, or any parts of "space" as their own, either as a permanent possession or as mere raw material that can be degraded or destroyed for human purposes. Seen in biblical perspective, trashing or polluting the earth, its air, and seas or other waters amounts to desecration.[2] All that is is good, and all belongs to God. There is no place in biblical tradition for the popular modernist notion that the proper task or destiny of humankind is the "conquest of nature" or the "conquest of space."

Biblical tradition consistently affirms that God is Sovereign over all creation. It is he who has dominion, which he exercises both over human affairs and over the creation or nature. This sovereignty often is represented in the form of God's compassionate care for the creation and for all creatures: for the earth, the land, for all that grows upon it, and for all living creatures, human and nonhuman alike. Water is another expression of God's compassionate care: whether as rain, streams, rivers, or however found, water is God's gift to the land and to all life. He also made or set apart the seas and created all kinds of marine creatures for his own purposes.

---

1. As has been noted, some NT texts represent Christ as the Creator, and certain texts affirm that all things were created for him. These texts at least implicitly affirm the goodness of all creation.

2. See Asamoah-Gyado, "Foreword," xii: "The Bible has much to say about ecotheology and that continued desacralization would spell the doom for the whole of humanity." Also at xiii: "In capitalism, profits remain the ultimate goal and therefore environmental exploitation in search of mineral wealth, harvesting precious trees, and the destruction of river bodies proceeds without much thought being given to the implications of these human activities for our future." See also Howell, "Reflections," 236.

The understanding that God is Sovereign over and compassionately cares for the land, the seas, and all living things has important implications for environmental ethics. Among these, that people who share this faith should recognize that God alone is Sovereign: that there is no biblical basis for the illusion that any particular people or generation of people—or even all of humankind—are entitled to treat themselves as masters or lords over God's creation or his creatures. Whatever "dominion" over other creatures the primordial human couple may have been granted, such dominion is limited, among other ways, by God's own continuing and ultimate dominion. Moreover, God's compassion for his creation and for all creatures indicates how humans, made in some way in "his own image," should relate themselves to the earth and other living species, whether flora or fauna. Namely, with appreciation, respect, and compassion.

Biblical traditions often say that not only humans but also many other creatures can and do call upon God for help in times of need, or in praise and thanks for his glories and for his care. That other creatures may do so is entirely in accord with the biblical understanding that God is the Giver of life and continues to care for all creatures. All creatures are precious in God's sight. Modern secular humanists sometimes dismiss any suggestion that humans and other creatures are similar as mere "anthropomorphism," as if humans had a monopoly on all desirable traits or characteristics found among known life-forms. As has been seen and will be recalled, biblical tradition sees many similarities between humans and other creatures. Recognizing such similarities means that other creatures are not so unlike "us" as to be regarded and treated casually as "its," mere mechanisms or lifeless "things."

At the same time, other creatures were not thought of as if they were human beings; nor does biblical tradition call for treating them as such. There is no suggestion that caring for wild or exotic species meant capturing and treating them as pets. Or putting them in zoos. Respect for living beings of other species meant recognizing them as the creatures they are and responding appropriately to their particular needs, including, in the case of wildlife, leaving them ample habitat of their own, undisturbed by human activity.

As the Genesis story is told, following the great flood, God instructed Noah and his sons to "be fruitful and multiply" and "fill the earth." Interpreters sometimes read these instructions as authorizing perpetual multiplication of humankind, to the exclusion and detriment of all other species. It turns out, however, that this instruction was given at a time when the human population had been reduced to a mere handful of persons: Noah and his immediate family. It was not repeated later in the biblical narrative; and various texts imply that the task of replenishing the human race already had been completed within biblical times. Moreover, not only early humankind was so instructed. The forebears of all kinds of creatures were also instructed or expected to "be fruitful and multiply." There is no biblical warrant for the idea that humans were to keep on being fruitful and multiplying, filling the land with their offspring and crowding out other species. Rather, earth's habitat was to be shared by the descendants of both Noah and all other creatures whose ancestors were on the "ark" or in the sea: in short, all kinds of living beings.

After the flood, the primordial era of vegetarianism came to an end. Now humans were authorized to eat other creatures. But with an important qualification: they were not to "eat flesh with its life, that is, its blood." The life of all creatures killed for food was to be respected. Later biblical laws provided that when creatures were sacrificed or otherwise killed for food, their blood was to be returned either to the ground or at YHWH/God's altar. Moreover, under biblical law, God's people might kill only "clean" animals for food. There was no authorization to kill animals for sport or trophies, or to demonstrate or augment personal prowess or man- (or woman-) hood.

Immediately following the account of God's telling Noah and his family to "be fruitful and multiply" and his granting them permission to kill animals for food comes the account of the covenant that God then made not only with Noah and his sons but also with all kinds of living creatures for all future generations. In this covenant, God promised never again to cause a flood that would "cut off all flesh" and "destroy the earth." That this covenant extended to all living creatures of all flesh is stated five distinct times, in order to emphasize this point. God's concern for all kinds of creatures was believed to extend throughout all time and beyond that, into the future messianic age. God was understood to value every kind of creature, that is, every animate species. Whatever position one might take as to the evolution of species, the biblical understanding is that no species was unimportant, let alone dispensable. Humans were not authorized to cause the extinction of any species. Rather, if God made his covenant with all species, humans also should respect all species, not just those that might serve human needs or interests.

Many biblical laws pertain to sacrificing animals as offerings to God. The initial dynamic may have been recognition that since all life comes from God, some animals or parts of animals killed for food should be returned to him. This recognition appears to underlie laws requiring the offering of firstborn animals and firstfruits of fields and orchards. Biblical laws specify, however, that when animals are sacrificed or killed for food, their blood—which was believed to constitute their life—should be returned to God in one way or another. Their lives came from God and should go back to him. Not only each species but each living creature was precious before God. Many biblical voices, moreover, protested that God did not need or desire animal sacrifices: all creatures already belonged to him; they were already his. In the course of time, biblical people—both Jews and Christians—abandoned the practice of offering animal sacrifices. Nevertheless, the underlying rationale for offering sacrifices, for requiring that the blood of sacrificial animals be returned to God, and for opposing sacrificial offerings remains instructive in our time. The rationale is this: that every single animal's life is valued by God and, therefore, to be respected. This rationale has many important implications. We sometimes say that animals should be treated "humanely." From a biblical standpoint, they should be treated as God's creatures, with respect and care. That would mean avoiding such practices as are common in factory farming, or in educational and scientific or commercial circles, such as repetition of unnecessary animal experiments.

Such experiments often kill or inflict unnecessary pain on laboratory animals, whether in biology and zoology classes, medical school instruction, and in drug and cosmetics research. It would mean consideration as to how domestic animals are raised, transported, and slaughtered for food. Hunting, trapping, and fishing techniques also would be of concern, as would many other matters, such as boating speeds in areas with marine mammals, turtles, or other vulnerable creatures; and constructing buildings in ways that minimize fatalities to migrating birds. In short, all kinds of decisions and actions known to cause other creatures pain or put their lives risk.

In the course of debates about evolution, as well as in modern discussions about relations between humans and other creatures, it has been commonplace for those who view "man" as the "measure of all things" to deny that humans and other creatures are in any way significantly alike. For centuries, various Western humanistic schools of thought have struggled to elevate the place of humans in the universe by denigrating other species. Biblical faith is not bothered by similarities between humans and other creatures. God made all alike from the same earth or ground and gave them all the same breath or spirit. Biblical faith also understood that humans and other creatures share a common fate: all return to the ground, whatever may become of their respective spirits afterwards. Moreover, all alike are subject to divine judgment: all experience or share similar consequences when humans violate the conditions of their existence before God. Human-made environmental catastrophes need not be attributed to divine judgment; yet, clearly, as in the case of global climate change and faulty oil drilling and transportation practices, ill-considered human activities can and do impact adversely—and fatally—both humans and many other species of living beings.

In accordance with the biblical prohibition as to making images of God, no biblical texts undertake to give a description of God's physical appearance. A few texts suggest that God was understood to have some human features; but at least as often, God is compared with nonhuman creatures. Sometimes humans are compared with other creatures, and in a very few instances, the other creatures are seen to be inferior in some respect. The comparisons often point to ways in which humans and other creatures alike are deficient; others to ways in which both are to be admired, so that the comparison to other creatures comes as a compliment to the human. Certain creatures are said to be much more powerful than people and thus not subject to human dominion or control. And sometimes wiser than humans.

In biblical times many people viewed other creatures with considerable interest. Biblical texts often report careful observations and show appreciation, or even awe, in regard to the ways and capabilities of other living things. A number of such texts hold up certain creatures as models for humans to imitate or emulate. Observation and appreciation of other creatures shows a positive evaluation of their importance. Such creatures are generally understood to have been endowed by their Creator with certain special gifts. These texts show that other creatures were respected. Despite occasional protestations by modern secular humanists that humans are—or surely *must be*—inherently superior to other creatures, it is common knowledge that life sciences consider other creatures so similar to humans that experiments performed, for instance, on mice, rats, rabbits, dogs, and pigs, can provide important information as to how humans may respond to similar treatment.[3] People in biblical times probably would not have been shocked or humiliated to learn that human beings and many other life-forms share much of the same DNA.

From these related considerations, people informed by biblical values might well conclude that humans should regard other creatures as fellow beings, similar in some ways, different in others, but in any case, worthy of respect for being the creatures they are, whether or not they may resemble humans. That many other creatures experience pain, pleasure, fear, and other emotions is now well established. As are the facts that many species live their lives in the context of highly developed social organizations and

---

3. Also animal organs as transplant replacements for human organs.

that members of many species effectively communicate with one another in ways humans are only beginning to comprehend.[4]

Many biblical texts either imply or explicitly call upon those faithful to God to care for his creation and for other creatures with consideration. Biblical tradition supports a "land ethic" that includes proper care for the land itself and for living things that grow upon it. That the land belongs to God means that it should be cared for and protected against overuse, pollution, or other forms of degradation. Like God's people, the land itself must be allowed to rest for its own good. God may grant people the use of his land, but all land remains his to take back if he so chooses. Modern forms of pollution are, to be sure, different and infinitely more toxic than in biblical times. But the principle remains the same: all the earth belongs to God; people must be careful not to defile or pollute it. In biblical perspective, humans are honored with the task of tilling or serving the soil and tending the garden. In modern times, such tending and care might be extended to mean soil conservation and protecting land—whether agricultural, forests, wilderness, or wetlands—from destructive development and harmful industrial activities.

That the land belongs to God also has certain implications for how people distribute its fruits. In various ways, biblical laws call for sharing the produce of fields and the fruit of vineyards and orchards with those in the community who are unable to provide for themselves. These laws could be seen as representing concern for what now sometimes is called eco-justice.

In biblical times, there was apparently no danger that human activities might result in loss of fields and prairies, forests and woodlands that sustained people and provided habitat for other creatures. Nor, of course, was anything known about the role of trees and other vegetation (and phytoplankton) in making the critically important carbon dioxide-oxygen cycle. There was, nevertheless, concern that trees should not be destroyed unless such destruction was necessary in time of war, for trees, like everything else, provide food and shelter for many life-forms. Moreover, trees

---

4. Conventional references to "dumb" animals often mean only that humans have not yet learned to understand their languages.

and plants, made by God who found them "good," belong to him. There is no biblical warrant for wanton destruction of trees or other vegetation.[5]

Many laws, along with other types of biblical tradition, provided people in biblical times with explicit guidelines for what Albert Schweitzer called "reverence" or "respect for life." The most dramatic narrative instance, of course, was Noah's role in constructing a huge ship in order to provide safe passage for all kinds of species that otherwise would have gone extinct because of the great flood. Biblical laws provided for humane treatment of domestic animals: special consideration was to be given to animal mothers and their newborn offspring; lost or distressed animals were to be assisted, oxen were to be free to graze or browse while treading out grain, and work animals were to be allowed to rest on the Sabbath day and the Sabbatical Year. Provisions also were made for wildlife: nesting mother birds were to be left free in order to preserve their species; and during Sabbatical Years some of the produce of fields, vineyards, and orchards was to be left for wildlife to "glean" or forage. Both Old and New Testament texts also show concern for the well-being of birds and other animals.

Contemporary ethicists tend to assume that ethics is concerned only with human agency. There are, of course, trained rescue and seeing-eye dogs, and stories about dogs or cats alerting and saving people from fires, or porpoises rescuing people from drowning. But generally, people look to other people for help. Biblical narratives, on the other hand, describe several instances where other creatures come to the aid of persons. The most notable example, of course, is in the parable of Jonah,[6] where the "great fish," acting on instructions from God, saves Jonah from drowning and helps send him on his mission to Nineveh. Likewise, ethicists usually suppose that only human beings can be agents for justice. Yet many wisdom texts, along with others, represent various creatures as agents of God's judgment against unrighteous individuals

---

5. Since early times, Christian ethicists have had strangely little to say about concern for the life and well-being of plants and trees. And not much to say about human activities resulting in the extinction of tree and plant species.

6. See Richard Hiers, *Reading the Bible*, 86–88.

or peoples. And many prophetic texts, along with others, declare that a wide range of creatures are or have acted as agents of God's judgment against the people of Israel and Judah, because of their transgressions, or will so act against them in the future, because of these people's failure to keep the terms of his covenants with them. Texts in the book of Revelation in the New Testament also anticipate that wild animals and "all the birds that fly in mid-heaven" will be called on to act as agents of divine judgment by devouring the flesh of the wicked. These texts substantially are in accord with the secular, commonplace wisdom clichés, e.g., "Nature bats last" or "has the last word."

Such texts as these appear to undermine the notion that, in biblical faith, humans were given permanent dominion over other creatures. It has been noted that God's authorizing the first man and the first women to "have dominion" over other creatures and to "subdue the earth" were not repeated to their descendants after the great flood. As the story is told, the flood destroyed nearly all humankind because the LORD had seen "that the wickedness of humankind was great in the earth, and that every imagination of the thoughts of their hearts was only evil continually." Although Noah himself was deemed "a righteous man," it seems that his descendants (all humankind, as the story is told) were not to be entrusted with such authority again. Many texts refer to God's care for wild creatures or to such creatures enjoying life in their own habitats, apart from human activity, much less "dominion." Such texts indicate that God intended many kinds of animals to be left alone, to range free. As has been seen, only God himself will have dominion in the coming age, and then his dominion will extend to all creation.

All Old Testament texts that look forward to the coming or messianic age visualize that era taking place on earth, albeit a radically transformed earth, sometimes referred to as the "new world." Jesus likewise evidently was looking for the establishment of God's kingdom on earth when he taught his followers to pray and prepare for the coming of God's kingdom. Then God's will will be done on earth, as it already is being done in heaven.

As portrayed in many biblical texts, the coming age will be that time when everything would be made right: where God's creation will at last be freed from all corrupting influences, most notably, human lust for power and glory. Or dominion. Then humans and all other creatures will, at last, live together in peace, everlasting peace. In this new world, people will no longer offer animal sacrifices. They might then continue to serve God by tilling the soil and tending vines and fruit trees, but now fields, vineyards, and orchards will yield abundant harvests. Several prophets anticipated that in this future era, various kinds of wildlife will have for their own permanent habitat some places formerly occupied by humans.

The expectation that flora and fauna will flourish in the coming age may seem strange to those who were brought up believing the Bible says that God cares only about humankind. Yet as expressed in Ps 145, quoted at the beginning of this book, the biblical God was believed to be "good to all" and to have compassion "over all that he has made." A late biblical wisdom saying likewise summed up the nature of divine compassion: "The compassion of man is for his neighbor, but the compassion of the Lord is for all living beings" (Sir 18:13). Recognition of God's compassion for all creation and all creatures is also attested by many other texts considered in this book. It should not, therefore, be surprising that biblical faith, which consistently affirms that God found everything he had made to be good, would include all creation and all creatures in that new age when he will bring to fulfillment his original purposes in calling into existence everything that was, and is, and is to be.

The relevance of this biblical hope and expectation for environmental ethics parallels and expresses core beliefs witnesses throughout biblical tradition: that because God made and values all that he has made, giving special care to living creatures, it follows that those who affirm this same God as the basis for faith, hope, and love should likewise extend their care to the whole of creation. No species, no creature is unworthy of respect and compassion and care—however problematic it may be for those who so believe to adjust their and our competing or conflicting interests in this world. The biblical hope is that in the future messianic age, God himself will somehow transform such conflicts and make things right for all creatures and the entire creation. Implicitly, these texts, along with the Genesis texts describing ancient paradise, provide standards of faith, hope, and love that could and should guide and human conduct in the long interim between the paradise lost and the future time of redemption and transformation.[7]

B. CONCLUDING REFLECTIONS

Although Native Americans and many other indigenous peoples have long been engaged in protecting the natural environment from degradation, most Americans and Europeans have only recently begun to realize how precarious life here on planet Earth has now become. Publication of Rachel Carson's *Silent Spring* marks the beginning of such recognition. A decade later, important studies like Meadows's *Limits to Growth* and Commoner's *Closing Circle* brought a series of critical issues to widespread public attention. A few decades earlier, Albert Schweitzer, writing about what he called the philosophy and ethics of "reverence for life" addressed many such concerns.[8] Schweitzer reviewed world religions and traditional philosophies and found them, for the most part, strangely indifferent to animals' suffering and cruel death at

---

7. See Murphy, *Haunted by Paradise*.

8. See Schweitzer's essay on "Ethics of Reverence." Schweitzer's term, *Ehrfurcht*, translated commonly as "reverence," can also be read to mean "respect" or "awe." As has been seen, many biblical texts express or call for respect or awe in regard to other creatures. By "reverence for life," Schweitzer affirmed the value of all living things, including, but not only, that of human beings.

Sometimes Schweitzer has been criticized for being concerned only about nonhuman beings. That is a profound misreading of his life and thought. Witness his long career in Africa as a medical doctor and his efforts, along with those by Albert Einstein, to prevent nuclear war—efforts for which both Alberts were awarded the Nobel Peace Prize. Schweitzer's contributions to modern environmental awareness are carefully examined by Ice, *Schweitzer*, 99–125. See also J. Cobb, *Is It Too Late*, 35–36.

See also Heide, *My Father's World*, 160: "I have to ask myself the question, 'If God loves this creation, shouldn't Christians also love it?' . . . Albert Schweitzer cared deeply for animals and humanity. He would often compare love for humanity with love for the whole creation. Understanding love as the heart of any concern shown humans or animals, he stated, 'Anyone who has accustomed himself to regard the life of any living creature as worthless is in danger of arriving at the idea of worthless human lives.'"

the hands of humans.[9] Somewhat more recently, the philosopher Mary Midgley developed a careful analysis and critique of typical rationalizations offered in justification of such indifference.[10] Contrary to defensive claims by those who see animal interests and human interests in conflict, as if they were mortal opponents in a zero-sum game, Schweitzer, Carson, Meadows, Commoner, Midgley, and many others[11] who shared their concerns cared deeply about both animal welfare and human welfare.

Now global warming and other catastrophic consequences of climate change have greatly accentuated the kinds of concerns already raised by Carson and others in regard to the future of the Earth as the critical habitat for living things. Albert Gore's *An Inconvenient Truth*—the film and the book alike—cites virtually unanimous scientific studies that leave no room for doubt that both human and nonhuman planetary populations are already in serious trouble, and that much worse is yet to come.[12] Gore correctly characterized global warming as fundamentally a moral issue, in that much, if not most, global warming is attributable to human activity. Moreover, humans have the capacity to do something about their contribution to this effect. Modern technology provides the means to slow, if not reverse, the pattern of rising temperatures and to reduce the outflow of toxic pollutants into the air and onto the Earth's surfaces and waters, and other environmentally destructive activities and their consequences. The critical question is *whether* humankind will choose to do what is necessary to avoid, or at least mitigate, these kinds of present and pending catastrophes. Human beings, who have so far managed to bring about the extinction of hundreds of thousands of species, and daily destroy millions of living organisms, have not yet been able to *create* even a single living cell.

What happens to people and what happens to other living things is a matter of moral concern—but only if there is some basis for making moral judgments. Western religions provide such

9. See also Blumenson, "Who Counts Morally?"
10. Midgley, *Animals*.
11. See above, preface to this book.
12. See also Gore's earlier book, *Earth in the Balance*.

basis.[13] And biblical tradition is the foundation for Judaism and Christianity. Biblical perceptions and affirmations as to nature and living things are more significant and relevant than either proponents or critics of Judaism and Christianity commonly assume.

Most modern Western philosophers[14] have tended to assume that moral judgments can and should be concerned solely with humans. What was deemed "right" or "good" was what was believed beneficial to human beings. What was deemed "wrong" or "bad" was what was thought harmful to humans. In short, the ethics of most such philosophy is humanistic or anthropocentric: that is to say, an ethics grounded upon the premise that human beings—but only human beings—are valuable and that what happens to them alone matters.[15] To the extent that only humans are valued, it is not surprising that other life-forms tend either to be ignored or regarded as having only instrumental value, that is, important or worthy of existence and care only if they happen to contribute to human well-being or might conceivably do so at some time in the future. From the standpoint of such anthropocentric ethics, humankind is the center of value or fundamental measure of worth. By way of contrast, from a theocentric perspective, all creation and all creatures or beings—including human beings—are perceived and affirmed as worthy of existence and care by virtue of their relation to God, the ultimate Source and Valuer of all that is.[16] The present study demonstrates that biblical ethics is fundamentally theocentric.

---

13. "Religious ideas and traditions may not be directly involved in the organization of a community. But they are the ultimate sources of the moral standards from which political principles are derived." Reinhold Niebuhr, *Children of Light*, 125. Other religious traditions also express concern for what we call environmental ethics. See, e.g., the series of articles in the online journal *Forum on Religion and Ecology* (http://fore.research.yale.edu/main.html) and the many references in Taylor et al., *Encyclopedia of Religion and Nature*.

14. Cf. recent so-called postmodernist philosophy, which urges (or presupposes) that there is no normative basis for making any kind of moral judgments, and that people can only have conversations about such matters.

15. For example, utilitarian ethics, where the "greatest good for the greatest number" implicitly refers to the greatest good for the greatest number *of human beings*.

16. For a fuller elaboration of relational value theory, see H. Richard Niebuhr's essay "The Center of Value," in *Radical Monotheism*, 100–113.

In our time, not even a humanistic or anthropocentric ethics can be taken for granted or assumed to be operative. It has become all too apparent in modern (and purportedly postmodern) times that human beings do not necessarily care about the well-being of other human beings. Filling this existential vacuum, many parochial or tribal systems of faith and ethics are alive and well. If not rampant. True-believing patriots or nationalists plan and act with a view to what they believe will protect or benefit their own tribe or nation. Those committed to the interests of their own class, race, ethnic, or religious group often, even typically, do not care about the well-being of persons associated with other commitments or communities, and may even regard them as enemies who must be defeated, destroyed, or at least suppressed. Moreover, in every era there are moral narcissists, practitioners of the ethics of autonomous individualism, who care only about protecting or promoting their own individual images and interests. In biblical times, too, there were many instances where nationalist or tribal and individual self-interests were asserted to the detriment—and sometimes destruction—of other peoples.[17] On the other hand, there are many biblical texts that make clear the belief that the God of Israel was also the God of all nations and peoples, and that this God's mercy and compassion embraced all humankind.[18]

Similarly, in biblical tradition, some texts represent a humanistic or anthropocentric ethic: urging, in effect, that what is good is what is good for people (whether Israelites or other human communities) and that animals and other living things either do not count at all or have value only to the extent that they can be eaten or otherwise used for the benefit of human beings.[19] Yet, as we

17. For instance, the *herem* practice described and seemingly approved in the book of Joshua, which called for the destruction of enemy or indigenous peoples. See, e.g., Josh 10:28–40; 11:10–20. Or the nationalistic enthusiasm articulated by the prophets Nahum and Obadiah. On the other hand, biblical traditions are sharply critical of the ethics of autonomous individualism. Its first exemplar was Cain, who killed his brother in order to become number one (Gen 4:10–16). See also, e.g., 2 Sam 12:7–12; Prov 16:2, 18; Amos 4:1–3; 8:4–6; Wis 1:16—2:24; 3:10–11.

18. See, e.g., Isa 19:18–25, and the entire book of Jonah. See generally Richard Hiers, *Trinity Guide to Bible*, 25–26, and *Nation of Immigrants*.

19. See, e.g., Gen 9:2–3, and Singer's somewhat scathing comment in *Animal*

have seen in the previous chapters of this book, most biblical texts affirm the value of other creatures without regard to any possible ways they might serve human interests.

It is largely to the credit of the historian Lynn White, whose important 1967 article blamed Christianity in general, and the Bible in particular, for the emerging environmental crisis,[20] that numbers of modern biblical scholars subsequently began to revisit the Bible in order to determine whether there was more to be said.[21]

Since then, considerable attention has been given to biblical themes and texts that express appreciation of nature and all kinds living things.[22] One might even say that since White, a consensus has emerged among biblical scholars and others who have found that much more is to be said.

Biblical tradition informs the faith-understanding of a great many Jews and Christians the world over.[23] The fundamental biblical premise is that God created all that is, cares for his creation, exercises dominion over it, and calls on those who are faithful to

---

Liberation, 95: "There is nothing [elsewhere in the OT] to challenge the overall view set down in Genesis, that man is the pinnacle of creation, that all the other creatures have been delivered into his hands, and that he has divine permission to kill and eat them." The present book has pointed to a great deal of biblical tradition that places significant limits on human dominion, and affirms the value of other creatures not only because of but also apart from their value for human beings.

20. White, "Historical Roots," and his article, "What Hath Man Wrought?," where he contends that Christianity maintains that nature exists only to serve human uses. For careful critiques of White's position, see Cone, *Redacted Dominionism*; and above, ch. 4A.

21. See excerpts and citations in Scharper and Cunningham, *Green Bible*, and other secondary literature cited in footnotes and bibliography at the end of this book.

22. An extended bibliography listing important studies during the past few decades is available at the *Forum on Religion and Ecology* website (Bakken, "Christianity and Ecology Bibliography"). See also Hessel, "Bibliography"; and Hessel, "Christianity and Ecology."

23. Biblical themes that might be categorized as affirming nature or "reverence for life" have long informed Christian worship. Such themes, for example, come to expression in many traditional as well as modern hymns. However, prayers for the well-being of other living beings or the creation as a whole are strangely absent in typical Christian worship services. As to Jewish reflections on environmental concerns, see Coalition on the Environment and the Jewish Life, "What's Jewish?," and other sources cited above.

him to act in accordance with his purposes.[24] Biblical morality is grounded upon such faith.

People in contemporary society generally look to science to "solve" our "problems." Unfortunately, science, as such, can contribute little in the way of guidance to such critical questions as: when is a particular situation or trend a "problem"; what constitutes a "problem" or a "solution"; or what people *should* or *should not* do in relation to the environment, to other species, or to individual creatures. Questions like these are normative, that is, moral questions.[25] Certainly, science can provide basic information regarding such critical matters as likely consequences of climate change, air and water pollution, genetic engineering, resource depletion, overfishing, and disposal of toxic chemicals and nuclear waste. Such matters are critical because they are deemed harmful to persons and other living beings who are valued for normative reasons.[26] In biblical times, all these beings are affirmed as good, among other reasons, because God created them, found them "good," and cares for them. Science, on the other hand, as such, provides no basis for

---

24. See Heide, *My Father's World*, 175: "We should view the whole creation as our sacred trust from God. We should wish to serve it and watch out for its best interests the best way we know how. We should seek to restore the harmony of creation as best we can until He returns to restore it completely."

25. See Jonas, "Technology and Responsibility," §4, para. 5 (emphasis in original): "And what if the new kind of human action would mean that more than the interest of man alone is to be considered—that our duty extends farther and the anthropocentric confinement of former ethics no longer holds? . . . It would mean to seek not only the human good, but also the good of things extra-human, that is, to extend the recognition of 'ends in themselves' beyond the sphere of man and make the human good include the care for them. For such a role of stewardship no previous ethics has prepared us—and the dominant, scientific view of *Nature* even less. Indeed, the latter emphatically denies us all conceptual means to think of Nature as something to be honored, having reduced it to the indifference of necessity and accident, and divested it of any dignity of ends."

26. See Wilson, *Creation*. Wilson's scientific account of life-forms in our time is informed by a profound ethic of biophilia or "love of life," a faith and ethic that resembles closely Schweitzer's "philosophy" or ethics of reverence for life. See Wilson, *Creation*, 62–69 and 170n63. From this normative basis, Wilson urges, e.g., "*Save the Creation, save all of it! No lesser goal is defensible. However biodiversity arose, it was not put on this planet to be erased by any one species.*" Wilson, *Creation*, 89 (emphasis in original). Also, Wilson, *Creation*, 91: "Humanity must make a decision, and make it right now: conserve Earth's natural heritage, or let future generations adjust to a biologically impoverished world."

concern as to the welfare of humans or other living beings, or for making any kinds of value judgments or normative claims. That many scientists in fact are so concerned derives from their commitments to religious, humanistic, or biophilic ethics, not from the canons of science as such.[27]

It is not assumed here that the biblical texts described and discussed here were written in order to tell "us" what "we" or anyone else should do with respect to environmental issues confronting twenty-first-century decision-makers. Most of these issues had not yet surfaced in biblical times. Nevertheless, the attitudes and ethical standards inherent in these texts may serve as guideposts for those whose beliefs and values are informed by biblical attitudes, affirmations, and hopes.

Even people who consider themselves and their values entirely secular may be interested—and probably surprised—to learn that biblical tradition and law present, with a high degree of consistency, a coherent and ecologically affirming worldview. According to this worldview (or faith-understanding) all things that exist—not only humankind but all other kinds of living beings, including "creeping things," things that "swarm," as well as plants and trees—are good in the "eyes" of the God, who is the Source and Power of all being. Accordingly, both by implication, and often by explicit "word" of command or promise, all things that exist should be treated with respect and loving care by humans as well.

Until recently, it was commonly said that people should be concerned about environmental issues for the sake of future generations, or at least for that of their own grandchildren. It is now all too clear that the devastating effects of human indifference to and exploitation of "the environment" are now upon us. Too long we have grown accustomed to thinking that concern for the environment was just a matter of interest to "environmentalists." As if environmentalists were some kind of special interest group. Whether we recognize it or not, all people and living beings depend upon the health of this Earth's environment for survival. Now we are called to act not only to protect the environment for the sake of

---

27. See Rolston, "Bible and Ecology." For further reflections on religion, values, and science, see essays in H. Richard Niebuhr, *Radical Monotheism*.

future generations, or even just our children's future, but our own lives and those of all our other animate companions in being. All too clearly, our and their survival depends upon on the well-being of this good planet that has been given to us and all other living things by God's good grace. Given to us to share and enjoy: but only if we honor the Creator of all that is and respond with care for his creation.

We may take comfort in recalling the covenant God made with Noah and every other living thing to all generations, never again to destroy life on earth by floodwaters. But there was no promise to prevent later generations of humanity from destroying life on earth all by ourselves, by our own cumulative acts of violence against nature—God's creation.

Though moving, along with the rest of our solar system, at tremendous speed through infinite space, our small planet Earth—light-years away from any other known life in the entire universe—is the place, the only place we humans and our fellow travelers here can hope to live. Only by God's amazing grace are we alive at all and privileged to call this incredibly wondrous world our home. It is ours to keep, or to lose.

Bibliography

Abrecht, Paul, et al. *Faith, Science and the Future*. Philadelphia: Fortress, 1979.
Ackerman, Susan. *Under Every Green Tree*. Chico, CA: Scholar's, 1992.
Anderson, Bernhard W. *Creation in the Old Testament*. Philadelphia: Fortress, 1984.
———. *From Creation to New Creation: Old Testament Perspectives*. Philadelphia: Fortress, 1994.
Asamoah-Gyado, J. Kwabena. "Foreword: 'The Earth is The Lord's': Mainstreaming Ecological Issues in African Theology." In *Essays on the Land, Ecotheology, and Traditions in Africa*, edited by Benjamin Abotchie Ntreh et al., xi–xx. Eugene, OR: Resource, 2019.
Associated Press. "Church Opens Doors to Dogs." *Independent Florida Alligator* (Oct. 7, 2008).
Austin, Richard C. *Hope for the Land: Nature in the Bible*. Louisville: John Knox, 1987.
Babbitt, Bruce. "Between the Flood and the Rainbow: Our Covenant to Protect the Whole Creation." *Animal Liberation* 2 (1996) 5.
Bainton, Roland H. *Here I Stand: A Life of Martin Luther*. Nashville: Abingdon-Cokesbury, 1950.
Bakken, Peter W. "Christianity and Ecology Bibliography." Yale, n.d. http://fore.research.yale.edu/religion//christianity/bibliography.html. Site suspended.
Barbour, Ian. *Ethics in an Age of Technology*. Gifford Lectures, 2nd ser. New York: HarperCollins, 1993.
———. *Religion in an Age of Science*. Gifford Lectures, 1st ser. San Francisco: Harper & Row, 1990.
Barlow, Chuck D. "Why the Christian Right Must Protect the Environment." *Boston College Environmental Affairs Law Review* 23 (1996) 781–802.
Barr, James. "Man and Nature: The Ecological Controversy and the Old Testament." *Bulletin of the John Rylands Library* 52 (1972) 9–32.
Baumer, Franklin L. *Modern European Thought: Continuity and Change in Ideas, 1600–1950*. New York: Macmillan, 1977.
Baur, Gene. *Farm Sanctuary: Changing Hearts and Minds about Animals and Food*. New York: Touchstone, 2008.
Begley, Sharon. "What the Spill Will Kill." *Newsweek* (June 14, 2021) 25–28.
Bentham, Jeremy. *An Introduction to the Principles of Morals and Legislation*. N.p.: N.p. 1789.
Bergant, Dianne. "Is the Biblical Worldview Anthropocentric?" *New Theology Review* 4 (1991) 5–14.

Berger, Peter L. *The Noise of Solemn Assemblies*. New York: Doubleday, 1961.
———. *The Sacred Canopy: Elements in a Sociological Theory of Religion*. New York: Doubleday, 1969.
Berry, Wendell. *The Gift of the Good Land: Further Essays, Cultural and Agricultural*. Albany, CA: North Point, 1981.
———. *Sex, Economy, Freedom & Community*. New York: Pantheon, 1993.
Bird, Phyllis A. "'Male and Female He Created Them': Genesis 1:27b in the Context of the Priestly Act of Creation." *Harvard Theological Review* 74 (1981) 137–44.
Bland, Dave, and Sean Patrick Webb. *Creation, Character, and Wisdom: Rethinking the Roots of Environmental Ethics*. Eugene, OR: Wipf & Stock, 2016.
Blumenson, Eric. "Who Counts Morally?" *Journal of Law and Religion* 14 (1999–2000) 1–40.
Bouma-Prediger, Steven. *For the Beauty of the Earth: A Christian Vision for Creation Care*. Rev. ed. Grand Rapids: Baker Academic, 2001.
Brabazon, James, ed. *Albert Schweitzer: Essential Writings*. Maryknoll, NY: Orbis, 2005.
Braun, Wernher von. "Responsible Scientific Investigation and Application." In *The Nature of a Humane Society: A Symposium on the Bicentennial of the United States of America*, edited by H. Ober Hess, 118–28. Philadelphia: Fortress, 1977.
Brouman, Simon, and Debbie Legge. *Law Relating to Animals*. London: Cavendish, 1997.
Buck, Holly Jean. "Carbon Removal Is Essential." *Sierra* (Summer 2022) 38–39.
Caldwell, Lynton Keith, and Kristin Shrader-Frechette. *Policy for Land: Law and Ethics*. Lanham, MD: Rowman & Littlefield, 1993.
Callicott, J. Baird. "Genesis and John Muir." In *Covenant for a New Creation: Ethics, Religion and Public Policy*, edited by Carol S. Robb and Carl J. Casebolt, 187–219. Maryknoll, NY: Orbis, 1991.
Campbell, Will D. *Providence*. Waco, TX: Baylor University Press, 2002.
Caras, Roger. "The Promised Land, Israel, for Biblical Beasts." *Wildlife* 3 (1973) 4–13.
Carr, Archie. *A Naturalist in Florida: A Celebration of Eden*. Edited by Marjorie Carr. New Haven, CT: Yale University Press, 1994.
Carson, Rachel. *The Edge of the Sea*. Boston: Houghton Mifflin, 1955.
———. *The Sea around Us*. New York: Oxford University Press, 1951.
———. *Silent Spring*. Boston: Houghton & Mifflin, 1962.
Carter, Jimmy. *Our Endangered Values: America's Moral Crisis*. New York: Simon & Schuster, 2005.
Charlesworth, James H. *The Old Testament Pseudepigrapha*. 2 vols. New York: Doubleday, 1983–85.
Clark, Henry. *The Ethical Mysticism of Albert Schweitzer*. Boston: Beacon, 1962.
Coalition on the Environment and the Jewish Life. "What's Jewish about Protecting the Environment?" COEJL, n.d. http://www.coejl.org/Jewviro.php. Site discontinued.
Cobb, John B., Jr. *Is It Too Late: A Theology of Ecology*. Minneapolis: Fortress, 2021.
———. *Sustainability, Economics, Ecology, and Justice*. Maryknoll, NY: Orbis, 1992.
Cobb, Nathan. "Black Lab Fights with Alligator to Save Flock of Ducks." *Gainesville Sun*, Sept. 26, 2021.
Cohen, Jeremy. "On Classical Judaism and Environmental Crisis." *Tikkun* 5 (1990) 74–77.
Cohn, Priscilla, ed. *Ethics and Wildlife*. Lewistown, NY: Mellen, 1999.

———. "Exploding the Hunting Myths." In *Ethics and Wildlife*, edited by Priscilla Cohn, 101–41. Lewistown, NY: Mellen, 1999.

Commoner, Barry. *The Closing Circle: Nature, Man, and Technology*. New York: Knopf, 1971.

Cone, Christopher. *Redacted Dominionism: A Biblical Approach to Grounding Environmental Responsibility*. Eugene, OR: Wipf and Stock, 2012.

Coogan, Michael D., ed. *The New Oxford Annotated Bible, New Revised Standard Version with the Apocrypha*. 3rd ed. New York: Oxford University Press, 2001.

Council on Environmental Quality, and Department of State. *The Global 2000 Report to the President: Entering the Twenty-First Century*. 3 vols. Washington, DC: Government Printing Office, 1980.

Dawson, J. W. *Nature and the Bible: A Course of Lectures Delivered in New York, in December, 1874, on the Morse Foundation of the Union Theological Seminary*. 1875. Reprint, Ann Arbor: Scholarly Publication Office, University of Michigan Press, 2021.

Derr, Thomas S. *Environmental Ethics and Christian Humanism*. Nashville: Abingdon, 1996.

———. "Religion's Responsibility for the Ecological Crisis: An Argument Run Amok." *World View* 18 (1975) 39–45.

De Vries, Barend A. *Champions of the Poor: The Economic Consequences of Judeo-Christian Values*. Washington, DC: Georgetown University Press, 1998.

DeWitt, Calvin B. "Behemoth and Batrachians in the Eyes of God: Responsibility to Other kinds in Biblical Perspective." In *Christianity and Ecology: Seeking the Well-Being of Earth and Humans*, edited by Dieter T. Hessel and Rosemary Radford Ruether, Religions of the World and Ecology, 291–316. Cambridge, MA: Harvard University Press, 2000.

Douma, J. *Environmental Stewardship*. Edited by Nelson D. Klosternan. Translated by Albert H. Oosterhoff. Eugene, OR: Wipf & Stock, 2015.

Drummond, William. *The Rights of Animals and Man's Obligation to Treat Them with Humanity (1838)*. Edited by Rod Preece and Chien-hui Li. Lewistown, NY: Mellon, 2005.

Dubos, Rene J. *A God Within*. New York: Scribner's, 1972.

Ehrenfeld, David. *The Arrogance of Humanism*. New York: Oxford University Press, 1978.

Episcopal Church. *Book of Common Prayer*. New York: Oxford University Press, 1928.

Evangelical Climate Initiative. "Climate Change: An Evangelical Call to Action." Influence Watch, n.d. https://www.influencewatch.org/app/uploads/2020/08/climate-change-an-evangelical-call-to-action.-08.20.pdf.

Feliks, Jehuda. "Animals in the Bible and Talmud." *Encyclopedia Judaica* 3 (1972) 7–19.

Ferre, Frederick. *Hellfire and Lightning Rods: Liberating Science, Technology, and Religion*. Eugene, OR: Wipf & Stock, 2017.

Fihavango, George. "Quest for Ecotheology in a Situation of Ecological Disaster." In *Christian Theology and Environmental Responsibility*, edited by J. N. K. Mugambi and Mika Vahakangas, 90–95. Nairobi: Action, 2001.

Fortin, Ernest L. "The Bible Made Me Do It: Christianity, Science, and the Environment." *Review of Politics* 57 (1995) 197–223.

Fowler, Robert Booth. *The Greening of Protestant Thought*. Chapel Hill: University of North Carolina Press, 1995.

Francione, Gary L. "Animals, Property and Legal Welfarism: 'Unnecessary' Suffering and the 'Humane' Treatment of Animals." *Rutgers Law Review* 46 (1994) 721–70.
———. *Animals, Property, and the Law.* Philadelphia: Temple University Press, 1995.
———. "Animal Rights and Animal Welfare." *Rutgers Law Review* 48 (1996) 397–469.
Francis of Assisi. "All Creatures of Our God and King." Paraphrased by William Draper. Hymnary, 1225. https://hymnary.org/text/all_creatures_of_our_god_and_king.
Friedman, Thomas L. "We're in the Age of Noah." *Gainesville Sun,* Dec. 26, 2007.
G. G. *The Creatures Praysing God, or The Religion of Dumbe Creatures.* 1622. Reprint, Norwood, NJ: Johnson, 1979.
Gaster, Theodor H. *Festivals of the Jewish Year.* Hudson, NY: Sloane, 1953.
———. *Myth, Legend, and Custom in the Old Testament.* New York: Harper & Row, 1969.
General Convention of The Episcopal Church. "Recognize Global Warming and Reaffirm Church's Environmental Responsibility." Archives of Episcopal Church, June 2006. From General Convention, *Journal of the General Convention of . . . The Episcopal Church, Columbus, 2006* (New York: General Convention, 2007), 484–85. https://www.episcopalarchives.org/cgi-bin/acts/acts_resolution-complete.pl?resolution=2006-C018.
George, Richard T de. "The Environment, Rights, and Future Generations." In *Responsibilities to Future Generations,* edited by Ernst Partridge, 157–65. New York: Prometheus, 1981.
Gore, Albert. *Earth in the Balance: Ecology and the Human Spirit.* New York: Houghton Mifflin, 1993.
———. *An Inconvenient Truth: The Planetary Emergency of Global Warming and What We Can Do about It.* Emmaus, PA: Rodale, 2006.
Gottfried, Robert R. *Economics, Ecology, and the Roots of Western Faith.* Lanham, MD: Rowman & Littlefield, 1995.
Graham, Frank. *Since Silent Spring.* New York: Houghton & Mifflin, 1970.
Granberg-Michaelson, Wesley. *A Worldly Spirituality: The Call to Redeem Life on Earth.* New York: Harper & Row, 1984.
Gray, Elizabeth Dodson. "A Critique of Dominion Theology." In *For Creation's Sake,* edited by Dieter T. Hessel, 71–83. Louisville: Geneva, 1985.
Gushee, David P. *The Sacredness of Human Life: Why Ancient Biblical Vision Is Key to the World's Survival.* Grand Rapids: Eerdmans, 2013.
Gustafson, James M. *Ethics from a Theocentric Perspective: Ethics and Theology.* 2 vols. Chicago: University of Chicago Press: 1983–84.
———. *A Sense of the Divine: The Natural Environment from a Theocentric Perspective.* Cleveland: Pilgrim, 1994.
Hall, Douglas John. *Imaging God: Dominion as Stewardship.* Washington, DC: Friendship, 1986.
Hardin, Garrett. "The Tragedy of the Commons." *Science* 162, new ser. (1968) 1243–48.
Hart, John. *Sacramental Commons: Christian Ecological Ethics.* Lanham, MD: Rowman & Littlefield, 2006.
———. *The Spirit of the Earth: A Theology of the Land.* Mahwah, NJ: Paulist, 1984.
Hayden, Tom. *The Lost Gospel of the Earth.* Dublin: Wolfhound, 1996.
Heide, Gale. *This Is My Father's World: A Unique Perspective on Environmental Ethics.* Eugene, OR: Wipf and Stock, 2008.
Herriott, James. *Dog Stories.* New York: St. Martin's: 1986.

———. *The Lord God Made Them All*. New York: Bantam, 1982.
Hess, H. Ober, ed. *The Nature of a Humane Society: A Symposium on the Bicentennial of the United States of America*. Philadelphia: Fortress, 1977.
Hessel, Dieter T. "Bibliography." In *Theology for Earth Community: A Field Guide*, 269–92. Eugene, OR: Wipf & Stock, 2003.
———. *For Creation's Sake*. Louisville: Geneva, 1985.
———. "Christianity and Ecology: Wholeness, Respect, Justice, Sustainability." Yale, n.d. http://fore.research.yale.edu/religion/christianity/index.html. Site suspended.
———, ed. *Theology for Earth Community: A Field Guide*. Eugene, OR: Wipf & Stock, 2003.
Hessel, Dieter T., and Rosemary Radford Ruether, eds. *Christianity and Ecology: Seeking the Well-Being of Earth and Humans*. Religions of the World and Ecology. Cambridge, MA: Harvard University Press, 2000.
Hiebert, Theodore. "The Human Vocation: Origins and Transformations in Christian Tradition." In *Christianity and Ecology: Seeking the Well-Being of Earth and Humans*, edited by Dieter T. Hessel and Rosemary Radford Ruether, Religions of the World and Ecology, 138–41. Cambridge, MA: Harvard University Press, 2000.
———. "Rethinking Traditional Approaches to Nature in the Bible." In *Theology for Earth Community: A Field Guide*, edited by Dieter T. Hessel, 29–30. Eugene, OR: Wipf & Stock, 2003.
Hiers, Rebecca H. "Water: A Human Right or a Human Responsibility?" *Willamette Law Review* 47 (2011) 467–93. https://willamette.edu/law/resources/journals/review/pdf/volume-47/wlr-47-3-hiers.pdf.
Hiers, Richard H. "Day of the Lord." In *Anchor Bible Dictionary*, edited by David Noel Freedman, 2: 82–83. New York: Doubleday, 1992.
———. "Ecology, Biblical Theology, and Methodology: Biblical Perspectives on the Environment." *Zygon, Journal of Science and Religion* 19 (1984) 43–59.
———. *Jesus and the Future*. Louisville: John Knox, 1981.
———. *Justice and Compassion in Biblical Law*. Harrisburg, PA: Continuum, 2009.
———. *A Nation of Immigrants: Sojourners in Biblical Israel's Tradition and Law*. Foreword by David P. Gushee. Eugene, OR: Resource 2021.
———. "Not the Season for Figs." *Journal of Biblical Literature* 87 (1968) 394–400.
———. *Reading the Bible Book by Book*. Philadelphia: Fortress, 1988.
———. "Reverence for Life and Environmental Ethics in Biblical Law and Covenant." *Journal of Law and Religion* 13 (1996–98) 127–88.
———. "Reverence for Life and Environmental Ethics in Biblical Law and Covenant." *Forum on Religion and Ecology*, 2001. http://fore.research.yale.edu/religion/christianity/essays/chris_hiers_index.html. Site suspended.
———. "Transfer of Property by Inheritance and Bequest in Biblical Law and Tradition." *Journal of Law and Religion* 10 (993–94) 121–55.
———. *Trinity Guide to the Bible*. Harrisburg, PA: Trinity, 2001.
———. *Women's Rights and the Bible: Implications for Christian Ethics and Social Policy*. Foreword by Lisa Sowle Cahill. Eugene, OR: Pickwick, 2012.
Hiers, Richard, and Charles A. Kennedy. "The Bread and Fish Eucharist in the Gospels and Early Christian Art." *Perspectives in Religious Studies* 3 (1976) 20–47.
Hill, Brennan R. *Christian Faith and the Environment: Making Vital Connections*. Maryknoll, NY: Orbis, 1998.

Hollands, Clive. "The Animal Kingdom and the Kingdom of God." In *The Animal Kingdom and the Kingdom of God*, Occasional Paper 26, 16–23. Edinburgh: University of Edinburgh Press, 1991.

Howell, Allison, M. "Reflections: A Ghanaian Christian View of Land Care." In *Essays on the Land, Ecotheology, and Traditions in Africa*, edited by Benjamin Abotchie Ntreh et al., 233–49. Eugene, OR: Resource, 2019.

Hughes, Bryan. "Foreword." In *This Is My Father's World: A Unique Perspective on Environmental Ethics*, by Gail Heide, unnumbered pages. Eugene, OR: Wipf and Stock, 2008.

Ice, Jackson Lee. *Schweitzer: Prophet of Radical Theology*. Philadelphia: Westminster, 1971.

"Is It Already 2050?" *The Week* (Aug. 19, 2022) 17.

Jacobson, Diane. "Biblical Bases for Eco-Justice Ethics." In *Theology for Earth Community: A Field Guide*, edited by Dieter T. Hessel, 45–52. Eugene, OR: Wipf & Stock, 2003.

Johnson, Elizabeth A. "Losing and Finding Creation in the Christian Tradition." In *Christianity and Ecology: Seeking the Well-Being of Earth and Humans*, edited by Dieter T. Hessel and Rosemary Radford Ruether, Religions of the World and Ecology, 3–22. Cambridge, MA: Harvard University Press, 2000.

Jonas, Hans. "Technology and Responsibility: Reflections on the New Tasks of Ethics." *Interdisciplinary Encyclopedia of Religion and Science*, 1972. From *Philosophical Essays: From Ancient Creed to Technological Man* (Chicago: University of Chicago Press, 1980), 3–20. https://inters.org/jonas-technology-responsability.

Kalugila, Leonidas. "Old Testament Insights and the Kagera Region, Tanzania." In *Christian Theology and Environmental Responsibility*, edited by J. N. K. Mugambi and Mika Vahakangas, 82–89. Nairobi: Action, 2001.

Kaplan, Zvi. "Animals, Cruelty To." In *Encyclopedia Judaica*, 3:5–6. New York: Macmillan, 1973.

Kay, Jeanne. "Concepts of Nature in the Hebrew Bible." *Environmental Ethics* 10 (1988) 309–17.

Keller, Catherine. "No More Sea: The Lost Chaos of the Eschaton." In *Christianity and Ecology: Seeking the Well-Being of Earth and Humans*, edited by Dieter T. Hessel and Rosemary Radford Ruether, Religions of the World and Ecology, 183–98. Cambridge, MA: Harvard University Press, 2000.

Ken, Thomas. "Praise God from Whom All Blessings Flow." Hymnary, 1674. https://hymnary.org/text/praise_god_from_whom_all_blessings_ken.

Kethe, William. "All People That on Earth Do Dwell." Hymnary, 1561. https://hymnary.org/text/all_people_that_on_earth_do_dwell.

Lagat, Daniel K. *Christian Faith and Environmental Stewardship: Ecological Foundations for Creation Care*. Eugene, OR: Resource, 2019.

Larsen, Dale, and Sandy Larsen. *While Creation Waits: A Christian Response to the Environmental Challenge*. Wheaton, IL: Shaw, 1992.

Lekachman, Robert. *Greed Is Not Enough: Reaganomics*. New York: Pantheon, 1983.

Leopold, Aldo. *The Sand County Almanac*. New York: Oxford University Press, 1970.

Lewis, C. S. *The Abolition of Man*. New York: Macmillan, 1947.

———. *That Hideous Strength: A Modern Fairy Tale for Grownups*. New York: Macmillan, 1965.

Lilburne, Geoffrey R. *A Sense of Place: A Christian Theology of the Land.* Nashville: Abingdon, 1989.

Limburg, James. "'The Way of an Eagle in the Sky: Reflections on the Bible and the Care of the Earth." *Catholic World* (July/Aug. 1990) 148–52.

Lin, Johnny Wei-Bing. *The Nature of Environmental Stewardship: Understanding Creation Care Solutions to Environmental Problems.* Eugene, OR: Pickwick, 2016.

Linzey, Andrew, and Dorothy Yamamoto, eds. *Animals on the Agenda.* Champaign: University of Illinois Press, 1998.

MacArthur, John F. *Genesis 1–11: Creation, Sin, and the Nature of God.* Nashville: Nelson, 2015.

Maguire, Daniel C. *A Moral Creed for All Christians.* Minneapolis: Augsburg Fortress, 2005.

Malchow, Bruce J. "Contrasting Views of Nature in the Hebrew Bible." *Dialog* 26 (1987) 40–43.

Marienfeld, Kya. "Missing the Forest for the Trees: How the BLM's Costly Practice of Vegetation Removal Still Threatens Ecosystems across the West." *Redrock Wilderness* (Summer 2022) 6–9.

Marshall, George, and Daniel Poling. *Schweitzer: A Biography.* New York: Albert Schweitzer Fellowship, 1975.

Martin-Schramm, James B., and Robert L. Stivers. *Christian Environmental Ethics: A Case Method Approach.* Maryhill, NY: Orbis, 2003.

Mason, Jim. *An Unnatural Order: Uncovering the Roots of Our Domination of Nature and Each Other.* New York: Simon & Schuster, 1993.

Massie, Bob. "The Moral Dilemma of Growth." *Reflections* (Fall 2012) 30–33.

Mastaler, James S. *Woven Together: Faith and Justice for the Earth and the Poor.* Eugene, OR: Cascade, 2019.

May, Herbert G., and Bruce M. Metzger, eds. *The Oxford Annotated Bible with the Apocrypha.* Revised Standard Version. New York: Oxford University Press, 1977.

McAfee, Gene. "Ecology and Biblical Studies." In *Theology for Earth Community: A Field Guide*, edited by Dieter T. Hessel, 31–44. Eugene, OR: Wipf & Stock, 2003.

McCoy, Charles S. "Creation and Covenant: A Comprehensive Vision for Environmental Ethics." In *Covenant for a New Creation: Ethics, Religion and Public Policy*, edited by Carol S. Robb and Carl J. Casebolt, 212–25. Maryknoll, NY: Orbis, 1991.

McDaniel, Jay B. "A God Who Loves Animals." In *Good News for Animals? Christian Approaches to Animal Well-Being*, edited by Charles Pinches and Jay B. McDaniel, 86–91. 1993. Reprint, Eugene, OR: Wipf & Stock, 2008.

McFague, Sallie. "Earth Economy: A Spirituality of Limits." *Reflections* (Spring 2010) 61–65.

———. "An Ecological Christianity: Does Christianity Have It?" In *Christianity and Ecology: Seeking the Well-Being of Earth and Humans*, edited by Dieter T. Hessel and Rosemary Radford Ruether, Religions of the World and Ecology, 29–43. Cambridge, MA: Harvard University Press, 2000.

McKibben, William. *The End of Nature.* New York: Random House, 1989.

Meadows, Donella H., et al. *The Limits to Growth: A Report for the Club of Rome on the Predicament of Mankind.* New York: Signet, 1972.

Midgley, Mary. *Animals and Why They Matter.* Athens: University of Georgia Press, 1984.

Milgrom, Jacob. *Leviticus 1–16.* AB 3A. New York: Doubleday, 1991.

Miller, Alan S. *A Planet to Choose: Value Studies in Political Ecology*. Cleveland: Pilgrim, 1978.

Montagu, Ashley, and Floyd W. Matson. *The Dehumanization of Man*. New York: McGraw Hill, 1983.

Mugambi, J. N. K., and Mika Vahakangas, eds. *Christian Theology and Environmental Responsibility*. Nairobi: Action, 2001.

Murphy, James Bernard. *Haunted by Paradise: A Philosopher's Quest for Biblical Answers to Key Moral Questions*. Eugene, OR: Cascade, 2021.

Mwombeki, Fidon R. "Ecology in the New Testament." In *Christian Theology and Environmental Responsibility*, edited by J. N. K. Mugambi and Mika Vahakangas, 96–111. Nairobi: Action, 2001.

Nash, James A. *Loving Nature: Ecological Integrity and Christian Responsibility*. Nashville: Abingdon, 1991.

Neale, John Mason, trans. "Good Christian Men, Rejoice." Hymnary, n.d. https://hymnary.org/text/good_christian_men_rejoice.

Niebuhr, H. Richard. *Radical Monotheism and Western Culture*. New York: Harper & Row, 1960.

Niebuhr, Reinhold. *The Children of Light and the Children of Darkness*. New York: Scribner's, 1944.

———. *Man's Nature and His Communities*. New York: Scribner's, 1965.

North, Gary. *The Dominion Covenant: Genesis 27–36*. Tyler, TX: Institution for Christian Economics, 1982.

Ntreh, Benjamin Abotchie. "Introduction: The Bible and Caring for the Land." In *Essays on the Land, Ecotheology, and Traditions in Africa*, edited by Benjamin Abotchie Ntreh et al., 1–14. Eugene, OR: Resource, 2019.

Ntreh, Benjamin Abotchie, et al., eds. *Essays on the Land, Ecotheology, and Traditions in Africa*. Eugene, OR: Resource, 2019.

Oelschlaeger, Max. *Caring for Creation*. New Haven, CT: Yale University Press, 1994.

Page, Ruth. "The Animal Kingdom and the Kingdom of God." In *The Animal Kingdom and the Kingdom of God*, Occasional Paper 26, 1–9. Edinburgh: University of Edinburgh Press, 1991.

Partridge, Ernest, ed. *Responsibilities to Future Generations: Environmental Ethics*. Buffalo: Prometheus, 1981.

Passmore, John. *Man's Responsibility for Nature: Ecological Problems and Western Traditions*. New York: Scribner's, 1974.

Peters, Sharon L. "Pets Have a Place in the Sickbed." *USA Today*, Oct. 29, 2008.

Petersen, Anna L. *Being Animal: Beasts and Boundaries in Nature Ethics*. New York: Columbia University Press, 2013.

Phan, Peter C. "Eschatology and Ecology: The Environment in the End-Time." Paper presented at the Inter-Religious Federation for World Peace conference, Seoul, August 20–27, 1995.

Pinches, Charles, and Jay B. McDaniel, eds. *Good News for Animals? Christian Approaches to Animal Well-Being*. 1993. Reprint, Eugene, OR: Wipf & Stock, 2008.

Pojman, Louis P. *Global Environmental Ethics*. Mountain View, CA: Mayfield, 1999.

Polt, Gabe. *50 Odd Couples*. NY: Scholastic, 2020.

Poole, Kristen. *Christianity in a Time of Climate Change: To Give a Future with Hope*. Eugene, OR: Wipf & Stock, 2020.

Preece, Rod, and Chien-hui Li, eds. *The Rights of Animals and Man's Obligation to Treat Them with Humanity (1838)*. By William Drummond. Lewistown, NY: Mellen, 2005.

Prochenau, Bill, and *Washington Post* Staff Writer, with contributions from Valarie Thomas. "The Watt Controversy." *Washington Post*, June 30, 1981. https://www.washingtonpost.com/archive/politics/1981/06/30/the-watt-controversy/d591699b-3bc2-46d2-9059-fb5d2513c3da/.

Pulver, Dinah Voles, and Doyle Rice. "Baked Up? Extreme Heat May Be Here to Stay." *Gainesville Sun*, Aug. 8, 2022.

Rad, Gerhard von. *Deuteronomy: A Commentary*. Philadelphia: Westminster, 1966.

———. *Old Testament Theology*. Vol. 1. New York: Harper, 1962.

Rasmussen, Larry L. *Earth Community, Earth Ethics*. Maryknoll, NY: Orbis, 1996.

Reformed Church in America. "Climate Change/Environment." RCA, n.d. https://www.rca.org/synod/statements/#climate.

Regan, Tom. "Philosophical Perspectives on Hunting." In *Ethics and Wildlife*, edited by Priscilla Cohn, 83–99. Lewistown, NY: Mellen, 1999.

Robb, Carol S. *Wind, Sun, Soil, Spirit: Biblical Ethics and Climate Change*. Minneapolis: Fortress, 2010.

———, and Carl J. Casebolt, eds. *Covenant for a New Creation: Ethics, Religion and Public Policy*. Maryknoll, NY: Orbis, 1991.

Rockefeller, Steven C., and John C. Elder, eds. *Spirit and Nature*. Boston: Beacon, 1992.

Rogerson, John W. "What Was the Meaning of Animal Sacrifice?" In *Animals on the Agenda*, edited by Andrew Linzey and Dorothy Yamamoto, 8–17. Champaign: University of Illinois Press, 1998.

Rolston, Holmes, III. "The Bible and Ecology." *Interpretation* 50 (1996) 16–26.

———. *Environmental Ethics: Duties to and Values in the Natural World*. Philadelphia: Temple University Press, 1988.

———. "Foreword: Weaving What Together?" In *Woven Together: Faith and Justice for the Earth and the Poor*, by James S. Mastaler, ix–xii. Eugene, OR: Cascade, 2019.

Rossing, Barbara R. "River of Life in God's New Jerusalem: An Eschatological Vision for Earth's Future." In *Christianity and Ecology: Seeking the Well-Being of Earth and Humans*, edited by Dieter T. Hessel and Rosemary Radford Ruether, *Christianity and Ecology*, Religions of the World and Ecology, 205–24. Cambridge, MA: Harvard University Press, 2000.

Russell, Colin A. *The Earth, Humanity, and God*. Los Angeles: UCLA Press, 1994.

Santmire, H. Paul. *Celebrating Nature by Faith: Studies in Reformation Theology in an Era of Global Emergency*. Eugene, OR: Cascade, 2020.

———. *The Travail of Nature: The Ambiguous Ecological Promise of Christian Theology*. Philadelphia: Fortress 1985.

Schaeffer, Francis A. *Pollution and the Death of Man: The Christian View of Ecology*. Carol Stream, CA: Tyndale, 1970.

Scharper, Stephen B., and Hilary Cunningham. *The Green Bible*. Maryknoll, NY: Orbis, 1993.

Schorsch, Ismar. "Learning to Live with Less: A Jewish Perspective." In *Spirit and Nature*, edited by Steven C. Rockefeller and John C. Elder, 25–38. Boston: Beacon, 1992.

Schwartz, Eilon. "Jewish Theory and the Environmental Crisis." In *Theology for Earth Community: A Field Guide*, edited by Dieter T. Hessel, 53–63. Eugene, OR: Wipf & Stock, 2003.

Schweitzer, Albert. "Civilization and Ethics." In *Philosophy of Civilization*, 85–345. New York: Macmillan, 1960.

———. "The Ethics of Reverence for Life." In *Albert Schweitzer: Essential Writings*, edited by James Brabazon, 164–65. Maryknoll, NY: Orbis, 2005.

———. *Out of My Life and Thought*. New York: Mentor, 1953.

Shepard, Paul. *Nature and Madness*. San Francisco: Sierra, 1982.

Simkins, Ronald A. *Creator and Creation: Nature in the Worldview of Ancient Israel*. Peabody, MA: Hendrickson, 1994.

Singer, Peter. *Animal Liberation: A New Ethics for the Treatment of Animals*. New York: Random House, 1977.

Smith, Walter C. "Immortal, Invisible, God Only Wise." Hymnary, 1867. https://hymnary.org/text/immortal_invisible_god_only_wise.

Steck, Odil H. *World and Environment*. Nashville: Abingdon, 1980.

Steffen, Lloyd H. "In Defense of Dominion." *Environmental Ethics* 14 (1992) 63–81.

Stendahl, Krister. "Biblical Theology, Contemporary." In *The Interpreter's Dictionary of the Bible*, edited by George Arthur Buttrich, 1:418–32. Nashville: Abingdon, 1962.

———. "Response to Wernher von Braun's 'Responsible Scientific Investigation and Application.'" In *The Nature of a Humane Society: A Symposium on the Bicentennial of the United States of America*, edited by H. Ober Hess, 147–61. Philadelphia: Fortress, 1977.

Sturm, Douglas. *Solidarity and Suffering: Toward a Politics of Relationality*. Albany: SUNY Press, 1998.

Taylor, Bron A., et al. eds. *The Encyclopedia of Religion and Nature*. 2 vols. London: Thoemmes Continuum, 2005.

Thompson, Thomas H. "Are We Obliged to Future Others?" In *Responsibilities to Future Generations*, edited by Ernst Partridge, 195–202. New York: Prometheus, 1981.

Tillich, Paul. *The Shaking of the Foundations*. New York: Scribner, 1948.

Towner, Sibley W. "The Future of Nature." *Interpretation* 50 (1996) 27–35.

Trible, Phyllis. "Ancient Priests and Modern Pollution." *Andover Newton Quarterly* 12 (1971) 74–79.

———. *God and the Rhetoric of Sexuality*. Philadelphia: Fortress, 1978.

Tubbs, James B., Jr. "Humble Dominion." *Theology Today* 50 (1994) 543–56.

Tucker, Gene M. "Rain on a Land Where No One Lives: The Hebrew Bible on the Environment." *Journal of Biblical Literature* 116 (1997) 3–17.

Tucker, Mary Evelyn. "The Role of Religion in Forming an Environmental Ethics: New Challenges for Interreligious Dialogue." In *Theology for Earth Community: A Field Guide*, edited by Dieter T. Hessel, 143–54. Eugene, OR: Wipf & Stock, 2003.

Tull, Patricia K. *Inhabiting Eden: Christians, the Bible, and the Ecological Crisis*. Louisville: Westminster John Knox, 2013.

Twum-Baah, Emmanuel Gyimah. "The Bible and Environment: Care for the Land." In *Essays on the Land, Ecotheology, and Traditions in Africa*, edited by Benjamin Abotchie Ntreh et al., 15–37. Eugene, OR: Resource, 2019.

Underwood, Anne. "10 Fixes for the Planet." *Newsweek* (Apr. 14, 2008) 56.

United Methodist Church. "Climate Change and the Church's Response." UMC Justice, 2016. From 2016 Book of Resolutions, no. 1035. https://www.umcjustice.org/who-we-are/social-principles-and-resolutions/climate-change-and-the-church-s-response-1035.

United States Conference of Catholic Bishops. *Global Climate Change: A Plea for Dialogue, Prudence, and the Common Good*. USCCB, 2001. https://www.usccb.org/resources/global-climate-change-plea-dialogue-prudence-and-common-good.

Vorster, Jacobus M. "The Ethics of Land Restitution." *Journal of Religious Ethics* 34 (2006) 685–707.

Warren, E. Janet. *All Things Wise and Wonderful: A Christian Understanding of How and Why Things Happen in Light of COVID-19*. Eugene, OR: Wipf & Stock, 2021.

Watts, Isaac. "Our God, Our Help in Ages Past." Hymnary, 1719. https://hymnary.org/text/our_god_our_help_in_ages_past_watts.

Wellhausen, Julius. *Prolegomenon to the History of Ancient Israel*. 1878. Reprint, Gloucester, MA: Smith, 1973.

Westbrook, Raymond. *Property and the Family in Biblical Law*. JSOTSup 113. Sheffield, UK: JSOT, 1991.

White, Lynn T., Jr. "The Historical Roots of Our Ecologic Crisis." *Science* 155 (1961) 1203–7.

———. "What Hath Man Wrought?" *Americas* 19 (May 1967) 11–19.

"Wildfire Mitigation." *Forest News* (Summer 2021) 4–6.

Wiley, Petroc, and Eldred Wiley. "Will Animals Be Redeemed?" In *Animals on the Agenda*, edited by Andrew Linzey and Dorothy Yamamoto, 190–200. Champaign: University of Illinois Press, 1998.

Wilkinson, Loren, ed. *Earthkeeping in the Nineties: Stewardship of Creation*. Rev. ed. Grand Rapids: Eerdmans, 1991.

Wilson, Edward O. *The Creation: An Appeal to Save Life on Earth*. New York: Norton, 2006.

Wise, Steven M. "The Legal Thinghood of Nonhuman Animals." *British Columbia Environmental Affairs Law Review* 23 (1996) 471–542.

Wolterstorff, Nicholas P. "Foreword." In *Haunted by Paradise: A Philosopher's Quest for Biblical Answers to Key Moral Questions*, by James Bernard Murphy, ix–xii. Eugene, OR: Cascade, 2021.

Wright, Christopher J. H. *Old Testament Ethics for the People of God*. Downers Grove, IL: InterVarsity, 2004.

Wright, G. Ernest. *Biblical Archeology*. Philadelphia: Westminster, 1960.